# Autism
## Spectrum
# Disorders

# Autism
## Spectrum
# Disorders

A HANDBOOK FOR PARENTS
AND PROFESSIONALS
Volume 2: P–Z

*Edited by*
*Brenda Smith Myles, Terri Cooper Swanson,*
*Jeanne Holverstott, and Megan Moore Duncan*

PRAEGER

**Westport, Connecticut**
**London**

**Library of Congress Cataloging-in-Publication Data**

Autism spectrum disorders : a handbook for parents and professionals /
edited by Brenda Smith Myles, Terri Cooper Swanson, Jeanne Holverstott,
and Megan Moore Duncan
    p. cm.
    Includes bibliographical references and index.
    ISBN-13: 978–0–313–33632–4 (set : alk. paper)
    ISBN-13: 978–0–313–34632–3 (v. 1 : alk. paper)
    ISBN-13: 978–0–313–34634–7 (v. 2 : alk. paper)
    1. Autism in children—Handbooks, manuals, etc.
    [DNLM: 1. Autistic Disorder—Handbooks. 2. Child Development
Disorders, Pervasive—Handbooks. WM 34 A939 2007] I. Myles, Brenda
Smith. II. Swanson, Terri Cooper. III. Holverstott, Jeanne. IV. Duncan,
Megan Moore.
    RJ506.A9A92377 2007
    618.92′85882—dc22        2007030685

British Library Cataloguing in Publication Data is available.

Library of Congress Catalog Card Number: 2007030685
ISBN-13: 978–0–313–33632–4 (set)
        978–0–313–34632–3 (vol. 1)
        978–0–313–34634–7 (vol. 2)

First published in 2007

Praeger Publishers, 88 Post Road West, Westport, CT 06881
An imprint of Greenwood Publishing Group, Inc.
www.praeger.com

Printed in the United States of America

∞

The paper used in this book complies with the
Permanent Paper Standard issued by the National
Information Standards Organization (Z39.48–1984).

10  9  8  7  6  5  4  3  2  1

# Contents

# P

## PATTERNING (DOMAN-DELACATO TREATMENT)

The Doman-Delacato patterning treatment is an intervention involving exercises aimed at forming or correcting neurological organization that has been damaged or never developed. Created by Doman and Delacato (The Institutes for the Achievement of Human Potential [IAHP], n.d.) in the 1960s, and carried out by the IAHP, this intervention is based on the belief that the development of a child mirrors that of human evolution (crawling, creeping, crude walking, and mature walking). IAHP believes that most disabilities are false labels, each representing only different symptoms of brain damage. Therefore all children with disabilities, from those in persistent vegetative states to those with mild learning disabilities, are referred to as brain-injured children (diagnoses then consist of where the brain injury is and to what extent). This therapy is thought to aid all children, regardless of their brain injury, with the goal that children "achieve intellectual, physical and social excellence" (IAHP Goals).

The first step is to determine the stage of development where injury took place or normal development ceased. A child is then taken through the steps or movements that a typically developing child would go through in that stage. The aim is to train the brain to go through the typical developmental process, believing that this will then lead to a return to normal development. IAHP states that once injury occurs, development at higher levels cannot occur; each level must be mastered before a child can move on to the next level. If a child is able, he or she performs the exercises alone. If the child is not able to perform the exercises, three adults cause the body to move through the exercises in a fluid manner. Patterning is an intensive therapy, used in conjunction with intensive programs covering reading, math, social skills, fitness, health, and so on.

Although several studies were carried out in the late 1960s–1970s, there was no evidence that patterning held any benefit above that of normal care. Despite these findings, as well as the rejection by science of this child development model and the ability to change development and structure of the brain through repetitive movements, this intervention continues to be practiced and claimed as a cure. Many organizations have issued statements of concern about patterning, including the American

Academy of Pediatrics (AAP), American Academy of Neurology, and the United Cerebral Palsy Association. In its statement the AAP says,

> Treatment programs that offer patterning remain unfounded … In most cases, improvement observed in patients undergoing this method of treatment can be accounted for based on growth and development, the intensive practice of certain isolated skills, or the nonspecific effects of intensive stimulation … On the basis of past and current analyses, studies, and reports, the AAP concludes that patterning treatment continues to offer no special merit, that the claims of its advocates remain unproved, and that the demands and expectations placed on families are so great that in some cases their financial resources may be depleted substantially and parental and sibling relationships could be stressed. (1999)

**REFERENCES**

American Academy of Pediatrics. (1999). The treatment of neurologically impaired children using patterning. *Pediatrics, 104*(5), 1149–1151.

The Institutes for the Achievement of Human Potential. (n.d.). Retrieved June 28, 2006, from www.iahp.org.

**FURTHER INFORMATION**

Novella, S. (1996). Psychomotor patterning. *The Connecticut Skeptic, 1*(4), 6. Retrieved June 28, 2005, from http://www.theness.com/articles/patterning-cs0104.html.

KATIE BASSITY


**PDD-NOS.** *See* Pervasive Developmental Disorder–Not Otherwise Specified


## PEDANTIC SPEECH

Pedantic speech is often characterized by expressive language that is overly formal, excessive in technical details, has an adult quality with sophisticated grammar, and is often precise in intonation.

*See also* Asperger's disorder.

KATHERINE E. COOK


## PEER REVIEWED

Peer reviewed (or refereed) refers to a process of subjecting work or ideas to experts in the field for review and critique. This process is designed to ensure that authors adhere to the standards of their field.

JEANNE HOLVERSTOTT


## PEPTIDE

Peptides aid in digestion. Digestive peptides assist the body in the breakdown of gluten, casein, and protein. Many individuals with autism have lower levels of amino acids in their body, which results in the buildup of opioid **peptides** that may mimic the effects of morphine. When there is a buildup of opioid peptides, one may observe that the individual may appear drunk or may have a more difficult time with behavioral self-control.

*See also* casein-free; gluten-free.

TERRI COOPER SWANSON

## PERCENTILE

Percentile is a value on a ranking scale from 1 (low) to 99 (high) and a median of 50 that specifies the percent of the distribution that falls equal to or below the norm. A percentile rank illustrates the percentage of a norm group obtaining the same score or scores lower than the test-taker's score.

A percentile score is often confused with percentages. It does not refer to the number of questions marked correctly. The 85th percentile, for example, indicates the score below which 85 percent of the scores fall in a particular distribution of scores.

RASCHELLE THEOHARRIS

## PERSEVERATION

Perseveration, manifested in speech, play, or other motoric actions, is characteristic of individuals with autism. Perseverative speech is the repetition of the same words or phrases, either spontaneously spoken or echoed (echolalia), which may or may not be functional in its purpose. Perseverative play is the repetition of the same motor or other behavioral activities used in play, such as the lining up of animals over and over, the exact same placement of an object in a container over and over, or repeating the script from a cartoon or movie included in any dramatic play.

*See also* echolalia: immediate, delayed, mitigated.

**FURTHER INFORMATION**
Quill, K. A. (2000). *Do-watch-listen-say: Social and communication intervention for children with autism*. Baltimore: Brookes Publishing Co.

ANN PILEWSKIE

## PERSEVERATIVE SCRIPTING

Perseverative scripting is a term used to describe the habit of repeatedly retelling an entire story line from a movie, television show, video game, etc. A common behavior among individuals with Asperger syndrome, this retelling can be very exact and detailed, complete with dialogue, speech inflections, and accents. In children, it might involve the repeated acting out of the story line, possibly with toys.

*See also* echolalia: immediate, delayed, mitigated.

**FURTHER INFORMATION**
Osborne, L. (June 18, 2000). The little professor syndrome. *The New York Times Magazine*. Retrieved September 3, 2006, from www.nytimes.com/library/magazine/home/20000618mag-asperger.html.

LISA BARRETT MANN

## PERSONAL PERSPECTIVES

Personal perspectives are an individual's narration about their own experiences. For more on personal perspectives related to autism spectrum disorders, see Appendix D.

TERRI COOPER SWANSON

## PERSON FIRST LANGUAGE

Person first language puts the person before his or her disability or supports (i.e., child with autism, not autistic child) in an effort to separate the person from the condition and retain his or her dignity. Some individuals on the autism spectrum dislike person first language, preferring autistic person to person with autism, because the diagnosis is critical to their self-concept.

JEANNE HOLVERSTOTT

## PERVASIVE DEVELOPMENTAL DISORDER–NOT OTHERWISE SPECIFIED

Pervasive Developmental Disorder–Not Otherwise Specified (PDD-NOS) is one of five disorders classified as **pervasive developmental disorders**. The other disorders include **autistic disorder, Asperger's disorder, Rett's disorder**, and **childhood disintegrative disorder**. An individual with a PDD-NOS diagnosis does not meet the diagnostic criteria for pervasive developmental disorders, yet clearly shows unusual development in the areas of communication, social interaction, and interests/attention.

PDD-NOS is a neurological disorder, and symptoms can range from mild to severe. Individuals with a PDD-NOS diagnosis have more intact social skills than individuals diagnosed with other pervasive developmental disorders. Sometimes this diagnosis is given to very young children with limited communication skills who also show characteristics of autism. As the child's communication skills increase, other symptoms of autism may become apparent (Chakrabarti & Fombonne, 2001). Some infants with PDD-NOS tend to avoid eye contact and demonstrate little interest in human voice. They do not usually put up their arms to be picked up in the way that typical children do. They may seem indifferent to affection and seldom show facial responsiveness. As a result, parents often think the child is deaf. In children with fewer delays, lack of social responsiveness may not be obvious until well into the second or third year of life (Tsai, 1998).

Children with PDD-NOS may continue to show lack of eye contact, but may enjoy physical contact. They do not develop typical attachment behavior, possibly indicating a failure to bond. Generally, they do not follow the parents around the house, do not show normal separation or stranger anxiety, may approach a stranger almost as readily as they do their parents, and may show a lack of interest in being with or playing with other children. They may even actively avoid other children (Tsai, 1998).

These children may develop a greater awareness or attachment to parents and other familiar adults. However, social difficulties continue with group games and forming relationships; albeit, some children with less-severe PDD-NOS may become involved in other children's games. As they grow older they may become affectionate and friendly with their parents or siblings. The social relationships may still be difficult to understand (Tsai, 1998).

Chakrabarti and Fombonne (2001) state that no two individuals diagnosed with PDD-NOS are exactly alike. However, many individuals with PDD-NOS have some characteristics in common including: deficits in social behavior; uneven skill development (strengths in some areas and significant delays in others); poorly developed speech and language comprehension and skills; difficulty with changes in environment; deficits in nonverbal communication; uncommon responses to taste, sight, sound, smell, and touch; repetitive or ritualistic behaviors (i.e., opening and closing doors repeatedly or switching a light on and off); and unusual likes and dislikes.

Current estimates are that 3–4 per 1,000 individuals may have PDD-NOS, often occurring with some degree of cognitive impairment. Individuals with PDD-NOS are found in all races, ethnicities, and social status (Chakrabarti & Fombonne, 2001).

REFERENCES

Chakrabarti, S., & Fombonne, E. (2001). Pervasive developmental disorders in preschool children. *Journal of the American Medical Association, 285*(24), 3093.

Tsai, L. Y. (1998). *Pervasive developmental disorders*. A briefing paper written for the publication of the National Dissemination Center for Children with Disabilities.

VIRGINIA L. COOK

## PERVASIVE DEVELOPMENTAL DISORDER–NOT OTHERWISE SPECIFIED DIAGNOSTIC CRITERIA (DIAGNOSTIC CRITERIA FOR 299.80, INCLUDING ATYPICAL AUTISM)

The essential features of PDD-NOS are: severe and pervasive impairment in the development of reciprocal social interaction or verbal and nonverbal communication skills; stereotyped behaviors, interests, and activities; and the criteria for **autistic disorder** are not met because of late age onset, and atypical and/or subthreshold symptomatology are present.

This category should be used when there is a severe and pervasive impairment in the development of reciprocal social interaction or verbal and nonverbal communication skills, or when stereotyped behavior, interests, and activities are present, but the criteria are not met for a specific **pervasive developmental disorder**, **schizophrenia**, schizotypical personality disorder, or avoidant personality disorder. For example, this category includes *atypical autism*—presentations that do not meet the criteria for autistic disorder because of late age of onset, atypical symptomatology, or subthreshold symptomatology, or all of these.

### FURTHER INFORMATION

American Psychiatric Association. (2000). *Diagnostic and statistical manual of mental disorders* (4th ed., text rev.). Washington, DC: Author.

JEANNE HOLVERSTOTT

## PERVASIVE DEVELOPMENTAL DISORDERS (PDD)

A pervasive developmental disorder (PDD) is a general term for a group of specific disorders characterized by pervasive (affecting multiple environments and domains) and significant impairments in the development of social interaction, imaginative activity, and verbal and nonverbal communication skills, as well as a limited number of interests and activities that tend to be repetitive (Tsai, 1998).

The ***Diagnostic and Statistical Manual of Mental Disorders*** (DSM-IV-TR; APA, 2000), identifies the following pervasive developmental disorders: **autistic disorder**, **Rett's disorder** (also known as Rett syndrome), **childhood disintegrative disorder** (CDD), **Asperger's disorder**, and **pervasive developmental disorder–not otherwise specified** (PDD-NOS). PDD is often misused as a reference to PDD-NOS. PDD-NOS refers to individuals demonstrating levels of impairment that do not meet the criteria for disorders within the PDD spectrum.

REFERENCES

American Psychiatric Association. (2000). *Diagnostic and statistical manual of mental disorders* (4th ed., text rev.). Washington, DC: Author.

Tsai, L. Y. (1998). *Pervasive developmental disorders*. A briefing paper written for the National Dissemination Center for Children with Disabilities.

VIRGINIA L. COOK

## PERVASIVE DEVELOPMENTAL DISORDER SCREENING TEST-II (PDDST-II)

The Pervasive Developmental Disorder Screening Test-II (PDDST-II; Siegel, 2004) is a questionnaire to be completed by parents for children between the ages of 18 months and 3 years. The questionnaire contains symptoms from the three diagnostic categories of communication, repetitive movements, and social interaction.

REFERENCE

Siegel, B. (2004). *Pervasive Developmental Disorder Screening Test II*. San Antonio, TX: Harcourt Assessment.

BROOKE YOUNG

## PESTICIDES

Pesticides are substances (often chemical or biological in nature) used to control or kill various insects, plants, animals, fungi, or bacteria that can bother and harm humans. Over the past decade the role of pesticides has been questioned as a possible causative agent for autism. Some researchers claim that pesticides such as maneb can cause neurological damage. However, the research on pesticides and autism remains very limited and increased scientific studies are needed.

FURTHER INFORMATION

Barlow, B. K., Lee, D. W., Cory-Slechta, D. A., & Opanashuk, L. A. (2005). Modulation of antioxidant defense systems by the environmental pesticide maneb in dopaminergic cells. *Neurotoxicology, 26*, 63–75.

PAUL G. LACAVA

## PHARMACOLOGY

Pharmacology is the systematic investigation of how chemicals interact with living organisms. When chemicals have medicinal effects, they are considered pharmaceuticals. At this time, there are no pharmaceuticals to cure or suppress autism, however there are pharmaceuticals that assist with controlling compulsion (SSRI), anxiety (SSRI), inattention (Dexadrine), aggression (towards self [SSRI], towards others [Clonidine]), sleep disturbance (Clonidine, Klonpin), and seizures (Tegretol).

*See also* anxiety disorders; mood disorders.

TERRI COOPER SWANSON

## PHENOTYPE

According to the National Human Genome Research Project (n.d.), phenotype is the "observable traits or characteristics of an organism, for example hair color, weight, or the presence or absence of a disease." In autism spectrum disorders, phenotypes could include social, cognition, language, and communication.

REFERENCE

National Human Genome Research Project. (n.d.). *Talking glossary*. Retrieved November 30, 2006, from www.genome.gov/glossary.cfm?key=phenotype.

TERRI COOPER SWANSON

## PHYSICAL THERAPIST

A physical therapist (PT) is a medical professional with a minimum of a master's degree in **physical therapy** from an accredited university, who has passed a national certification exam. A PT specializes in remediation, prevention, or slowing the regression of physical conditions that may result from physical injury, chronic disease, or other causes. The PT provides services to people of all ages, including mobility training, range of motion, strengthening, balance, coordination, and modalities.

Two different professional designations exist in the physical therapy community. A physical therapist has graduated from a master's degree program in physical therapy and has received a license to practice in the state of their choice (if required). A licensed physical therapist (PT) will evaluate and treat individuals with specific motor impairments. A physical therapist assistant (PTA) must complete the education program at an approved university and be supervised by a licensed physical therapist. A PTA may carry out interventions after the physical therapist has evaluated the patient and created the treatment plan. The PTA may neither evaluate nor make modifications in the treatment plan and must work under the supervision of a PT.

Physical therapists work in a variety of settings including private practices, hospitals, nursing homes, schools and development centers, and universities. Those physical therapists that work with children who have yet to develop a certain skill are referred to as developmental therapists. Physical therapists that help individuals regain skills or strength after an injury or illness are sometimes referred to as rehabilitation therapists. Other specialties in physical therapy include pediatrics, orthopedics, sports medicine, and rehabilitation.

FURTHER INFORMATION

American Physical Therapy Association: www.apta.org.

LYNN DUDEK AND KELLY M. PRESTIA

## PHYSICAL THERAPY

Physical therapy (PT) is the treatment delivered by a licensed practitioner (**physical therapist** or physical therapist assistant) to treat the physical aspects of illnesses or injuries. Therapy may involve the use of exercises and specific activities to maintain and restore function and strength as well as condition muscles.

When an individual has sustained an injury, has surgery, or has movement difficulties because of a disability, illness, or disease, their physician may recommend physical therapy. Physical therapy is an effective treatment for people of any age. A physical therapist uses many different methods of exercises and modalities to improve functioning and decrease pain. These include stretching, strength training, therapeutic exercise, play activities, aquatic therapy (water), electrical stimulation, transcutaneous electrical nerve stimulation (TENS), interferential current (IFC), iontophoresis, ultrasound, phonophoresis, hot or cold therapy, and massage. Other treatment interventions include gait training, balance activities, range of motion, joint mobilization, and wound care.

FURTHER INFORMATION
American Physical Therapy Association: www.apta.org.

LYNN DUDEK

## PICA

Pica is listed in the *Diagnostic and Statistical Manual of Mental Disorders* (DSM-IV-TR; APA, 2000; 307.52 Pica) as an eating disorder. It is not pathological in all situations, as it has a lengthy history that has been well documented among most cultures since ancient times. Therefore, it must meet four guidelines as outlined in the DSM-IV-TR:

Persist for at least one month duration.
Developmentally inappropriate behavior.
Not associated with cultural practices.
If pica persists with individuals who have a concurrent developmental disorder, treatment may need to be targeted just for the pica behavior.

By definition, pica (pronounced pike-a) is the eating of nonnutritive items, such as dried paint, candles, wax, soap, rust, burnt matchsticks, feces, needles, light bulbs, dirt, used coffee grounds, and so on. Because babies frequently mouth, taste, lick, and chew nonedible items, this behavior becomes a problem when exhibited for at least 1 month after the age of 18 months, although some say after age 3 years.

Historical evidence links the practice of pica as a medicinal treatment of stomach ailments and by pregnant women who may be nutritionally deficient due to the pregnancy. It has been hypothesized that the compulsion is caused by the body's natural instinct to supplement missing nutrients not taken in by food alone. However, pica also has been used ritualistically, even magically, to promote healing, fertility, and other curatives. It has also been used during times of famine as a way to "bulk up" available food, such as clay baked with bread, or cooked into potatoes. Even today, Haitian women make mud pies of clay and water, baking them in the sun and selling them as a way to "put something in the belly."

Pica has elements of being a compulsive behavior and therefore needs prompt attention when displayed by children or adults with developmental disorders such as **autism**, **mental retardation**, or mental health disorders such as **schizophrenia**.

While the human body can be marvelously resilient, there are many assaults that it cannot withstand, such as the ingestion of lead-based paint, which can cause a multitude of health and behavior disorders, and substances such as animal feces that can cause serious intestinal diseases, or items that can pierce the intestinal walls or cause bowel obstructions. Another danger is that once this behavior begins, it may become a compulsion that the individual may not be able to quit.

Further, in some instances, people resort to pica because they do have certain mineral deficiencies, such as iron. For these people, treatment with a change in diet to meet these nutritional requirements may be enough to change the behavior.

If pica exists as part of an obsessive-compulsive disorder, multiple steps will likely be needed to change this behavior, including behavioral intervention, nutritional monitoring or instruction, and even environmental controls. When pica is first diagnosed during early childhood, chances for successful treatment are higher than when it first occurs later on.

REFERENCE

American Psychiatric Association. (2000). *Diagnostic and statistical manual of mental disorders* (4th ed., text rev.). Washington, DC: Author.

ANN PILEWSKIE

## PICTURE EXCHANGE COMMUNICATION SYSTEM (PECS)

The Picture Exchange Communication System (PECS) is a functional, expressive communication system designed for children and adults who do not use speech as their primary means of communication (Frost & Bondy, 2002). PECS is a low-tech alternative or augmentative communication system. It can be implemented as a primary communication system or to enhance current speech skills. PECS can be rapidly acquired because the only prerequisite is being able to identify powerful **reinforcers**. Users are not required to establish and maintain eye contact, discriminate among pictures, be a certain age, or have a predetermined level of cognitive ability prior to beginning PECS. Research has shown that the use of PECS as an alternative or augmentative communication system enhances the development of speech rather than inhibiting it (see Mirenda, 2003, for review of the relationship between augmentative/ alternative systems, including PECS, and speech development.) In addition, when given an effective communication system, most people's inappropriate behaviors greatly decrease (Charlop-Christy, Carpenter, Le, LeBlanc, & Kelley, 2002).

Bondy and Frost began developing PECS in 1985, and it is based on the Pyramid Approach to Education in Autism (Bondy & Sulzer-Azaroff, 2002). The Pyramid Approach to Education encompasses the principles of broad-spectrum **applied behavior analysis** and stresses the importance of functional activities, powerful reinforcement systems, functional communication, and behavior management plans. PECS uses a variety of lesson formats, teaching strategies, error correction procedures, and plans for generalization of skills from the start.

Prior to beginning PECS, an extensive reinforcer assessment must be conducted to determine what the student prefers. This assessment is ongoing and should result in a hierarchy of most preferred to least preferred items.

The PECS protocol is comprised of six phases. Individuals begin PECS with Phase I and move forward in a linear fashion. The early phases parallel typical language development by first teaching students to communicate in a nonvocal manner, just as typical infants and toddlers do before they use speech. Very young children are able to initiate communication by doing something that gains someone's attention (e.g., looking at an object and then the person), acting in some manner that influences the communicative partner (e.g., gesture), and then receiving some type of reinforcement (social or direct) via that person. Therefore, Phase I teaches what to do with the picture rather than trying to teach the meaning of the picture. In later phases, picture discrimination is taught, which is comparable to the first spoken words of typical students. PECS is then expanded to include the use of simple sentences, adjectives, pronouns, prepositions, verbs, and other parts of speech. Students are also taught to answer simple questions and comment via PECS. Each phase systematically builds upon skills acquired in earlier phases.

### PHASE I: HOW TO COMMUNICATE

The goal in Phase I is to teach the student "how" to communicate by socially approaching a listener to initiate communication by giving a picture in exchange for a desired reinforcer. The student is provided with only one picture at a time, as picture discrimination is not required at this time. This phase involves two trainers: a communicative partner and a physical prompter. The communicative partner's role is to entice with a desired item, wait for the student to initiate (usually a reach for the item), and deliver the reinforcer immediately once the picture is placed into the trainer's hand. The role of the physical prompter is to wait for initiation and then physically prompt the exchange of the picture. Over time, the physical prompter fades prompts to minimize prompt dependency. Phase I is taught across settings, using various reinforcers and different trainers to increase generalization. The student has mastered Phase I when, upon seeing a desired item, he independently exchanges the picture.

### PHASE II: DISTANCE AND PERSISTENCE

The goal in Phase II is to teach the student to generalize the use of PECS to more communicative partners in many settings while also increasing the distance traveled to both communicative partners and to the communication book. In this phase, one picture at a time is displayed on the front of a communication book; no picture discrimination is required. Two trainers will speed acquisition of this phase. The teaching strategy of shaping is the primary teaching strategy used. A physical prompter is "standing by" in case the student needs a gestural prompt to facilitate traveling.

### PHASE III: PICTURE DISCRIMINATION

The goal in Phase III is to teach the student to discriminate among many pictures that are included in a communication book. Phase IIIA begins by teaching the student to discriminate between a preferred picture and a nonpreferred/contextually irrelevant picture. This is known as simple discrimination. If the preferred picture is exchanged, the outcome is immediately reinforcing. If the nonpreferred picture is exchanged, an error correction procedure is initiated to improve discrimination. The student should be able to discriminate between two pictures at least 80 percent of the time. If the student is having difficulty with picture discrimination, a variety of alternative discrimination strategies can be implemented by manipulating the size, color, dimension, or image of the icon.

Phase IIIB requires the student to discriminate between two preferred pictures. This is known as conditional discrimination. The communicative partner conducts correspondence checks to be sure that the student is making the correct correspondence between the picture that is exchanged and the item that is chosen. If the student makes an incorrect correspondence, the trainer uses an error correction procedure to teach about the picture of the desired item. Discrimination among three, four, and five pictures is also taught. At the end of this phase, the student will be able to find her communication book, flip through the pages of reinforcer pictures, find a desired picture, and then travel to a communicative partner to deliver the message.

## PHASE IV: SENTENCE STRUCTURE

The goal in Phase IV is to teach the student to make a request using a simple sentence. The sentence starter "I want" is introduced and paired with a picture of a reinforcer to construct a two-picture sentence on a separate sentence strip to make a request. This sequential lesson is taught using backward **chaining**, that is, teaching the last step in the chain first and then the second to the last step and so on. Once the student is able to independently construct a two-picture sentence, he is taught to tap the pictures as the communicative partner reads the sentence. To facilitate speech without demanding it, a pause is inserted when reading the sentence to the student, and the student is differentially reinforced for speaking. If the student does not speak, the exchange is honored and the reinforcer is delivered. At this point in the training, many preschool students begin to vocalize (Frost & Bondy, 1998; Ganz & Simpson, 2004).

### Attributes

Once Phase IV is mastered, the teaching of attributes starts. The student's current reinforcers are assessed to determine which attributes might be taught. For example, if the student likes markers, the trainer can develop a color lesson. Other attributes to be taught include size, shape, and quantity or specific aspects of things such as body parts, animals, and toys. By learning additional vocabulary, the student gains more opportunities to deliver a clear message. It is impossible to have a picture for every item. By teaching attributes, the student will be able to describe a desired item, such as "I want brown, square cracker," to indicate the desire for a graham cracker even when that specific picture is not available.

## PHASE V: RESPONDING TO A REQUESTING QUESTION (WHAT DO YOU WANT?)

The goal of Phase V is to teach the student to respond to the simple question, "What do you want?" This is the first time in the protocol that the student is taught to respond to the trainer's communication. A time-delay prompt strategy is used to teach this lesson. It is imperative that trainers not ask questions all day, because this could undermine spontaneous requesting.

## PHASE VI: COMMENTING

The goal in Phase VI is to teach the student to comment in response to questions such as, "What do you see?" or "What do you hear?" and eventually to make spontaneous comments about events in the environment. This function of language is often difficult for students on the autism spectrum because the student does not receive a tangible reinforcer, as when making a request such as, "I want book." Instead, the reinforcer for commenting is social.

Phase VI is taught using the same time-delay prompt strategy as in Phase V. The trainer asks the student a commenting question such as "What do you see?" and the student answers the question by constructing a sentence using the "I see" sentence starter and a picture of the corresponding item. Students are also taught to discriminate among many sentence starters as these will serve as the means for the listener to know if the student is making a request or a comment.

### RESEARCH ON PECS

Bondy and Frost (1994) first reported outcome data regarding a large proportion of preschool children with autism who learned PECS and subsequently displayed speech. A preliminary controlled group study from England (Magiati & Howlin, 2003) demonstrated successful implementation of PECS in a variety of classroom settings. Single-subject studies also have demonstrated not only acquisition of PECS, but significant improvement in speech acquisition, social orientation, and reductions in behavior management problems (Charlop-Christy et al., 2002; Ganz & Simpson, 2004; Kravits, Kamps, & Kemmerer, 2002). Research continues in an effort to ensure quality implementation as well as to improve teaching strategies.

### SUMMARY

The Picture Exchange Communication System can be a valuable tool for both parents and educators. It is a relatively easy **augmentative and alternative communication** system to teach, and an effective approach to use with individuals who are not yet speaking or who speak without spontaneity. PECS is a good place to start intervention because there are virtually no prerequisite skills required for its use. Many students have gone beyond PECS to use speech as their primary modality for communication; others have transitioned to a higher-tech voice output device. It is important to help students communicate effectively with people in their surroundings. Having an effective communication system that everyone can understand is a necessary component in reaching this goal.

### REFERENCES

Bondy, A., & Frost, L. (1994). The Picture Exchange Communication System. *Focus on Autistic Behavior, 9*, 1–19.

Bondy, A., & Sulzer-Azaroff, B. (2002). *The pyramid approach to education in autism*. Newark, DE: Pyramid Educational Products.

Charlop-Christy, M. H., Carpenter, M., Le, L., LeBlanc, L., & Kelley, K. (2002). Using the Picture Exchange Communication System (PECS) with children with autism: Assessment of PECS acquisition, speech, social-communicative behavior, and problem behaviors. *Journal of Applied Behavior Analysis, 35*, 213–231.

Frost, L. A., & Bondy, A. S. (1998). The Picture Exchange Communication System. *Seminars in Speech and Language, 19*, 373–389.

Frost, L., & Bondy, A. (2002). *The Picture Exchange Communication System training manual* (2nd ed.). Newark, DE: Pyramid Educational Products.

Ganz, J., & Simpson, R. (2004). Effects on communicative requesting and speech development of the Picture Exchange Communication System in children with characteristics of autism. *Journal of Autism and Developmental Disabilities, 34*, 395–409.

Kravits, T. R., Kamps, D. M., & Kemmerer, K. (2002). Brief report: Increasing communication skills for an elementary-aged student with autism using the Picture Exchange Communication System. *Journal of Autism and Developmental Disorders, 32*, 225–230.

Magiati, I., & Howlin, P. (2003). A pilot evaluation study of the Picture Exchange Communication System (PECS) for children with autistic spectrum disorders. *The International Journal of Autism, 7*, 297–320.

Mirenda, P. (2003). Toward functional augmentative and alternative communication for students with autism: Manual signs, graphic symbols, and voice output communication aids. *Language, Speech, and Hearing Services in Schools, 34*, 203–216.

JO-ANNE B. MATTEO

## PIVOTAL RESPONSE TRAINING

Children with autism spectrum disorders (ASD) display characteristics of impaired social interactions, restricted repetitive patterns of behavior, and difficulties in verbal and/or nonverbal communication (APA, 2000). Pivotal response training (PRT) is a naturalistic intervention that has been implemented to promote appropriate social interactions and communicative skills in children with ASD (Humphries, 2003). As opposed to traditional behavioral interventions, PRT places great emphasis on the child's environment using natural prompts. In addition, the procedures of this intervention are child- and family-centered (Humphries, 2003).

In the 1990s, researchers at the University of California, Santa Barbara, identified four pivotal areas of child functioning, including: (a) responding to multiple cues and stimuli, (b) improving motivation, (c) increasing self-management capacity, and (d) increasing self-initiations (Koegel & Koegel, 1995). The purpose of PRT is to provide children with ASD with adequate social and communicative skills that would lead them to function independently in natural environments.

PRT is suitable for individuals with ASD across a range of ages; however, it focuses primarily on early intervention. The cognitive ability of candidates for PRT ranges from mild cognitive challenges to average intelligence (Simpson et al., 2004), and minimal receptive and expressive language is required (Simpson et al., 2004). To be successful, children have to show interest in objects and be able to demonstrate imitation skills (Humphries, 2003). Since PRT occurs in the most inclusive settings, the best implementers of PRT are those who work with the children on a regular basis, such as general and special education teachers, therapists, and other professionals. Further, family members should be part of the intervention (Simpson et al., 2004).

### RESPONDING TO MULTIPLE STIMULI

The first pivotal area is responding to multiple cues and stimuli. Children with ASD have a habit of responding to very limited and irrelevant cues in their environments, called *stimulus overselectivity* (Lovaas, Schreibman, Koegel, & Rehm, 1971). One example of such stimulus overselectivity may be that a child with ASD only notices tiny telephone numbers on a small commercial sign in a background of a picture. In the light of this characteristic, two approaches to the intervention in this pivotal area are suggested. The first approach is within-stimulus prompting (Schreibman, 1975), whereby an important feature of a stimulus item is greatly exaggerated to show the relevance between the object and its components. After this differentiation has been made, the exaggerated feature is faded away gradually (Dunlap, Koegel, & Burke, 1981; Rosenblatt, Bloom, & Koegel, 1995). For example, to teach a child to distinguish pennies from quarters, the size of coins could be exaggerated. After the child has learned the differences, the original sizes of the pennies and quarters are reintroduced.

The second approach is to directly teach the child to respond to multiple cues and components by arranging activities and environments (Koegel & Schreibman, 1977; Schreibman, 1988; Schreibman, Stahmer, & Pierce, 1996). There are many concurrent cues and stimuli in everyday life, and being able to respond to them is necessary for successful social interactions. Thus, teachers and parents can focus on a few stimuli at a time and arrange for these selected stimuli to stand out against other stimuli in the environment. An example would be to ask the child to sort toys into colored baskets. If the child is asked to put the toy car into the red basket while there are other baskets of different colors, the child has to respond to those colors and make a correct differentiation. Therefore, the first pivotal area focuses on teaching children with ASD to be responsive to multiple cues in an effort to teach them to generalize the skill to various settings, such as home, school, and community, and to facilitate learning.

## MOTIVATION

The second pivotal area is improving child motivation. Improving motivation is associated with increasing responsiveness to environmental stimuli, decreasing response latency, and changing emotions (Koegel, Koegel, & Carter, 1999). Lack of motivation is one of the characteristics of children with ASD that interferes with everyday learning and social interactions. In the light of this, the second pivotal area encompasses several procedures for improving child motivation. First, the child should be allowed to choose materials, topics, and toys during interactions. When learning communicative skills, for instance, if the child is allowed to select her favorite toys as stimulus or reinforcement items, chances are that she will have a sense of engagement in learning activities. Besides increasing motivation, studies have indicated a decrease in challenging behaviors (Sigafoos, 1998). In addition, the use of natural and direct **reinforcers** benefits target behaviors and other functional activities (Koegel et al., 1999). The third way to improve child motivation is to intersperse previously learned tasks with newly acquired tasks (Dunlap, 1984; Dunlap & Koegel, 1980; Koegel & Koegel, 1986; Koegel & Johnson, 1989). Thus, the child maintains the level of competence and at the same time gains new skills based upon what he has learned. Thus, a strong possibility of completing tasks results in high motivation and increased responses. The other important motivational technique is to reinforce any clear and goal-directed attempts made by the child (Koegel & Johnson, 1989; Koegel & Mentis, 1985; Koegel, O'Dell, & Dunlap, 1988). That is, the child is more motivated to attend tasks if he receives encouragement when making any attempts to respond.

## SELF-MANAGEMENT

The third pivotal area is increasing self-management capacity. Having self-management skills helps children with ASD to: (a) be more independent from their intervention providers, (b) minimize the services of practitioners, and (c) reduce the supervision of the implementers. Using this approach, the intervention providers teach the child daily-living tasks and activities within the child's natural environments and encourage the child to be actively involved in the intervention.

Several general procedures are suggested to the use of self-management intervention (Koegel, Koegel, & Surratt, 1992). First, the intervention provider and the child identify a target behavior they are going to work on. For example, it could be a socially valid behavior that needs to be taught or an inappropriate behavior that needs to be reduced. The second step is to identify reinforcers. In order to improve self-management, it is better to use self-recruit reinforcement instead of external rewards. The third step is to select a self-monitoring device. Fourth, the intervention provider can teach the child how to monitor the occurrence or absence of the target behavior using the selected self-monitoring device. The final step is to see whether the child can generalize the self-management procedures to real-life situations. An example of incorporating these procedures is using self-management strategies to modulate the feelings. The intervention provider can start by assisting the child in identifying the behavior the child demonstrates when feeling angry. Worksheets or visual reminders, such as feeling thermometers, could be used as self-monitoring device. Then the child is taught how to use the monitoring device independently. For reinforcements the child can earn extra time doing his favorite activity to calm down. The goal of these intervention procedures is to enable children with ASD to internalize the self-monitoring device and foster behavioral management responsibility and use self-administered rewards.

## SELF-INITIATION

The fourth pivotal area focuses on increasing self-initiations. A lack of spontaneous language expression is a major characteristic of children with ASD. Koegel and her colleagues (1988) found that children with ASD could learn to generalize the skill of initiating simple questions. Several self-initiations include why-questions; assistance-seeking questions and information-seeking questions are also important (Houghton, Bronicki, & Guess, 1987; Koegel et al., 1999; Shukla, Surratt, Horner, & Albin, 1995).

To increase self-initiation, the intervention provider can start by having the child engage in his preferred activity and then create a teaching situation where these self-initiating questions occur. At first, the child is prompted and reinforced to ask questions. Gradually, the prompts are faded after the child is able to generalize these skills across settings. Teaching children with ASD how to initiate questions not only increases their language expressions but also improves their social communicative competence.

There are no documented risks of implementing PRT interventions (Simpson et al., 2004), and since most materials come from the child's natural environments, it is not costly. Further, PRT incorporates teaching sessions into the child's daily activities and, therefore, reduces the need for intensive intervention hours. However, the intervention provider should be careful about arranging teaching and learning environments, especially when introducing multiple components and stimuli into the intervention process. Thus, the instruction should be clear and uninterrupted.

Some areas that children with ASD have difficulties with are not included in PRT, such as sensory processing and motor planning (Simpson et al., 2004). In general, PRT focuses on teaching children to be responsive to the many learning opportunities and social interactions that occur in natural environments, as well as increasing motivation and improving self-initiation. The ultimate goal of PRT intervention is to help children generalize the behaviors they have learned in these four pivotal areas to other natural environments.

## REFERENCES

American Psychiatric Association. (2000). *Diagnostic and statistical manual of mental disorders* (4th ed., text rev.). Washington, DC: Author.

Dunlap, G. (1984). The influence of task variation and maintenance tasks on the learning and affect of autistic children. *Journal of Experimental Child Psychology, 37,* 41–64.

Dunlap, G., & Koegel, R. L. (1980). Motivating autistic children through stimulus variation. *Journal of Applied Behavior Analysis, 13,* 619–627.

Dunlap, G., Koegel, R. L., & Burke, J. C. (1981). Educational implications of stimulus overselectivity in autistic children. *Exceptional Education Quarterly, 20*, 37–49.

Houghton, J., Bronicki, G. B., & Guess, D. (1987). Opportunities to express preferences and make choices among students with severe disabilities in classroom settings. *Journal of the Association for Persons with Severe Handicaps, 12*, 18–27.

Humphries, T. (2003). Effectiveness of pivotal response training as a behavioral intervention for young children with autism spectrum disorders. *Bridges, 2*(4), 1–10.

Koegel, L. K., & Koegel, R. L. (1986). The effects of interspersed maintenance tasks on academic performance and motivation in a severe childhood stroke victim. *Journal of Applied Behavior Analysis, 19*, 425–430.

Koegel, L. K., & Koegel, R. L. (1995). Motivating communication in children with autism. In E. Schopler & G. B. Mesibov (Eds.), *Learning and cognition in autism* (pp. 73–87). New York: Plenum.

Koegel, R. L., & Johnson, J. (1989). Motivating language use in autistic children. In G. Dawson (Ed.), *Autism: Nature, diagnosis, and treatment* (pp. 310–325). New York: Guilford.

Koegel, R. L., Koegel, L. K., & Carter, C. M. (1999). Pivotal teaching interactions for children with autism. *School Psychology Review, 28*(4), 576–594.

Koegel, R. L., Koegel, L. K., & Surratt, A. (1992). Language intervention and disruptive behavior in children with autism. *Journal of Autism and Developmental Disorders, 22*, 141–152.

Koegel, R. L., & Mentis, M. (1985). Motivation in childhood autism: Can they or won't they? *Journal of Child Psychology and Psychiatry, 26*, 185–191.

Koegel, R. L., O'Dell, M. C., & Dunlap, G. (1988). Producing speech use in nonverbal autistic children by reinforcing attempts. *Journal of Autism and Developmental Disorders, 18*, 525–538.

Koegel, R. L., & Schreibman, L. (1977). Teaching autistic children to respond to simultaneous multiple cues. *Journal of Experimental Child Psychology, 24*(2), 299–311.

Lovaas, O. L., Schreibman, L., Koegel, R., & Rehm, R. (1971). Selective responding by autistic children to multiple sensory input. *Journal of Abnormal Psychology, 77*(3), 211–222.

Rosenblatt, J., Bloom, P., & Koegel, R. L. (1995). Overselective responding: Description, implications, and intervention. In R. L. Koegel & L. K. Koegel (Eds.), *Teaching children with autism: Strategies for initiating positive interactions and improving learning opportunities* (pp. 33–42). Baltimore: Brookes Publishing Co.

Schreibman, L. (1975). Effects of within-stimulus and extrastimulus prompting on discrimination learning in autistic children. *Journal of Applied Behavior Analysis, 8*, 91–112.

Schreibman, L. (1988). *Autism*. Newbury Park, CA: Sage.

Schreibman, L., Stahmer, A., & Pierce, K. (1996). Alternative applications of pivotal response training: Teaching symbolic play and social interaction skills. In L. K. Koegel, R. L. Koegel, & G. Dunlap (Eds.), *Positive behavioral support: Including people with difficult behavior in the community* (pp. 353–371). Baltimore: Brookes Publishing Co.

Shukla, S., Surratt, A. V., Horner, R. H., & Albin, R. W. (1995). Examining the relationship between self-initiations of an individual with disabilities and directive behavior of staff persons in a residential setting. *Behavioral Interventions, 10*, 101–110.

Sigafoos, J. (1998). Choice making and personal selection strategies. In J. K. Luiselli & M. J. Cameron (Eds.), *Antecedent control: Innovative approaches to behavioral support* (pp. 187–221). Baltimore: Brookes Publishing Co.

Simpson, R. L., Adams, L. G., Ben-Arieh, J., Byrd, S. E., Cook, K. T., de Boer-Ott, et al. (2004). *Autism spectrum disorders: Interventions and treatments for children and youth.* Thousand Oaks, CA: Corwin Press.

## FURTHER INFORMATION

Koegel, L. K., Camarata, S. M., Valdez-Menchaca, M. C., & Koegel, R. L. (1998). Setting generalization of question-asking by children with autism. *American Journal on Mental Retardation, 102*, 346–357.

Koegel, L. K., Koegel, R. L., & Dunlap, G. (Eds.). (1996). *Positive behavioral support: Including people with difficult behavior in the community.* Baltimore: Brookes Publishing Co.

Koegel, L. K., Koegel, R. L., Hurley, C., & Frea, W. D. (1992). Improving social skills and disruptive behavior in children with autism though self-management. *Journal of Applied Behavior Analysis*, 25(2), 341–353.

YU-CHI CHOU

## PLACEBO

A placebo is a pill that contains no active ingredients and is given to individuals in control groups in medication research studies. Although the placebo is made to look like an actual drug intended to help patients, it is used to help discover if the real drug provides better benefits than the placebo. The placebo effect is when a subject's behavior improves or gets better because they think they are taking a real drug.

PAUL G. LACAVA

## PLAY-ORIENTED THERAPIES

Play-oriented therapies and interventions are among the wide range of educational and treatment options available for children with autism spectrum disorders (ASD; Boucher & Wolfberg, 2003). These approaches greatly vary with respect to theoretical orientations, as well as the goals, methods, and contexts in which they are applied. While many utilize play as a vehicle to achieve goals that are not play-specific (e.g., social skills, positive behavior, communication, and language), others are explicitly designed to support children in learning how to play. Those interventions with the goal of promoting play often target specific aspects of play behavior focusing on cognitive and/or social domains. With regard to methods, play-oriented approaches vary in degree of structure, the kinds of materials used, whether they are situated in a clinic versus natural play setting, whether they involve play with an adult versus with other children, and the age and ability ranges of peers. Theoretical orientations also run the gamut of psychodynamic, developmental, and behavioral with offshoots and combinations of each. The following gives an overview of an assortment of play-oriented therapies and interventions that are geared to children with ASD.

### TRADITIONAL PLAY THERAPY

Traditional forms of play therapy are rooted in the psychoanalytic tradition (Freud, 1946), which prevailed in the early treatment of children with ASD, who were classified among children with a wide range of psychological problems (Axline, 1947; Klein, 1955). In general, play therapy focuses on resolving emotional and behavioral problems by establishing communication between therapist and child utilizing a variety of play activities—such as puppets, a dollhouse, sand, or clay. The idea is that play allows the child to express emotions that would otherwise be too difficult to verbalize or discuss with another person. An underlying premise of the psychoanalytic approach is that the child's problems reflect unresolved internal conflicts that arise from past experience, all of which may be represented in play. In its original application to children with ASD, play therapy focused on drawing the child out of his or her "autistic-state" by working through inner struggles that were interpreted as stemming from a dysfunctional mother-child relationship (Mahler, 1952). As theories of autism shifted from psychogenic to organic explanations for the disorder, traditional psychoanalytic play therapy was no longer considered a treatment of choice. While contemporary

259

versions of psychodynamic play therapy are now widely practiced with children who have diverse emotional issues, little research exists to determine its explicit benefits to children with ASD (Mittledorf, Hendricks, & Landreth, 2001). Nevertheless, play therapy may offer benefits to higher-functioning children who are experiencing emotional difficulties coupled with or as a by-product of ASD.

### ADULT-DIRECTED APPROACHES

Many play-oriented interventions for children with ASD are adult-directed, based on the principles of **applied behavior analysis** (for a review, see Stahmer, Ingersoll, & Carter, 2003). These interventions focus on the use of systematic reinforcement to increase target play behaviors. One such approach that is commonly practiced today is **discrete trial training** (DTT) as associated with the work of Lovaas (1987) and colleagues (Leaf & McEachin, 1999; Maurice, Green, & Luce, 1996). In DTT, target play behaviors are broken down into a discrete set of subskills, which are taught through a series of repeated teaching trials. The environment is highly structured and controlled by the adult who relies on prompting, shaping, and reinforcement to elicit the target response. **Pivotal response training** (PRT) uses an adult-directed approach to promote play that capitalizes on the child's motivation (Stahmer, 1995; Thorp, Stahmer, & Schreibman, 1995). PRT involves presenting the child with choices of preferred play activities, modeling the desired action, reinforcing the child for reasonable attempts at correct responding, and directly prompting the child to give the correct response (Koegel, Koegel, Harrower, & Carter, 1999).

Also based on the principles of applied behavior analysis are in vivo modeling (Tryon & Keane, 1986) and **video modeling** techniques (Schwandt et al., 2002; Taylor, Levin, & Jasper, 1999) to promote play in children with ASD. In each approach, the child is systematically reinforced for imitating an adult or peer who models or performs a predictable sequence of desired play behaviors (live or on video).

Self-monitoring techniques are also being used to support children with ASD in independent play (Stahmer & Schreibman, 1992) and social play with peers (Shearer, Kohler, Buchan, & McCullough, 1996). This involves training the child to monitor and deliver self-reinforcement for appropriate behavior as adult support is systematically withdrawn.

### CHILD-CENTERED APPROACHES

Many play-oriented therapies and interventions for children with ASD involve child-centered approaches that primarily operate within a developmental framework. In general, the adult follows the child's lead to stimulate, expand, and scaffold play along a continuum that mirrors typical development. Van Berckelaer-Onnes (2003) designed a play intervention that supports children in developing early forms of manipulative, relational, and functional play with objects. This intervention is carried out by an adult who offers and models toy play that is matched to the child's interest and developmental level. Beyer and Gammeltoft (1999) devised a more comprehensive intervention whereby an adult supports the child in following a series of play sequences that are patterned after typical development, as well as adapted to the child's developmental level. Each play sequence is carefully planned with respect to selecting motivating themes and materials and setting up the visual organization and structure of the play at the table where activities take place.

"Floor time" is part of **developmental individual-difference relation-based intervention** that supports children with ASD in reciprocal forms of play (Wieder & Greenspan, 2003). In floor time sessions, the adult follows the child's lead utilizing gestures, words, and affect to establish joint attention and increasingly complex social-communicative exchanges. Sherrat (2002) developed a systematic classroom-based approach that similarly involves elements of structure, affect, and repetition to stimulate symbolic play in children with ASD. The **SCERTS model** (Social Communication, Emotional Regulation and Transactional Support) also incorporates a variety of child-centered practices that support children with ASD in social and symbolic forms of play (Prizant, Wetherby, Rubin, Rydell, & Laurent, 2003).

## PEER-MEDIATED APPROACHES

Play-oriented interventions for children with ASD also include a variety of peer-mediated approaches. Odom and Strain (1984) were among the first to document peer-mediated interventions based on behavioral methods. Accordingly, typical peers are trained through modeling, prompting, and reinforcement to increase the play initiations and responses of the child with ASD. Extensions of this approach include a dual focus on providing explicit instruction to both the typical peers and the children with ASD applying ABA procedures (Haring & Lovinger, 1989; Oke & Schreibman, 1990). Similar methods have also been used for sociodramatic script training (Goldstein & Cisar, 1992). This procedure involves modeling, prompting, and reinforcing triads (consisting of one child with autism and two typically developing peers) to act out specific actions and dialogue in play scenarios that are scripted in advance for the children.

A number of peer-mediated approaches for children with ASD incorporate a variety of child-centered practices that are consistent with a developmental orientation. Documentation of early efforts shares a common focus on promoting spontaneous reciprocal play between small groups of children with ASD and typical peers in natural contexts (Bednersh & Peck, 1986; Casner & Marks, 1984; Lord & Hopkins, 1986). There is also an emphasis on facilitating social, communicative, and play exchanges with minimal adult intrusion (Meyer et al., 1987). Further, attention is focused on engineering the play environment by arranging the physical space and providing intrinsically motivating activities that are highly conducive to interactive as opposed to isolated play (Beckman and Kohl, 1984).

These early influences have carried over into current models of supported peer play. The Denver model (Rogers, Hall, Osaki, Reaven, & Herbison, 2000) applies child-centered practices to engage children with ASD in "sensory social exchanges" that revolve around toy preferences and social initiations with typical peers. This approach teaches children to initiate, imitate, and engage each other in social games and routines. The **integrated play group model** is a comprehensive intervention that uses guided participation to support children with ASD and typical peers in mutually engaging play experiences (Wolfberg, 1999; 2003). Routines, rituals, and visual supports are incorporated into play sessions that revolve around highly motivating social play activities. The adult facilitates by monitoring play initiations, scaffolding, and guiding social communication and play geared to each child's unique interests, ability, and experience. Extensions of this approach include combining integrated play groups with **sensory integration** therapy to enhance play (Fuge and Berry, 2004).

The selection of play-oriented therapies and interventions described herein includes a wide range of promising practices for children with ASD. It should be noted that this selection is by no means comprehensive, as there are undoubtedly other noteworthy play therapy and intervention models not mentioned here. It is also of interest to point out that despite apparent conceptual and methodological differences among these different approaches, there are actually some common threads that may be helpful for guiding parents and professionals in their efforts to support their children in play. First, there is a growing appreciation for the importance of including play in the lives of children with ASD. This is consistent with the recommendations of the National Research Council (2001) who ranked the teaching of play skills with peers among the six types of interventions that should have priority in the design and delivery of effective educational programs for children with ASD. Further, there is a general consensus that play interventions need to be adapted to each child's unique interests, developmental levels, and learning style (see for example, Kok, Kong, & Bernard-Opitz, 2002; Quill, 2000). Another common focus is on identifying and responding to what is intrinsically motivating for the child. There is also a growing trend toward more naturalistic approaches, which includes providing opportunities and support for children with ASD and typical peers to play together as play partners. Finally, there is a greater openness to blending best practices to ensure that every child with ASD is given the opportunity and means to reach his or her full potential for play.

## REFERENCES

Axline, V. (1947). *Play therapy*. New York: Ballantine Books.

Beckman, P. J., & Kohl, F. L. (1984). The effects of social and isolate toys on the interactions and play of integrated and nonintegrated groups of preschoolers. *Education and Training of the Mentally Retarded, 19*, 169–175.

Bednersh, F., & Peck, C. A. (1986). Assessing social environments: Effects of peer characteristics on the social behavior of children with severe handicaps. *Child Study Journal, 16*(4), 315–329.

Beyer, J., & Gammeltoft, L. (1999). *Autism and play*. London: Jessica Kingsley Publishers.

Boucher, J., & Wolfberg, P. J. (Eds.). (2003). Special issue on play. *Autism: The International Journal of Research and Practice, 7*(4), 339–346.

Casner, M. W., & Marks, S. F. (1984). *Playing with autistic children*. Paper presented at the annual convention of the Council for Exceptional Children, Washington, DC.

Freud, A. (1946). *The psychoanalytic treatment of children*. London: Imago (originally published 1926).

Fuge, G., & Berry, R. (2004). *Pathways to play! Combining sensory integration and integrated play groups*. Shawnee Mission, KS: Autism Asperger Publishing Company.

Goldstein, H., & Cisar, C. L. (1992). Promoting interaction during sociodramatic play: Teaching scripts to typical preschoolers and classmates with disabilities. *Journal of Applied Behavior Analysis, 25*, 265–280.

Haring, T. G., & Lovinger, L. (1989). Promoting social interaction through teaching generalized play initiation responses to preschool children with autism. *Journal of the Association for Persons with Severe Handicaps, 14*(1), 58–67.

Klein, M. (1955). The psychoanalytic play technique. *American Journal of Orthopsychiatry, 25*, 223–237.

Koegel, L. K., Koegel, R. L., Harrower, J. K., & Carter, C. M. (1999). Pivotal response intervention I: Overview of approach. *Journal of the Association for Persons with Severe Handicaps, 24*, 174–185.

Kok, A. J., Kong, T. Y., & Bernard-Opitz, V. (2002). A comparison of the effects of structured play and facilitated play approaches on preschoolers with autism: A case study. *Autism: The International Journal of Research and Practice, 6*, 181–196.

Leaf, R., & McEachin, J. (1999). *A work in progress: Behavior management strategies and a curriculum for intensive behavioral treatment of autism.* New York: DRL.

Lord, C., & Hopkins, M. J. (1986). The social behavior of autistic children with younger and same-age nonhandicapped peers. *Journal of Autism and Developmental Disorders, 16*(3), 249–262.

Lovaas, O. I. (1987). Behavioral treatment and normal educational and intellectual functioning in young autistic children. *Journal of Consulting and Clinical Psychology, 55*, 3–9.

Mahler, M. (1952). On child psychosis in schizophrenia: Autistic and symbiotic infantile psychosis. In R. S. Eissler, A. Freud, H. Hartmann, & K. Kris (Eds.), *Psychoanalytic study of the child* (pp. 265–305). New York: International University Press.

Maurice, C., Green, G., & Luce, S .C. (1996). *Behavioral intervention for young children with autism: A manual for parents and professionals.* Austin, TX: Pro-Ed.

Meyer, L. H., Fox, A., Schermer, A., Ketelsen, D., Montan, N., Maley, K., et al. (1987). The effects of teacher intrusion on social play interactions between children with autism and their nonhandicapped peers. *Journal of Autism and Developmental Disorders, 17*(3), 315–332.

Mittledorf, W., Hendricks, S., & Landreth, G. L. (2001). Play therapy with autistic children. In G. L. Landreth (Ed.), *Innovations in play therapy* (pp. 257–270). New York: Routledge.

National Research Council. (2001). *Educating children with autism.* Washington, DC: National Academy Press.

Odom, S., & Strain, P. (1984). Peer-mediated approaches to promoting children's social interaction: A review. *American Journal of Orthopsychiatry, 54*(4), 544–557.

Oke, N. J., & Schreibman, L. (1990). Training social initiations to a high-functioning autistic child: Assessment of collateral behavior change and generalization in a case study. *Journal of Autism and Developmental Disorders, 20*, 479–497.

Prizant, B., Wetherby, A., Rubin, E., Rydell, P., & Laurent, A. (2003). The SCERTS Model: A family-centered, transactional approach to enhancing communication and socioemotional abilities of young children with ASD. *Infants and Young Children, 16*(4), 296–316.

Quill, K. (2000). *Do-watch-listen-say: Social and communication intervention for children with autism.* Baltimore: Brookes Publishing Co.

Rogers, S. J., Hall, T., Osaki, D., Reaven, J., & Herbison, J. (2000). The Denver model: A comprehensive, integrated educational approach to young children with autism and their families. In J. S. Handleman & S. L. Harris (Eds.), *Preschool education programs for children with autism* (2nd ed., pp. 95–133). Austin, TX: Pro-Ed.

Schwandt, W. L., Pieropan, K., Glesne, H., Lundahl, A., Foley, D., & Larsson, E. V. (2002). *Using video modeling to teach generalized toy play.* Paper presented at the annual meeting of the Association for Behavior Analysis, Toronto, Canada.

Shearer, D. D., Kohler, F. W., Buchan, K. A., & McCullough, K. M. (1996). Promoting independent interactions between preschoolers with autism and their nondisabled peers: An analysis of self-monitoring. *Early Education and Development, 7*, 205–220.

Sherrat, D. (2002). Developing pretend play in children with autism: A case study. *Autism: The International Journal of Research and Practice, 6*(2), 169–179.

Stahmer, A. C. (1995). Teaching symbolic play to children with autism using pivotal response training. *Journal of Autism and Developmental Disorders, 25*, 123–141.

Stahmer, A. C., Ingersoll, B., & Carter, C. (2003). Behavioral approaches to promoting play. *Autism: The International Journal of Research and Practice, 7*(4), 401–413.

Stahmer, A. C., & Schreibman, L. (1992). Teaching children with autism appropriate play in unsupervised environments: Using a self-management treatment package. *Journal of Applied Behavior Analysis, 25*, 447–459.

Taylor, B. A., Levin, L., & Jasper, S. (1999). Increasing play-related statements in children with autism toward siblings: Effects of video modeling. *Journal of Developmental and Physical Disabilities, 11*, 253–264.

Thorp, D. M., Stahmer, A. C., & Schreibman, L. (1995). Teaching sociodramatic play to children with autism using pivotal response training. *Journal of Autism and Developmental Disorders, 25*, 265–282.

Tryon, A. S., & Keane, S. P. (1986). Promoting imitative play through generalized observational learning in autistic-like children. *Journal of Abnormal Child Psychology, 14*, 537–549.

Van Berckelaer-Onnes, I. A. (2003). Promoting early play. *Autism: The International Journal of Research and Practice, 7*(4), 415–423.

Wieder, S., & Greenspan, S. I. (2003). Climbing the symbolic ladder in the DIR model through floor time/interactive play. *Autism: The International Journal of Research and Practice, 7*(4), 425–435.

Wolfberg, P. J. (1999). *Play and imagination in children with autism.* New York: Teachers College Press, Columbia University.

Wolfberg, P. J. (2003). *Peer play and the autism spectrum: The art of guiding children's socialization and imagination.* Shawnee Mission, KS: Autism Asperger Publishing Company.

**FURTHER INFORMATION**
Autism Institute on Peer Relations and Play: www.autisminstitute.com.

PAMELA WOLFBERG

## POSITIVE BEHAVIOR SUPPORT (PBS)

Positive behavior support (PBS) is an empirically validated process for addressing problem behaviors and enhancing the lives of people with autism spectrum disorders (ASD). PBS is based on scientific principles, including **applied behavioral analysis** and humanistic theory. However, it is broader in that it is not a specific strategy, but a foundation for building effective interventions based on an understanding of the person's behavior and preferred lifestyle. PBS takes a functional approach to behavior and is considered an effective practice for students with ASD by several respected groups, including the National Research Council (2001), and others (Hurth, Shaw, Izeman, Whaley, & Rogers, 1999; Iovannone, Dunlap, Huber, & Kincaid, 2003).

### CHARACTERISTICS

Although PBS is an individualized approach, it is made up of a set of components:

1. the gathering and use of functional behavior assessment information to develop hypotheses about the purposes of behaviors;
2. the development of a multicomponent support plan based on the assessment data that includes:
   (a) strategies to *prevent* behavior from occurring,
   (b) strategies to *teach* the person a replacement skill for effectively interacting within various settings, or an appropriate communicative replacement behavior that will get the person the same outcome as did the problem behavior, and
   (c) strategies that change the way others *respond* to problem behavior so that it is no longer reinforced and to desired behaviors so that they are repeated.
3. the design of an evaluation and monitoring plan that documents the effectiveness of the interventions and provides data for making decisions about next steps.

Additional components characterize effective PBS. First, PBS works best when a collaborative team approach is used throughout the process of assessment and intervention. At a minimum, the teams should include the family members/caregivers, teachers, school staff, agency staff, and the student when appropriate. Each team member contributes his or her expertise and perspective of the person with autism spectrum disorder (ASD) and assists in developing a socially valid support plan.

Second, PBS is an ongoing process that addresses both long-term and short-term goals. Although problem behavior is usually the reason why the PBS process is initiated, enhancing the quality of life for the person with ASD is a crucial goal of the support plan. Specifically, inclusion in typical environments in both the school and the community is an objective underlying the entire process. The PBS process, therefore, continues even when the problem behavior is extinguished and new appropriate behaviors consistently occur.

## EXAMPLES OF USE

Generally, PBS consists of five steps: (a) establishing goals of intervention; (b) gathering information; (c) developing a hypothesis; (d) building a support plan; and (e) designing an evaluation, monitoring, and follow-up plan (Hieneman et al., 1999).

### Establishing Goals of Intervention

Identifying the appropriate short- and long-term goals is typically done by a support team. Team members must have a vested interest in the person with ASD and be committed to achieving the long- and short-term goals established.

The team develops goals based on the preferences, desires, abilities, and unique characteristics of the person with ASD. Goals should include reducing problem behaviors, increasing pro-social and academic skills, and improving the quality of the person's life, including increased inclusion in school, social, and community activities (Carr et al., 2002). *Person-centered planning* is one method that can help the team establish goals (Kincaid, 1996). A person-centered plan provides a foundation for understanding the person's vision for his or her life, the conditions that currently exist, and the resources that need to be accessed to help the person fulfill their vision. Outcomes of person-centered plans not only include long- and short-term goals, but also action steps for each team member to pursue throughout the process. Figures 11 and 12 present graphic examples of person-centered planning activities revolving around a vision and goals for Hannah, a 5-year-old girl with ASD who has limited verbal language.

### Gathering Information

Functional behavior assessment information may be gathered through indirect measures such as interviews, questionnaires, and rating scales, or through direct observational measures in various environments. The assessment is used to help the team understand the circumstances surrounding the problem behavior and provide insight into possible purposes, or functions, for engaging in the behavior. Examples of environmental circumstances may include demands, transitions, removal of a preferred object or activity, or the presence of a specific peer or adult. Most behavior serves two main purposes: (a) escaping or avoiding, or (b) obtaining (e.g., attention, tangible object, etc.). The assessment also explores the responses from others that follow the problem behavior. Typical responses following problem behavior include reprimands, redirects, removal of items, time-out, etc. The information gathered is reviewed by the team to identify patterns of circumstances (where, when, what, with whom) related to the behavior.

**Figure 11 Sample Dream Frame from Hannah's Person-Centered Plan**

### Developing a Hypothesis

Hypotheses or summary statements are made based on the data gathered. At a minimum, hypothesis statements should address the context or circumstances related to the behavior, the description of the behavior, and the function served by the behavior (O'Neill et al., 1997).

An example of a hypothesis statement for Hannah is as follows: *When presented with a demand/request/instruction by an adult, particularly when the demand takes Hannah away from a preferred activity, Hannah screams loudly to avoid and protest the demand and to keep access to her preferred activity.* The context most often related to Hannah's behavior is being presented with *demands*, particularly when they take her away from activities she likes. The *behavior* Hannah engages in under the conditions of demands is screaming with marked intensity (loudly). Finally, the *purpose* that is surmised from the data is that Hannah screams during demand conditions to escape the demand and continue to keep doing her favored activity and express her feelings about the situation. In other words, Hannah is communicating in the most effective and efficient way that is currently in her repertoire.

### Building a Support Plan

The hypothesis statement is important because it provides the foundation upon which interventions are built. Hypotheses are vital, particularly with people with ASD and deficient verbal skills, in that they provide a viewpoint of what the person

**Figure 12 Sample Goal Frame from Hannah's Person-Centered Plan**

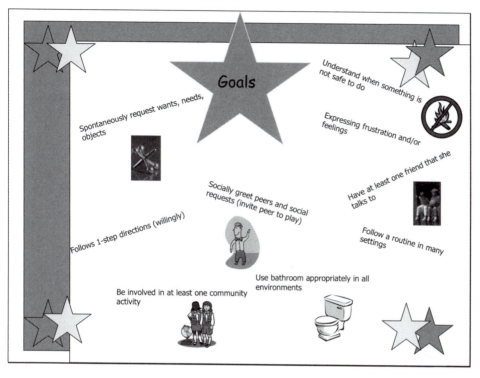

is trying to say with the behavior. By modifying the events under which behavior predictably occurs, the behavior can be prevented and made irrelevant (i.e., no longer necessary). Further, by teaching an appropriate, socially valid way to obtain the same outcome with the same or better effectiveness and efficiency, the problem behavior becomes inefficient and ineffective (O'Neill et al., 1997).

Examples of interventions designed to prevent problem behavior include choices, curricular modifications, transition cues, and environmental and **visual supports**. Interventions that teach new skills can either be strategies that provide the person a functional communicative replacement behavior (e.g., teach the person to ask for a break rather than screaming to avoid something) and/or an alternative skill (e.g., self-management, problem-solving strategies). Since the new behavior must be as efficient or better than the problem behavior in getting a desired outcome, it is important to select a behavior that is already in the person's repertoire. For example, if the person is nonverbal and the strategy is to teach her to ask for a break, the communicative method must be easy to use and one that others can respond to efficiently. Finally, the support plan should include different ways for adults and others to respond to the person's new replacement behaviors and old problem behaviors. The responding interventions should include a way to (a) reinforce the replacement or alternative behavior so that it is used instead of the problem behavior and (b) no longer reinforces the problem behavior.

An example of a PBS plan for Hannah that includes the three minimum components of interventions (i.e., prevent, teach new skills, respond in new ways to behavior) is shown in Figure 13. Because Hannah has minimal verbal language, the team selected one word and sign, *wait*, both already in her repertoire, to replace her

Figure 13  Positive Behavior Support Plan for Hannah

Hypothesis: When presented with a demand/request/instruction by an adult, particularly when the demand takes Hannah away from a preferred activity, she will scream loudly to avoid and protest the demand and to keep access to her preferred activity.

| Preventative Interventions | Replacement Behaviors Alternative Behaviors | Responding Behaviors | Other Strategies |
|---|---|---|---|
| • Rearrange problem environments to make bathroom more enticing (e.g., provide music, textures on wall, texture books in basket) <br>• Give a transition warning when switching from preferred to non-preferred; provide music/routine/warning 3 minutes prior to change <br>• Provide a "First/Then" for transitions (with choice); e.g., first bathroom then "choice." <br>• Set visual timer to provide Hannah with a display of time before she has to go to the transitions <br>• Provide a visual schedule; balance preferred and unpreferred activities <br>• Provide choices—what book to take in the bathroom and who should go into the bathroom with her | • Teach Hannah to say/sign "wait" <br>• Allow Hannah to use "wait" one time to delay transition to next activity <br>• Once Hannah says/signs "wait," provide her with one additional minute before she has to come to next activity <br>• Provide antecedent interventions to increase the likelihood that Hannah will go to non-preferred activity without problem behavior | • Honor "wait" each time Hannah uses it during allowed times <br>• Reinforce Hannah for using her words/signs <br>• When Hannah comes to non-preferred activity, provide reinforcement <br>• If Hannah screams, show her visual (big red X over picture of someone screaming) to indicate "no screaming" paired with a photograph of Hannah signing "wait" to indicate what she should do— minimal attention provided <br>• When Hannah stops screaming, represent the request/demand with antecedent interventions and immediately prompt Hannah to use "wait" (if she hadn't used it already) | • Have Hannah identify feelings in herself and match feelings to others <br>• Teach Hannah to ask "Can I play?" to Head Start <br>• Peers selected to be her buddies <br>• Identify at least one community activity in which she may participate <br>• Use safety signal (red X) <br>• Conduct a home visit to go over the plan with Hannah's mom |

Figure 14  Evaluation Plan for Evaluating Change to Hannah's Problem Behavior

## Hannah's Transition to Toilet Time: Evaluation Plan

| 3 | 2 | 1 | 0 |
|---|---|---|---|
| Goes 3 times without screaming loudly | Goes 2 times without screaming loudly | Goes 1 time without screaming loudly | Screams loudly each time she transitions to the toilet |

Week of:_____

| MONDAY | TUESDAY | WEDNESDAY | THURSDAY | FRIDAY |
|--------|---------|-----------|----------|--------|
| 3 | 3 | 3 | 3 | 3 |
| 2 | 2 | 2 | 2 | 2 |
| 1 | 1 | 1 | 1 | 1 |
| 0 | 0 | 0 | 0 | 0 |

Week of:_____

| MONDAY | TUESDAY | WEDNESDAY | THURSDAY | FRIDAY |
|--------|---------|-----------|----------|--------|
| 3 | 3 | 3 | 3 | 3 |
| 2 | 2 | 2 | 2 | 2 |
| 1 | 1 | 1 | 1 | 1 |
| 0 | 0 | 0 | 0 | 0 |

Week of:_____

| MONDAY | TUESDAY | WEDNESDAY | THURSDAY | FRIDAY |
|--------|---------|-----------|----------|--------|
| 3 | 3 | 3 | 3 | 3 |
| 2 | 2 | 2 | 2 | 2 |
| 1 | 1 | 1 | 1 | 1 |
| 0 | 0 | 0 | 0 | 0 |

screaming behavior. The team also selected several prevention strategies to make the demand to transition less aversive to Hannah. Finally, the team carefully agreed upon how they were going to respond when Hannah used her new behavior and how they would respond if she engaged in her problem behavior.

The additional strategies in the fourth column in Hannah's support plan relate to some of the goals that were developed during the person-centered plan. The intent of

Figure 15  Hannah's Evaluation Plan

**Behavior Rating Scale**

Student Name *Hannah*

| Behavior | | Date | 9/3/05 | 9/4/05 | 9/5/05 | 9/6/05 | 9/7/05 | 9/10/05 | 9/11/05 | 9/12/05 | 9/13/05 | 9/14/05 | 9/17/05 | 9/18/05 | 9/19/05 | 9/20/05 | 9/21/05 | 9/24/05 | 9/25/05 | 9/26/05 | 9/27/05 | 9/28/05 |
|---|---|---|---|---|---|---|---|---|---|---|---|---|---|---|---|---|---|---|---|---|---|---|
| Screaming | Frequent screams | | 5 4 3 2 1 | 5 4 3 2 1 | 5 4 3 2 1 | 5 4 3 2 1 | 5 4 3 2 1 | 5 4 3 2 1 | 5 4 3 2 1 | 5 4 3 2 1 | 5 4 3 2 1 | 5 4 3 2 1 | 5 4 3 2 1 | 5 4 3 2 1 | 5 4 3 2 1 | 5 4 3 2 1 | 5 4 3 2 1 | 5 4 3 2 1 | 5 4 3 2 1 | 5 4 3 2 1 | 5 4 3 2 1 | 5 4 3 2 1 |
| | No screams | | | | | | | | | | | | | | | | | | | | | |
| Asking "wait" | Regular use of wait | | 5 4 3 2 1 | 5 4 3 2 1 | 5 4 3 2 1 | 5 4 3 2 1 | 5 4 3 2 1 | 5 4 3 2 1 | 5 4 3 2 1 | 5 4 3 2 1 | 5 4 3 2 1 | 5 4 3 2 1 | 5 4 3 2 1 | 5 4 3 2 1 | 5 4 3 2 1 | 5 4 3 2 1 | 5 4 3 2 1 | 5 4 3 2 1 | 5 4 3 2 1 | 5 4 3 2 1 | 5 4 3 2 1 | 5 4 3 2 1 |
| | Never used wait | | | | | | | | | | | | | | | | | | | | | |
| Transitions | Transitioned easily | | 5 4 3 2 1 | 5 4 3 2 1 | 5 4 3 2 1 | 5 4 3 2 1 | 5 4 3 2 1 | 5 4 3 2 1 | 5 4 3 2 1 | 5 4 3 2 1 | 5 4 3 2 1 | 5 4 3 2 1 | 5 4 3 2 1 | 5 4 3 2 1 | 5 4 3 2 1 | 5 4 3 2 1 | 5 4 3 2 1 | 5 4 3 2 1 | 5 4 3 2 1 | 5 4 3 2 1 | 5 4 3 2 1 | 5 4 3 2 1 |
| | Protested | | | | | | | | | | | | | | | | | | | | | |

the strategies is to improve Hannah's quality of life by expanding her social relationships and community activities.

Once a support plan is developed, it is important for the team to make an action plan that outlines how the interventions will be implemented. The action plan should include the steps to be taken, training to be delivered, and resources to be accessed.

## Monitoring and Evaluation

Once the support plan is implemented, the team gathers information to evaluate the effectiveness of the supports and to make decisions for future activities (Dunlap & Hieneman, 2005). Information to be collected should include ways to evaluate behavior changes, including the person's use of replacement or alternative behaviors. Finally, an evaluation plan should be developed to assess quality-of-life changes for the individual (e.g., having more friends, being included in more community events).

Several data methods may be used to measure change in behavior, ranging from frequency recording to perceptual ratings. The important thing to consider when choosing a data method is whether the person collecting the data can use the method with minimal intrusiveness to the daily routine. A sample evaluation plan to assess whether Hannah's screaming behavior changes is shown in Figures 14 and 15.

The team chose this method because the teacher felt that something as simple as circling a number once a day would make it more likely that she would do so consistently than taking interval or frequency data. Once Hannah's screaming behavior decreased, the team developed another evaluation method that would provide information on Hannah's use of her new behavior as well as the occurrence of problem behavior. This form measures the teacher's perception of the occurrence of Hannah's problem behavior and replacement behavior.

*See also* empiricism.

## References

Carr, E. G., Dunlap, G., Horner, R. H., Koegel, R. L., Turnbull, A. P., Sailor, W., et al. (2002). Positive behavior support: Evolution of an applied science. *Journal of Positive Behavior Interventions, 4*(1), 4–16.

Dunlap, G., & Hieneman, M. (2005). Positive behavior support. In G. Sugai & R. Horner (Eds.), *Encyclopedia of behavior modification and cognitive behavior therapy (Vol. 3): Educational applications* (pp. 1421–1428). Thousand Oaks, CA: Sage Publications.

Hieneman, M., Nolan, M., Presley, J., DeTuro, L., Gayler, W., & Dunlap, G. (1999). *Facilitator's guide, positive behavioral support.* Tallahassee: Florida Department of Education, Bureau of Instructional Support and Community Services.

Hurth, J., Shaw, E., Izeman, S. G., Whaley, K., & Rogers, S. J. (1999). Areas of agreement about effective practices among programs serving young children with autism spectrum disorders. *Infants and Young Children, 12*(2), 17–26.

Iovannone, R., Dunlap, G., Huber, H., & Kincaid, D. (2003). Effective educational practices for students with autism spectrum disorders. *Focus on Autism and Other Developmental Disabilities, 18*(3), 150–165.

Kincaid, D. (1996). Person-centered planning. In L. K. Koegel, R. L. Koegel, & G. Dunlap (Eds.), *Positive behavioral support: Including people with difficult behavior in the community* (pp. 439–465). Baltimore: Brookes Publishing Co.

National Research Council. (2001). *Educating children with autism.* Washington, DC: National Academy Press.

O'Neill, R. E., Horner, R. H., Albin, R. W., Sprague, J. R., Storey, K., & Newton, J. S. (1997). *Functional assessment and program development for problem behavior: A practical handbook* (2nd ed.). Pacific Grove, CA: Brooks Cole Publishing Company.

FURTHER INFORMATION

Carr, E. G., Horner, R. H., Turnbull, A. P., Marquis, J., Magito-McLaughlin, D., McAtee, M. L., et al. (1999). *Positive behavior support for people with developmental disabilities: A research synthesis.* Washington, DC: American Association on Mental Retardation.

Koegel, L. K., Koegel, R. L., & Dunlap, G. (Eds.). (1996). *Positive behavioral support: Including people with difficult behavior in the community.* Baltimore: Brookes Publishing Co.

ROSE IOVANNONE

## POSITRON EMISSION TOMOGRAPHY (PET)

Positron Emission Tomography (PET) is an imaging technique that utilizes tiny amounts of injected, radio-labeled compounds. The photon emissions are then recorded like x-rays in a **CAT scan**. The accumulation of these compounds in certain areas of the body may show glucose use, blood flow, oxygen, or dopamine transport depending on the type of compound injected.

BRUCE BASSITY

## POSTSECONDARY EDUCATION

Postsecondary education occurs after graduation from high school. Postsecondary education can be provided in a variety of settings: continuing education, vocational technical school training, community college education, technical college education, and traditional four-year university training. Placement in one of these settings is determined based on eligibility and meeting the policy requirements of the institution to which the individual applies.

Individuals with disabilities who have applied to and been accepted by an institution may be eligible for reasonable **accommodations** in the educational setting. The individual will need to seek out the support services office to determine eligibility and the type of reasonable accommodations for which the student may be eligible. It is important for individuals with disabilities and their parents to understand that the accommodations and modifications received in high school will not automatically transfer to reasonable accommodations in the postsecondary setting. Therefore, the student needs to self-disclose his or her disability if the student wants assistance in the educational setting. The student will also need to be reassessed to determine what accommodations for the disability will be reasonable in the postsecondary setting.

*See also* Americans with Disabilities Act; Section 504 of the Rehabilitation Act of 1973; self-advocacy; self-determination.

BETH CLAVENNA-DEANE

## POSTTRAUMATIC STRESS DISORDER (PTSD)

According to the ***Diagnostic and Statistical Manual of Mental Disorders*** (DSM-IV-TR; APA, 2000), posttraumatic stress disorder typically develops following exposure to an extreme traumatic event that involved actual or threatened death or serious injury or a threat to the physical integrity of self or others. The reaction is extreme fear, helplessness, or horror; in children it may be expressed by disorganized or agitated behavior.

## SYMPTOMS

### The Traumatic Event Is Reexperienced

The person has repeated painful memories, dreams, or flashbacks in which the event seems to be recurring. Sometimes the patient experiences bodily reactions to stimuli or situations that resemble the traumatic event. Children may engage in repetitive play in which they reflect the themes or elements of the trauma.

### Constant Avoidance of Stimuli Related with the Trauma and Emotional Numbing

Efforts to avoid feelings, thoughts, activities, places, or people associated with the trauma are constant with an inability to recall important aspects of the event. Some patients demonstrate a detachment from others; others express lack of interest or participation in activities that they previously enjoyed and a feeling of no future.

### Persistent Symptoms of Increased Arousal That Were Not Present before the Trauma

The person can experience persistent symptoms of anxiety, difficulty falling asleep or staying asleep, and nightmares. Some persons report difficulty concentrating and being in a constant state of vigilance. Also irritability and outburst of anger and exaggerated startle response can occur.

## DURATION AND COURSE OF THE SYMPTOMS

This disorder causes clinically significant distress or impairment in social, occupational, and other important areas of functioning. Symptoms are classified as *acute*, if the length is less than 3 months, *chronic*, if the symptoms last 3 months or longer, and *with delayed onset*, if at least 6 months have passed between the traumatic event and the onset of symptoms.

Posttraumatic stress disorder can occur at any age and symptoms usually begin within the first 3 months after the traumatic event. The disorder can develop in any person without predisposing conditions, especially if the stressor was particularly extreme; however, there is evidence of a heritable susceptibility to the transmission of the disorder.

## REFERENCE

American Psychiatric Association. (2000). *Diagnostic and statistical manual of mental disorders* (4th ed., text rev.). Washington, DC: Author.

## FURTHER INFORMATION

Breslau, N., Chilcoat, H. D., Kessler, R. C., Peterson, E. L., & Lucia, V. C. (1999). Vulnerability to assaultive violence: Further specification of the sex difference in post-traumatic stress disorder. *Psychological Medicine, 29,* 813–821.

Davison, J. R. T., Book, S. W., Colket, J. T., Tupler, L. A., Roth, S., David, D., et al. (1997). Assessment of a new self-rating scale for post-traumatic stress disorder. *Psychological Medicine, 27,* 153–160.

Yule, W. (1999). Posttraumatic stress disorder. *Archives of Disease in Childhood, 80,* 107–109.

SUSANA BERNAD-RIPOLL

## POWER CARD STRATEGY

Power Cards, created by Gagnon (2001), are a visual aid that uses the child's interests in teaching appropriate social interactions, routines, behavior expectations, and the meaning of language. Using a hero or special interest serves several purposes: easy to "buy into" idea, capitalizes on the relationship between the hero and the child, and has generalization built into the strategy. Moreover, Power Cards are a quick, portable, low cost, and nonthreatening motivator for children. To develop a Power Card, the teacher or parent writes a short scenario in first person (from the child's point of view) on a single sheet or booklet form, describing how the hero or special interests solves a problem.

In the first paragraph of this scenario, the hero attempts a solution to the problem and experiences success. The second paragraph encourages the student to try the new behavior, which is broken down in three to five steps. The Power Card is about the size of a business card, bookmark, or trading card, includes a small picture or special interest, and summarizes the problem-solving steps. This card is carried with the student to aid in generalization. For an example of a Power Card see Figure 16.

To use the Power Card in a school setting, follow these steps: identify the problem behavior and special interest, conduct a functional assessment, collect baseline data, write and introduce scenario/Power Card, take data, evaluate, modify if needed, and fade scenario/Power Card and let student help with the decision to continue use. The same steps can be taken when used at home.

When used appropriately, Power Cards address sensory needs to help students realize when sensory input is needed, *not* to help tolerate sensory needs. To use a Power Card, a child must understand spoken language at a sentence or paragraph level, must exhibit behaviors frequently, and must have a well-developed interest. The Power Card is not a punishment, so the presenter should have a good relationship with the student.

*See also* visual strategies.

**Figure 16  Power Card Example: Barbie and Her Markers**

Barbie and Her Markers

When Barbie finishes her school assignments, she loves to draw and color with markers. She has learned that it is important to take care of her markers so that they will last a long time. When she is getting ready to draw, Barbie puts the marker cap on the opposite end of the marker so she won't lose it. She is always careful to draw only on the paper so her desk and body stay clean. When she is finished with a marker, she carefully puts the cap back on. *Barbie wants every girl and boy to take good care of their markers. She has learned that it is important to have markers with caps so her favorite colors won't dry up.*

*Barbie wants you to remember these three things:*

*Put the cap on the end of your markers before you draw.*

*Be careful to only draw on the paper.*

*Put the cap back on the marker when you are finished.*

*Try your best to remember these three things so you can draw just like Barbie!*

## REFERENCE

Gagnon, E. (2001). *Power Cards: Using special interests to motivate children and youth with Asperger syndrome and autism.* Shawnee Mission, KS: Autism Asperger Publishing Company.

## FURTHER INFORMATION

Gagnon, E., Keeling, K., Myles, B. S., & Simpson, R. L. (2003). Using the Power Card strategy to teach sportsmanship skills to a child with autism. *Focus on Autism and Other Developmental Disabilities, 18*(2), 105–107.

JEANNE HOLVERSTOTT

## PRAGMATICS

Pragmatics involves the ability to use practical components of language to enhance the communicative message. Components of pragmatics are similar to the rules of nonverbal language, including the use of eye contact between communicative partners, the distance between speaker and listener, and gestures to enhance meaning and turn-taking and topic selection within a conversation. Pragmatics is often based on one's cultural experiences or background.

KATHERINE E. COOK

## PRAXIS

Praxis is the ability to plan, organize, and carry out a physical, motor action.
*See also* sensory integration.

KELLY M. PRESTIA

## PRECISION TEACHING

Precision teaching, an "instructional decision-making method" (Cooper, Heron, & Heward, 1987) under the realm of **applied behavior analysis** principles, is founded in several theories. First, those who use precision teaching believe that the best way to assure learning has occurred is to measure a difference in the rate of learning responses. Second, they believe that "learning most often occurs through proportional changes in behavior" (Cooper et al., 1987). Finally, future learning has a positive correlation with past performance gains or losses.

## REFERENCE

Cooper, J. O., Heron, T. E., & Heward, W. L. (1987). *Applied behavior analysis.* Upper Saddle River, NJ: Prentice Hall.

## FURTHER INFORMATION

Athabasca University Online Precision Teaching Training Module, http://psych.athabascau.ca/html/387/OpenModules/Lindsley.
The Standard Celeration Society: www.celeration.org.

TARA MIHOK

## PRESENT LEVEL OF EDUCATIONAL PERFORMANCE (PLEP)

The present level of educational performance (PLEP), also referred to as the present level, is an integral part of an **Individualized Education Program** (IEP) that shares current information about the student's functioning. The present level is the corner stone to which all areas of the IEP should connect by summarizing the basic information related to a student's needs in one place. All goals and short-term objectives written later in the IEP process must relate directly to a need in the present level (Nebraska Department of Education Special Populations Office, n.d.). The PLEP covers all areas of development such as academics, daily living skills, social issues, behavior concerns, sensory needs, communication concerns, mobility issues, and vocational training. It also includes strengths, weaknesses, and learning styles of the individual (Rebhorn, 2002).

There are a variety of ways that an IEP team can gain information regarding the PLEP of a student. These include evaluation information (in district and independently done), information shared by parents, regular education teacher reports, grades, examples of student work, special education teacher observations, information from therapists' data collection, and, as appropriate, the information shared directly by the student (Massanari, 2002). The more information available, the more useful the present level will be to the IEP team. All information used must be current.

There are specific items that should be included in a present level. Information regarding the impact of the child's disability and how it pertains to progress within the general education setting is an absolute necessity when it comes to planning an appropriate IEP. This also pertains to how the preschool-aged child is involved in preschool activities and how their participation is affected by their disability (Rebhorn, 2002). When addressing how the child's disability affects their participation in the general education curriculum, it is necessary to understand the requirements of the grade-level classroom. This would include what the student's typical peers are required to learn and in what ways they are required to do so. The concerns related to the individual needs can be compared to the expectation of general education curriculum (Massanari, 2002).

A student's strengths should be directly addressed in the PLEP. These strengths can include academic skills, social skills, communication skills, or any other area the child shows as a strength (Rebhorn, 2002) or a relative strength. Strong abilities are important because they give the team a baseline of what a child can do well (LD Online, n.d.). These aptitudes are the foundations of instructional programming for individuals. By building on strengths through the creation of goals and objects based on abilities, success can be gained.

Parental concerns should be placed directly within the present level (3rd Cycle Special Education Special Education Self-Assessment [SEMSA] Training, 2004). These concerns may relate to home, school, or long-term issues. Concerns may relate to academics, social skills, or behavior issues that are individual to their child. If appropriate, later items within the IEP may address these concerns through a goal, objective, or behavior intervention plan if necessary.

The PLEP should contain information related to the most recent evaluations. This would include initial testing as well as 3-year reevaluation information. Specific test names and scores may be noted if appropriate. Information for an independent evaluation may also be included (Rebhorn, 2002). However, it is not necessary to list every test and score given. Often a statement of the child meeting the criteria for a specific diagnosis is included.

Changes in the student's functioning since the last IEP should be included in the present level of educational performance. This may include: met IEP goals and objectives, a change in placement, a change in school or living arrangement, or a change in health. Any change that affects the child and is relevant to education may be included.

State and district-wide **assessments** should be addressed within the present level. This includes what assessments will be taken and modifications that will be used if necessary. A statement of exemption from certain tests may also be included. Scores received on state and district testing should be summarized and explained clearly in relation to the strengths and weaknesses of the student (3rd Cycle SEMSA Training, 2004).

If a student is of an age to receive transition services, the present level should also contain information about employment and independent living issues and other final outcomes. Specific considerations should include academic and occupational skills the student will require, social and communication skills for success in a social setting, and personal management skills for independent living (LD Online, n.d.).

Within the present level, there are items that should not be included. These include statements of when, where, or how services will be provided. This information cannot be determined until goals are set (LD Online, n.d.). These items will be acknowledged after the IEP goals and objectives are written in a later part of the IEP.

The PLEP is an integral part of the IEP. It is the basis for goals and short-term objectives, modifications, behavior intervention plans, related services, and finally placement. It is imperative that the PLEP be measurable, include baseline data, include strengths and concerns, and include both academic and nonacademic information (WI Family Assistance Center for Education, Training, and Support, n.d.). The present level should be written in such a way that it would explain the needs of an individual child even to someone that did not know the child personally.

## References

LD Online. (1999). *IEP: The process*. Retrieved December 7, 2006, from www.ldonline.org/article/6277.

Massanari, C. B. (2002). *Connecting the IEP to the general curriculum: A talking paper*. Des Moines, IA: Mountain Plains Regional Resource Center.

Nebraska Department of Education Special Populations Office. (n.d.). *Present level of educational performance (PLEP)*. Retrieved June 6, 2005, from www.nde.state.ne.us/SPED/iepproj/develop/pre.html.

Rebhorn, T. (2002). *Developing your child's IEP: A parent's guide*. Washington, DC: National Information Center for Children and Youth with Disabilities.

Tennessee State Department of Education, Nashville. Division of Special Education. (2001). *Individualized Education Program (IEP)*. Nashville: Author.

3rd Cycle Special Education Special Education Self-Assessment (SEMSA) Training. (2004). *Special Education Compliance MoDESE*. Retrieved June 8, 2005, from http://dese.mo.gov/divspeced/Compliance/MSIP_Monitoring/3rdCycleSpecEd_FY06_files/slide0028.htm.

WI Family Assistance Center for Education, Training, and Support. (n.d.). *The IEP process & product*. Retrieved June 9, 2005, from www.wifacets.org/learning/IEPProc&Prod.ppt.

## Further Information

Gibb, G. S., & Dyches, T. T. (2000). *Guide to writing quality individualized education programs: What's best for students with disabilities?* Needham Heights, MA: Allyn & Bacon.

Tillmann, J. D., & Ford, L. (2001). *Analysis of transition services of individualized education programs for high school students with special needs*. Eric Document Reproduction Service ED 456608.

Trainor, A. A., Patton, J. R., & Clark, G. M. (2006). *Case studies in assessment for transition planning*. Austin, TX: Pro-Ed.

VALERIE JANKE REXIN

## PRESYMBOLIC THOUGHT

Presymbolic thought is the developmental and emotional stage, generally present between 8 and 24 months, that precedes **symbolic thought**. Presymbolic thought is manifested through gestures, such as pointing; vocalizations, such as "ma-ma" and "wa-wa"; reciprocity, the back and forth behavior communicated between an infant and caregiver; and affect signaling, such as smiling, frowning, or crying. Presymbolic thought is the formation of the sense of "self." A toddler's ability to see cause and effect, discover patterns, and learn to discriminate are all part of presymbolic thought processes.

### FURTHER INFORMATION

Greenspan, S., & Shanker, S. (2004). *The first idea, how symbols, language, and intelligence evolved from our primate ancestors to modern humans*. Cambridge, MA: Da Capo Press.

Quill, K. A. (2000). *Do-watch-listen-say: Social and communication intervention for children with autism*. Baltimore: Brookes Publishing Co.

ANN PILEWSKIE

## PREVALENCE

Prevalence is the rate of occurrence of a condition, disease, or characteristic within a specified population group. To obtain prevalence, one takes all the persons in a group, country, etc. and counts the number of persons with a specific condition at that time. The prevalence for autism has been and continues to be controversial. From the 1960s to the 1980s, the prevalence rate for autism was considered to be 4 or 5 per 10,000. In the 1990s, the rate rose to 10 per 10,000. Current prevalence rates for autism spectrum disorders are between 1 in 500 (20/10,000) and 1 in 166 children (60/10,000; Centers for Disease Control and Prevention, 2006; Chakrabarti & Fombonne, 2005; Fombonne, 2003; Department of Health and Human Services, n.d.).

### REFERENCES

Centers for Disease Control and Prevention. (2006, May 4). *Fact sheet: CDC autism research*. Retrieved May 16, 2006, from http://www.cdc.gov/od/oc/media/ transcripts/AutismResearch FactSheet.pdf.

Chakrabarti, S., & Fombonne, E. (2005). Pervasive developmental disorders in preschool children: Confirmation of high prevalence. *American Journal of Psychiatry, 162*, 1133–1141.

Department of Health and Human Services, Centers for Disease Control and Prevention. (n.d.) *How common are Autism Spectrum Disorders (ASD)?* Retrieved May 17, 2006, from http://www.cdc.gov/ncbddd/autism/asd_common.htm.

Fombonne, E. (2003). The prevalence of autism. *The Journal of the American Medical Association, 289*, 87–89. Retrieved May 16, 2006, from www.jama.com.

PAUL G. LaCAVA

## PRIMING

Priming is a strategy that helps prepare children for an upcoming activity or event with which they normally have difficulty. This intervention can be used with children with exceptionalities who engage in avoidance behaviors when materials or tasks are presented, require extensive exploration time before they can participate with a material, need help with social interactions, or have trouble transitioning in their environment (Wilde, Koegel, & Koegel, 1992). It can occur at home or in the classroom and is most effective if it is built into the child's routine. The actual priming session is short and concise and typically involves using the actual materials that will be used in the lesson or activity. Priming can occur the day before the activity, the morning of, or right before the activity (Zanolli, Daggett, & Adams, 1996). It can be performed by anyone that works with the child at home or at school. The purpose of priming is to introduce predictability into the information or activity, thereby reducing frustration and anxiety. It is not meant to teach the material, but only to familiarize the child with the material or the event in a nonthreatening and exploratory manner, increasing the probability of success.

The first step in priming is to determine who is going to prime and what activities are going to be involved. It is important that everyone working with the child (home and school) be involved in this process. This can be done at an **Individualized Education Program** meeting or conference. A classroom teacher, resource room teacher, paraprofessional, parent, or even a peer may prime the student.

Once the teacher, support staff, and parents have decided who will prime, it is important for open communication to exist between the teacher and family as to upcoming situations that may require priming. The following items must be addressed:

1. Who will prepare the priming materials?
2. Where and when can the primer access the priming materials?
3. How will the primer notify the teacher that the priming has occurred?
4. How will it be determined that priming is an effective strategy?
5. How will the problems be addressed?
6. How will documentation of priming session results be shared?

After communication and collaboration strategies have been implemented, the actual priming session can take place. Develop a routine by choosing a specific time and place to hold the priming sessions. Familiarize (not teach!) the student with the new material. During the priming session, be patient and encouraging and always reward the student for all attempts to participate in the session. Remember, this is supposed to be a positive experience! Students have more motivation to complete tasks if they feel they have some control over their environment. If possible, allow the student to be involved in deciding where the priming session will be held and what reinforcements will be used.

### EXAMPLE OF PRIMING

Bryan is having difficulty paying attention during circle time in kindergarten. He often disrupts other children particularly when the teacher is reading their daily story.

During a parent conference, Bryan's teacher and mother decided to use priming techniques at home to reduce his off-task behavior while in circle time.

Bryan's teacher gave his mother the book they were going to read the next day in circle time. Bryan's mother read the book to Bryan as part of his bedtime routine that evening. She asked him general questions along the way, but did not interrupt the story. By doing this, Bryan became familiar with the pictures and the text in a comfortable setting.

Because Bryan had heard the story the night before and knew what to expect from the story, he was able to focus on the book during circle time the following day. By familiarizing him with the book, Bryan attended to the story without disrupting the teacher or his peers.

This example can be used at all grade levels for upcoming events and academic subjects.

Communication between the teacher and the priming implementer continues after the priming session. After each session the priming implementer should notify the teacher of the results of the priming activity. Documentation as to whether the priming session had an impact on the student's behavior is necessary to determine if the intervention is effective.

*See also* accommodation.

### REFERENCES

Wilde, L. D., Koegel, L. K., & Koegel, R. L. (1992). *Increasing success in school through priming: A training manual.* Santa Barbara: University of California.

Zanolli, K., Daggett, J., & Adams, R. (1996). Teaching preschool age autistic children to make spontaneous initiations to peers using priming. *Journal of Autism and Developmental Disorders, 26*(4), 407–422.

### FURTHER INFORMATION

Bainbridge, N., & Myles, B. S. (1999). The use of priming to introduce toilet training to a child with autism. *Focus on Autism and Other Developmental Disabilities, 14*(2), 106–109.

Koegel, L. K., Koegel, R. L., Frea, W., & Hopkins, I. G. (2003). Priming as a method of coordinating educational services for students with autism. *Language, Speech, and Hearing Services in Schools, 34*(3), 28–35.

Moore, S. T. (2002). *Asperger syndrome and the elementary school experience: Practical solutions for academic and social difficulties.* Shawnee Mission, KS: Autism Asperger Publishing Company.

Roy, D., & Mukherjee, N. (2005). Towards situated speech understanding: Visual context priming of language models. *Computer Speech and Language, 19*(2), 227–248.

Schreibman, L., Whalen, C., & Stahmer, A. (2000). The use of video priming to reduce disruptive transition behavior in children with autism. *Journal of Positive Behavior Interventions, 2*(1), 3–11.

CYNTHIA K. VAN HORN AND KARLA DENNIS

## PROBE

Probes are assessments of small samples of behavior or skills under natural conditions, without teacher assistance or reinforcement. A probe evaluates how well a child learned a target skill. Some educators probe a student's performance on a skill prior to each instructional sitting. The results are then used to guide instruction.

*See also* assessment; reinforcer; single-subject design.

FURTHER INFORMATION

Salvia, J., & Ysseldyke, J. E. (2007). *Assessment: In special and inclusive education* (10th ed.). Boston: Houghton Mifflin Company.

Scheuermann, B., & Webber, J. (2002). *Autism: Teaching does make a difference.* Belmont, CA: Wadsworth/Thomson Learning.

Westling, D. L., & Fox, L. (2004). *Teaching students with severe disabilities* (3rd ed.). Upper Saddle River, NJ: Prentice Hall.

THERESA L. EARLES-VOLLRATH

## PROCEDURAL SAFEGUARDS

Procedural safeguards are the protections that federal law, the **Individuals with Disabilities Education Improvement Act** of 2004 (IDEA), affords to all students and their caregivers as they navigate the educational system. Some of the procedural safeguards include the right to inspect records, receive prior written notice before meetings, participate in meetings, register complaints, and obtain an outside independent evaluation.

REFERENCE

Individuals with Disabilities Education Improvement Act of 2004. Public Law No. 109-446, § 20 U.S.C. (2004).

FURTHER INFORMATION

Wright, P. W. D. (2004). *The individuals with disabilities education improvement act of 2004: Overview, explanation, and comparison, IDEA 2004 v. IDEA 97.* Retrieved May 26, 2006, from http://www.wrightslaw.com.

PAUL G. LACAVA

## PROMPT DEPENDENCE

Prompt dependence is an individual's reliance on prompts rather than attempting independence. This most often occurs when prompts have been overused (highly invasive prompts being used when less invasive ones are appropriate) or not faded quickly enough as the individual becomes capable of independent success. For example, when learning writing, a student may hold a pencil but not attempt to write, instead waiting for an adult to do the writing through prompts. Allowing a student to remain dependent on prompts in several areas of functioning can also lead to learned helplessness. Over time, the student may begin to believe he or she is not capable of completing a task independently.

*See also* graduated guidance; guided compliance; prompt hierarchy; prompting.

KATIE BASSITY

## PROMPT HIERARCHY

A prompt hierarchy is a series of supports provided to help a learner perform new skills and behaviors. The prompts are arranged by the level of support they provide. From least to most supportive, these prompts generally include natural environmental stimuli, gesturing, verbal prompting, modeling, and physical assistance. A decreasing prompt technique initially provides a prompt that ensures a correct response and systematically fades the prompt down the hierarchy until the learner achieves independence. For example, in teaching a child to touch his head when instructed, the teacher will first give the instruction, "Touch your head," paired with moving the child's hand to touch his head. Then the teacher will repeat the instruction while touching his elbow and moving the hand up to his head. Following this, the teacher will repeat the instruction while modeling the correct response or pointing to the child's head. Finally, after some repetition and this prompt fading, the child should be able to touch his head when given the verbal instruction.

In contrast, an increasing prompt technique allows the learner to first attempt the behavior and increases the level of prompt as needed until the learner successfully performs the behavior. In least-to-most prompting, the child is given the chance to increase his or her spontaneous responses for skills already mastered. If the child does not respond spontaneously, then the teacher would prompt from the least intrusive prompt to the most intrusive prompt to reach a correct response from the child (Anderson, Taras, & Cannon, 1996).

*See also* graduated guidance; guided compliance; prompt dependence; prompting.

**REFERENCES**
Anderson, S. R., Taras, M., & Cannon, B. O. (1996). Teaching new skills to young children with autism. In C. Maurice, G. Green, & S. L. Luce (Eds.), *Behavioral intervention for young children with autism* (pp.181–194). Austin, TX: Pro-Ed.

TARA MIHOK AND ANDREA HOPF

## PROMPTING

Prompting is any physical, verbal, or gestural assistance given to an individual to aid in the completion of or successful response to a given task. Prompts are generally used in the initial teaching stages of a new task or behavior. Within each type of prompting (physical, verbal, or gestural) there are several different levels of prompts. For example, physical prompts range from highly intrusive (such as **hand-over-hand assistance**) to least intrusive (such as placing a correct response closer to the student or a light touch to the body part needed for a successful response). It is preferable to use the least intrusive prompt necessary for the individual to succeed. For example, the intrusive hand-over-hand prompt would only be used if the individual could not succeed supported by a less invasive prompt. In addition, it is important to fade prompts as quickly as possible to allow the student to complete as much of the task independently as possible. It is important to use the form of prompting, which can most easily be faded, while ensuring the student's success. As always, it is also important to maintain consistency, particularly across individuals working on the same skills.

*See also* graduated guidance; guided compliance; no-no prompt procedure; prompt dependence.

KATIE BASSITY

## PRONOUN ERRORS

A common speech characteristic for individuals with autism is pronoun error or pronoun reversal. This is when an individual substitutes various pronouns such as saying "You" when "I" should be used. An early myth of autism was that pronoun difficulties were the child's misunderstanding of their own identity. Research has clearly shown that this is not the case, as pronoun errors are common in typical child development. However, most children develop more sophisticated language over time while those with autism may not. Children with autism may exhibit pronoun errors due to their echolalic use of language. That is, if they hear someone say, "Do you want ice cream?" they may repeat back "you want ice cream." Pronoun errors may also be due to confusion over when to use the correct tenses.

*See also* echolalia: immediate, delayed, mitigated.

**FURTHER INFORMATION**
Frith, U. (1989). *Autism: Explaining the enigma.* Oxford, UK: Blackwell Publishers.

PAUL G. LACAVA

## PROPRIOCEPTION

Muscle, joint, and tendon movements activate the receptors of the proprioceptive system, making carrying multiple objects down a packed hallway possible by providing information about the location and movement of a body part. For some individuals with autism spectrum disorder, these movements are not automatic, resulting in poor posture, incoordination, and chronic fatigue accompanying physical activity.

*See also* sensory integration; vestibular.

KELLY M. PRESTIA

## PROSODY

Prosody is an overall term used to describe the rhythm, intonation, and stress during speech production—that is, the importance of how something is said as opposed to the content of the speech. Both are essential to understanding and communicating language, emotion, intent, and so on. Some of the difficulties facing those with autism spectrum disorders (ASD) include producing understandable tone of voice, pitch, voice volume, pauses between syllables and words, speech rate, and so forth. Although not a characteristic of all, many with ASD have prosodic challenges that may or may not be changed over time. This communication challenge with both expressing and understanding prosody may contribute to social and relationship difficulties.

**FURTHER INFORMATION**
Gerken, L., & McGregor, K. (1998). An overview of prosody and its role in normal and disordered child language. *American Journal of Speech-Language Pathology, 7,* 38–48.
Prosody and Autism Spectrum Disorders. (n.d.). Retrieved July 21, 2006, from http://www.qmuc.ac.uk/ssrc/prosodyinASD/.
Shriberg, L. D., Paul, R., McSweeny, J. L., Klin, A., Cohen, D. J., & Volkmar, F. R. (2001). Speech and prosody characteristics of adolescents and adults with high-functioning autism and Asperger syndrome. *Journal of Speech, Language, and Hearing Research, 44,* 1097–1115.

PAUL G. LACAVA

## PROTO-DECLARATIVE

Proto-declarative pointing is when a baby or toddler uses their index finger/hand to point to an object to indicate that they have an interest in something and that they want another person to share in their attention. The key to this joint attention behavior is that the baby/toddler is indicating communicative intent with another person. Proto-declarative pointing is a behavior that typically developing youngsters begin to use around 14 months of age and is often delayed or absent in toddlers with autism. The absence of three behaviors (proto-declarative pointing, gaze response, and pretend-play) in toddlers at 18 months of age is often highly predictive of a future autism diagnosis.

*See also* autistic disorder; theory of mind.

**FURTHER INFORMATION**

Baird, G., Charman, T., Baron-Cohen, S., Cox, A., Swettenham, J., Wheelwright, S., et al. (2000). A screening instrument for autism at 18 months of age: A 6-year follow-up study. *Journal of the American Academy of Child and Adolescent Psychiatry, 39,* 694–702.

Baron-Cohen, S. (1995). *Mindblindness: An essay on autism and theory of mind.* Cambridge, MA: MIT Press.

Frith, U. (1989). *Autism: Explaining the enigma.* Oxford, UK: Blackwell Publishers.

Gerrans, P. (1998). The norms of cognitive development. *Mind and Language, 13,* 56–75.

PAUL G. LaCAVA

## PROTO-IMPERATIVE

Proto-imperative pointing is when an infant attempts to obtain something by using their index finger/hand to point to an object while verbalizing and alternating looking at their parent/caregiver. This behavior often begins around 1 year of age in typically developing youngsters. The child points to an object that they want and then looks to another person to indicate that they want it. The child is indicating what they want by verbalizing, pointing, and alternating looking at the adult. This behavior is developmentally part of joint attention behaviors, and toddlers with autism typically use this behavior but sometimes without eye contact or by pushing/taking the adult to the object they want.

**FURTHER INFORMATION**

American Academy of Pediatrics, Committee on Children with Disabilities. (2001). Technical report: The pediatrician's role in the diagnosis and management of autistic spectrum disorder in children [Electronic version]. *Pediatrics, 107.*

Baird, G., Charman, T., Baron-Cohen, S., Cox, A., Swettenham, J., Wheelwright, S., et al. (2000). A screening instrument for autism at 18 months of age: A 6-year follow-up study. *Journal of the American Academy of Child and Adolescent Psychiatry, 39,* 694–702.

Gerrans, P. (1998). The norms of cognitive development. *Mind and Language, 13,* 56–75.

PAUL G. LaCAVA

## PROTOTYPE FORMATION

Prototype formation involves the integration of information and the **generalization** of previously learned concepts to new situations. To assess prototype formation, utilize learning tasks that can be solved using a rule-based approach and a second set of tasks in which rules did not govern category membership (prototype tasks). Individuals with autism spectrum disorders have difficulty categorizing new information by forming prototypes and, instead, tend to rely on a rule-based approach to learning.

JEANNE HOLVERSTOTT

## PSYCHIATRIST

A psychiatrist is a medical doctor who specializes in the diagnosis, treatment, and prevention of mental and emotional disorders. Psychiatrists can diagnose individuals with an autism spectrum disorder and can prescribe medication.

STEVE CHAMBERLAIN

## PSYCHOACTIVE MEDICATIONS. *See* Antipsychotic Medications

## PSYCHOBIOLOGY

Psychobiology refers to the scientific study of the biological bases of behavior and mental states. Psychobiology and neuroscience both study the central nervous system, using techniques such as **functional magnetic resonance imaging** (fMRI), making it difficult to establish if the two are branches or one in the same study. As such, the terms are often used interchangeably. Psychobiology has been criticized because of its reductionist approach to the development of a disorder, which reduces human behavior to genetics; this position is contrasted by researchers who adopt a functionalist approach, which seeks to use psychological concepts to explain disorders of the mind.

*See also* genetic factors/heredity.

JEANNE HOLVERSTOTT

## PSYCHOEDUCATIONAL PROFILE–THIRD EDITION (PEP-3)

The Psychoeducational Profile–Third Edition (PEP-3; Schopler, Lansing, Reichler, & Marcus, 2005) is an evaluation that addresses the unique strengths and needs for those with autism and other related disabilities. The PEP-3 can be used to diagnose, chart developmental levels, and develop programming goals. The PEP-3 has a standardized, norm-referenced section that is administered to children and an informal report that is completed by the parent/caregiver. Some key features of the PEP-3 are its flexibility in administration and ability to be used with students who have severe cognitive and language impairments. The PEP-3 is appropriate for children ages 2 through $7\frac{1}{2}$ or for those who are older but functioning at lower levels.

*See also* norm-referenced assessment; standardization.

### REFERENCES

Schopler, E., Lansing, M. D., Reichler, R. J., & Marcus, L. M. (2005). *PEP-3: Psychoeducational Profile* (3rd ed.): *TEACCH Individualized Psychoeducational Assessment for Children with Autism Spectrum Disorders*. Austin, TX: Pro-Ed.

PAUL G. LACAVA

## PSYCHOLOGIST

A psychologist is a scientist who studies psychology, the study of human behavior and mental processes. Psychologists provide mental health care services, such as individual and family counseling, and contribute to the research base on human behavior/mental processing. Psychologists can diagnose autism and are major contributors to the autism research base.

STEVE CHAMBERLAIN

## PSYCHOMETRICS

Psychometrics is the field of study concerned with the design, administration, and interpretation of tests that measure the psychological characteristics (i.e., knowledge, skills, abilities, and personality traits) of an individual.

THERESA L. EARLES-VOLLRATH

## PSYCHOPHARMACOLOGY

Psychopharmacology broadly refers to the branch of science that studies the effect of drugs on brain chemistry and human behavior. It is also a term used to describe treatment with medications for those with emotional, psychiatric, or mental disorders. Psychopharmacology has been used for over 50 years to treat those with autism spectrum disorders (ASD). However, prescriptions for those with ASD have increased over the last decades. It has been estimated that 50 percent of those with an ASD are taking at least one prescription medication to help with the various symptoms. To date, little research has concluded the effectiveness of many psychotropic medications for use with children.

### FURTHER INFORMATION

Aman, M. G., Lam, K. S., & Collier-Crespin, A. (2003). Prevalence and patterns of use of psychoactive medicines among individuals with autism in the Autism Society of Ohio. *Journal of Autism and Developmental Disorders, 33*, 527–534.

Tsai, L. (2000). Children with autism spectrum disorder: Medicine today and in the new millennium. *Focus on Autism and Other Developmental Disabilities, 15*, 138–145.

Tsai, L. (2002). *Taking the mystery out of medications in autism/Asperger syndromes: A guide for parents and non-medical professionals*. Arlington, TX: Future Horizons.

PAUL G. LaCAVA

## PSYCHOSOCIAL

Psychosocial refers to psychological development pertaining to relationships with others and the adjustments necessary to navigate social situations. Psychosocial treatments involve a licensed **psychiatrist**, **psychologist**, social worker, or counselor, with the therapist and psychiatrist sometimes working together as the psychiatrist prescribes medications and the therapist monitors the individual's progress.

JEANNE HOLVERSTOTT

## PUNISHMENT

Punishment is an aversive **stimulus** contingent on a behavior that decreases the likelihood that the behavior will occur in the future (Azrin & Holz, 1966). Positive punishment consists of applying an aversive stimulus. Examples of positive punishment include giving a child detention for talking in class or spanking a child for violent behavior. Negative punishment consists of removing a positive **reinforcer**. Examples of negative punishment include grounding a teenager for breaking curfew or taking away a video game system for poor grades. **Response cost** is a form of negative punishment (Alberto & Troutman, 1999). Contrary to popular use of the term, punishment does not have to be aversive to the person to whom it is being applied. The consequence is punishing simply because the frequency of the behavior will be lessened in the future (Cooper, Heron, & Heward, 1996).

*See also* applied behavior analysis.

## REFERENCES

Alberto, P. A., & Troutman, A. C. (1999). *Applied behavior analysis for teachers*. Upper Saddle River, NJ: Merrill.

Azrin, N. H., & Holz, W. C. (1966). Punishment. In W. K. Honig (Ed.), *Operant behavior: Areas of research and application* (pp. 380–447). New York: Appleton-Century-Crofts.

Cooper, J. O., Heron, T. E., & Heward, W. L. (1987). *Applied behavior analysis*. Upper Saddle River, NJ: Prentice Hall.

TARA MIHOK AND JESSICA KATE PETERS

# R

## RDI PROGRAM

The RDI Program educates and guides parents and teachers of children with autism spectrum disorders (ASD) and others who interact and work with the child. It is a "mission oriented" program. This means that it is not wedded to any specific techniques. The mission of the RDI Program is to develop the most effective methods, whatever they might be, to remediate those specific deficits that impede people on the autism spectrum from productive employment, independent living, marriage, and intimate social relationships. Current treatment and intervention services do not address the abilities that ASD people need to attain a good quality of life. RDI strives to develop "real-world" dynamic abilities that will translate into future success.

Remediation is a gradual, systematic process of correcting a deficit, to the point where it no longer constitutes an obstacle to reaching one's potential. Remediation is a developmental process. It involves addressing early areas that, due to the neurological disorder, were never mastered. We search for the period in development where the child "hit a wall" and was not able to progress further. We go back and build competence from that point.

Ongoing program evolution is critical if we are to help increasing numbers of individuals on the autism spectrum to attain a quality of life. The latest findings from developmental psychology and autism research are carefully "engineered" to provide clinical methods that improve effectiveness. Continual program evaluation critically determines which program components are effective and highlights areas of necessary modification.

RDI empowers families and those who are primarily involved in caring for and educating the child. The bulk of resources are invested in preparing parents and teachers to act as participant guides, creating daily opportunities for the child to respond in more flexible, thoughtful ways to novel, challenging, and increasingly unpredictable settings and problems. Both fathers and mothers are essential participants in the treatment process.

Preliminary research indicates that the RDI Program is a powerful, effective means for increasing children's capacity and motivation for experience sharing, as well as their flexibility and adaptation. Parents engaged in RDI overwhelmingly report significant improvement in the quality of life of the ASD child, their own quality of life, as well as the lives of their nonaffected children (Gutstein, 2005; Gutstein, in press; Gutstein, Burgess, & Montfort, in press; Gutstein, Gutstein, & Baird, 2006). While family is central to the RDI model, treatment success also depends upon the commitment of school staff and other professionals to implement essential principles of remediation.

Real-world competence emerges from children participating as active, but junior partners—"apprentices," who are carefully guided by parents and other adults. Guides have access to a comprehensive system of over 1,200 developmentally staged objectives, which they use to carefully provide increasingly complex problems and challenges. Guides help the child capture and stockpile critical memories that build an experiential repository of success in gradually more complex environments. Parents are taught to rethink their daily lifestyle, structuring activities throughout the day to provide safe, but challenging opportunities for discovery.

## WHAT IS THE RDI PROGRAM?

- Systematic, long-term remediation of specific deficits that define autism spectrum disorders and limit the quality of life of people on the autism spectrum
- Preparing parents and teachers to act as participant guides. Restoring the critical early guided-participation relationship damaged by ASD
- Creating numerous daily opportunities for the child to respond in more flexible, thoughtful ways
- Helping children capture and stockpile critical memories that build a repository of competence, in gradually more complex environments

Education and coaching is implemented through the following methods:

- Small-group, intensive parent education
- Customized, balanced remediation planning, emphasizing a biopsychosocial model
- Careful selection and evaluation of developmentally based objectives. Each objective has clear criteria for cognitive mastery
- Individualized consultation sessions with parents
- Regular video-taped review of samples of parent-child performance in the home
- School staff training and consultation

### SELECTING THE FOCUS OF REMEDIATION

Over 200 research studies have, over the past 15 years, attempted to determine what deficit areas are unique and universal to individuals on the autism spectrum. In performing a comprehensive analysis of these studies we came to some important conclusions:

1. Autism spectrum disorders cannot be defined by "discrete" skills, such as speech, social skills, academic skills, or behavioral compliance (Hobson, 2002; Klin, Jones, Schultz, & Volkmar, 2003; Mayes & Calhoun, 2001; McGovern & Sigman, 2005). Rather, they appear to be related to "continuous process" abilities (Fogel, 1993).
2. Standard forms of measuring intelligence do not predict the severity of the autism itself (Howlin, 2003; Howlin & Goode, 2000).
3. Research results overwhelmingly support the idea that ASDs involve a wide range of neurological vulnerabilities that lead to more homogeneous deficits in certain types of complex information processing, which then lead to difficulties in all aspects of life (Belmonte et al., 2004; Just, Cherkassky, Keller, & Minshew, 2004; Minshew, Johnson, & Luna, 2001; Minshew, Williams, & Goldstein, 2004; Minshew, Goldstein, & Siegel, 1997).

The deficits universally found in ASD appear to belong to what is termed *Dynamic Intelligence* (Day & Cordon, 1993; Grigorenko & Sternberg, 1998; Sternberg, Forsythe, Hedlund, & Horvath, 2000). The ability to maintain employment, friendship, marriage, and most aspects of daily life are dependent on dynamic abilities. The dynamic elements of settings provide us with opportunities for growth, discovery, integration, and collaboration. We go to hear someone lecture not because we want them to repeat what they have written in a book, but to hear something new. When we have a conversation, we certainly do not ask to, once again talk about what we spoke about last week. We choose friends and mates who will encourage us to develop and grow. We spend much of our lives choosing to enter situations of greater dynamic potential. You are probably more familiar with *static* intelligence, such as the abilities measured in IQ tests. Think of static intelligence as measuring what you know, while dynamic intelligence measures what you can do with what you know in the real world. The following chart outlines some critical distinctions between dynamic and static forms of intelligence:

**Dynamic**
Continuous processing
Regulating and adapting
Flexible problem-solving
Dynamic analysis
Episodic memory
Experience sharing
Self-evaluation and self-regulation
Simultaneous
Flexible and contextual content use

**Static**
Discrete processing
Performing
Absolute problem-solving
Static analysis
Rote-procedural memory
Instrumental communication
Behavioral compliance
Sequential
Content accumulation

Almost all human communication and interaction occurs in dynamic encounters. The term *dynamic* implies the continual introduction of new information as well as the ongoing transformation of current information based upon changed contexts and relationships (Gaussen, 2001; Granic & Hollenstein, 2003; Lewis, 2000).

The dynamic elements of settings provide us with opportunities for growth, discovery, integration, and collaboration. Dynamic encounters provide an enormous payoff, but require a good deal of effort and different types of abilities than static environments. Because dynamic environments require continual evaluation and adaptation, they are referred to as *regulatory*. In more static settings, success accrues from accumulating enough *right* answers and *correct* solutions and applying them in association with specific setting cues. In other words, if I pick the right response, formula, or solution and apply it in the way I was taught, I will be successful. In contrast, the application of any single response or formula is a guarantee of failure in dynamic settings. Instead of absolute thinking, they require *relative* or *regulatory* functioning.

Regulation involves making continual adjustments to maintain optimal states of functioning in dynamic, constantly evolving systems. Regulation requires ongoing monitoring of the system and detection of important changes. It also requires the ability to rapidly distinguish important (central) from unimportant (peripheral) changes in the system and to rapidly adapt actions to maintain functioning given system changes.

By the end of their second year, typical infants have gone a long way towards learning to manage the difficulties inherent in dynamic systems. The 12-month-old actually prefers dynamic encounters because he feels competent in managing the tension inherent in such challenges and has already learned that the "edge" of his competence is the most rewarding place to be (Sroufe, 1996). Children with ASDs leave the pathway of dynamic learning somewhere in the first two years of life and are thus deprived of further opportunities for dynamic learning.

### Domains of Dynamic Intelligence

In order to develop a systematic progression of objectives, from rudimentary to highly sophisticated cognitive abilities, we have separated the elements of dynamic intelligence into five "processes."

### Creative-Flexible Thinking

Creative thinking involves altering problem solutions and ways of perceiving a problem, based on ongoing monitoring of current effectiveness. Flexible problem-solving involves finding "work arounds" when running into unexpected problems, or lacking the typical resources to solve problems. This is a critical problem for people with ASD (Berger, Aerts, van Spaendonck, & Cools, 2003; Channon, Charman, Heap, Crawford, & Rios, 2001; Craig & Baron-Cohen, 1999; Emerich, Creaghead, Grether, Murray, & Grasha, 2003; Jarrold, 2003).

- Think of how often in a typical way problems arise that require flexibility?
- Consider how rare it is for you to feel completely certain about your decisions?
- Are the proper tools and resources always available when you need them? How do you manage?

### Dynamic Analysis

Environments present many potential ways we can organize, relate, and prioritize information. Dynamic analysis is the act of evaluating the adaptational significance of our environment on a moment-to-moment basis. It entails actively searching for opportunities for growth and goal attainment. We integrate the realities of environmental demands, constraints and resources, with personal interests. Dynamic analysis is only possible when we learn that there are multiple ways we can organize meaning from any particular event or setting. Research has confirmed problems in dynamic analysis as a core aspect of ASDs (Burack, 1994; Dawson et al., 2004; Goldstein, Johnson, & Minshew, 2001; Hoeksma, Kemner, Verbaten, & Van Engeland, 2004; Hughes & Russell, 1993; Landry & Bryson, 2004; Lopez & Leekam, 2003; Mann & Walker, 2003).

- How many times in a day do you employ "good enough" thinking?
- How do you know when a change is central or peripheral?
- How well would you function if you did not analyze contextual information?

## Episodic Memory

Episodic memory involves more than just remembering details of a past episode. It entails extracting something that is personally important, different, changed, or that stands out and has personal meaning to us. Without episodic memories, you do not have access to your personal past in a manner that allows you to project into the future. You do not develop the ability to anticipate and think in a hypothetical sense about what might happen in your future. You do not learn to dream, create goals, plans, and really tie the past in with the future. Over 20 research studies confirm that episodic memory deficits appear to be universal in ASD (Bowler, Gardiner, & Grice, 2000; Bowler, Gardiner, & Berthollier, 2004; Millward, Powell, Mewwer, & Jordan, 2000; Shalom, 2003).

- What would your life would be like if you could not mentally prepare yourself for potential future events?
- How would you motivate yourself to reach goals if you could not "preview" the feeling of success prior to reaching it?
- How successful would you be if you were unable to learn from your own mistakes?

## Experience Sharing

Human communication differs from all other species in that it offers the opportunity to share our subjective experiences of the world. The essence of all human communication entails sharing and integrating experiences, combining something from you with something from me with the hope that something unique and unexpected emerges. As we become proficient communicators we learn that we can fluidly share our internal and external experiences as well as linking our past, present, and future. Experience sharing requires ongoing "continuous process" monitoring and evaluation of mutual comprehension and interest. Researchers have noted a lack of experience-sharing communication in individuals on the spectrum, regardless of their cognitive or language abilities. In fact, the single best predictor of future language for young children on the autism spectrum is the degree to which they develop the earliest manifestations of experience sharing (Baron-Cohen, Baldwin, & Crowson, 1997; Berger, 2006; Bono, Daley, & Sigman, 2004; Camaioni, Perucchini, Muratori, Parrini, & Cesari, 2003; Downs & Smith, 2004; Geller, 1998; Gutstein, 2000; Gutstein & Whitney, 2002; Hobson, 1989; Hobson & Lee, 1998; Keen, 2003).

- What is the role of language in communication? Can you communicate without words? What happens to adults who have a stroke and lose their language? Are "non-verbal" ASD children really only "non-verbal" or are they also "non-communicative"?
- Imagine a conversation that did not include the desire to create bridges between minds. What is there to talk about?

## Self Awareness

Self awareness involves developing a coherent sense of self; a "me" that we perceive as unique and coherent, even as it continues to grow and develop. The self becomes the primary organizing principle for appraisal and evaluation. The lack of a self in autism proves devastating in terms of the problem-solving capability of individuals; as they are unable to develop memories of themselves as problem-solving agents, they are therefore unable to build up stores of remembered skills in such a way that they can reflect on them strategically. We develop our sense of self through contrast and comparison with others. ASD individuals appear to have striking deficits in self-development (Dawson & McKissick, 1984; Gomez & Baird, 2005; Hill & Russell, 2002; Klein, Chan, & Loftus, 1999; Lee, Hobson, & Chiat, 1994; Nair, 2004; Powell & Jordan, 1993; Russell & Hill, 2001; Toichi, Kamio, Okada, Sakihama, Youngstrom, et al., 2002).

## THE INTERSUBJECTIVE RELATIONSHIP

The Intersubjective Relationship (IR) is perceived by developmental psychologists as the essential lab for learning to function in dynamic systems—environments in which new information is continually introduced and where success requires ongoing monitoring of the meaning of information in a contextual manner (Tomasello, 1999; Trevarthen & Aitken, 2001). For information, ideas, and mental skills to move from the social-interactive plane to the internal-thinking plane, the adult and child must strive for a common approach to the situation. In the IR each participant in the dialogue strives to grasp the subjective perspective of the other, an effort that results in a "meeting of minds" in which the partner's thoughts make contact, connect, and coincide. In a sense, through participating in the IR, children are able to temporarily "appropriate" their parents' mental processes—their ways of analyzing, evaluating, and reacting to the changes in their world.

ASD children's early failure to develop intersubjectivity is the most documented deficit in the autism research (Bacon, Fein, Morris, Waterhouse, & Allen, 1998; Charman et al., 1997; Dawson, Hill, Spencer, Galpert, & Watson, 1990; Gipps, 2004; Mundy, 1995; Mundy, Kasari, & Sigman, 1992; Mundy & Sigman, 1989; Robertson, Tanguay, L'Ecuyer, Sims, & Waltrip, 1999; Trevarthen, Aitken, Papoudi, & Robarts, 1996). It has also been found by researchers to be the deficit that is most persistent and resistant to change over time (Sigman, 1998; Sigman & McGovern, 2005). A primary focus for RDI consultants is helping parents and their children restore the critical IR that is inherently damaged by ASD. Our hope is that through reengaging the IR, the child, through parental guidance, can begin to develop on the pathway of dynamic learning opportunities and can internalize the complex mental processes that are essential to attaining a quality of life.

## PARENTS LEARN TO BE COMPETENT GUIDES

Guided participation, a term associated with psychologist Barbara Rogoff, describes the way that adults teach children to become competent in real-world thinking and problem solving (Rogoff, 1990, 1991, 1993). When we study societies and cultures all over the world, it is very clear that the way in which children learn to function in dynamic systems is not through direct instruction. You have never taken a course in any of the areas of dynamic intelligence. Rather we learn through acting as an inexperienced apprentice with an adult guide who gradually introduces us to more and more complexity in the world. Our guides also gradually require us to become more of a partner in maintaining the regularity of the system.

The underlying "engine" of guided participation is intersubjectivity: a sharing of focus and purpose between children and their more skilled partners (Harding, Weissmann, Kromelow, & Stilson, 1997; Hodapp, Goldfield, & Boyatzis, 1984; Kaye, 1982;

Tronick & Gianino, 1986). By participating in thousands of carefully constructed encounters involving shared understanding and problem solving, children appropriate an increasingly advanced understanding of and skill in managing the intellectual problems of their community. The aim of The RDI Program is to restore the guided participation relationship that is universally lost due to the ASD child's neurological vulnerabilities.

Support and challenge have to be in balance for parent-child interactions to be optimal for the child's development. Parents are taught to combine support with setting of challenging action goals to assist the child to achieve beyond his or her current level of mastery. Parents learn to focus their support on those aspects of tasks that are just beyond the level of mastery currently attained by their children (one-step-ahead strategy). Such a strategy is optimal for maintaining a functional balance between challenging a child's developmental potential and balancing for its weaknesses.

As children gain in mastery, parents learn to transfer greater responsibility for problem-solving and regulatory monitoring to the child. The parent objective is not just to maximize the number of their child's successes by balancing for their weaknesses, but, additionally, to sustain a level of challenge that they deem to be most promoting their children's development of competence.

In summary, adults learn to encourage and advise their child to attain the level of performance just beyond their current mastery and avoid providing superfluous assistance or clues so as not to be overfacilitative to the child's performance. They confront the child with additional cognitive demands for attaining a new level of performance when lesser challenges have been mastered, and they gradually transfer the responsibility for problem-solving, regulating, evaluating, and managing progressively more complex real-world problems and settings.

## REFERENCES

Bacon, A., Fein, D., Morris, R., Waterhouse, L., & Allen, D. (1998). The responses of autistic children to the distress of others. *Journal of Autism and Developmental Disorders, 28,* 129–142.

Baron-Cohen, S., Baldwin, D., & Crowson, M. (1997). Do children with autism use the speaker's direction of gaze strategy to crack the code of language? *Child Development, 68,* 48–57.

Belmonte, M., Cook, E., Anderson, G., Rubenstein, J., Greenough, W., Beckel-Mitchener, A., et al. (2004). Autism as a disorder of neural information processing: Directions for research and targets for therapy. *Molecular Psychiatry, 9,* 646–663.

Berger, H., Aerts, F., van Spaendonck, K., & Cools, A. (2003). Central coherence and cognitive shifting in relation to social improvement in high-functioning young adults with autism. *Journal of Clinical & Experimental Neuropsychology, 25,* 502–511.

Berger, M. (2006). A model of preverbal social development and its application to social dysfunctions in autism. *Journal of Child Psychology and Psychiatry, 47,* 338–371.

Bono, M. Daley, T., & Sigman, M. (2004). Relations among joint attention, amount of intervention and language gain in autism. *Journal of Autism & Developmental Disorders, 34,* 495–505.

Bowler, D., Gardiner, J., & Berthollier, N. (2004). Source memory in adolescents and adults with Asperger's syndrome. *Journal of Autism & Developmental Disorders, 34,* 533–542.

Bowler, D., Gardiner, J., & Grice, S. (2000). Episodic memory and remembering in adults with Asperger's syndrome. *Journal of Autism and Developmental Disorders, 30,* 305–316.

Burack, J. (1994). Selective attention deficits in persons with autism: Preliminary evidence of an inefficient attentional lens. *Journal of Abnormal Psychology, 103,* 535–543.

Camaioni, L., Perucchini, P., Muratori, F., Parrini, B., & Cesari, A. (2003). The communicative use of pointing in autism: Developmental profile and factors related to change. *European Psychiatry, 18*, 6–12.

Channon, S., Charman, T., Heap, J., Crawford, S., & Rios, P. (2001). Real-life-type problem-solving in Asperger's syndrome. *Journal of Autism & Developmental Disorders, 31*, 461–469.

Charman, T., Swettenham, J., Baron-Cohen, S., Cox, A., Baird, G., & Drew, A. (1997). Infants with autism: An investigation of empathy, pretend play, joint attention, and imitation. *Developmental Psychology, 5*, 782–789.

Craig, J., & Baron-Cohen, S. (1999). Creativity and imagination in autism and Asperger syndrome. *Journal of Autism and Developmental Disorders, 29*, 319–326.

Dawson, G., Hill, D., Spencer, A., Galpert, L., & Watson, L. (1990). Affective exchanges between young autistic children and their mothers. *Journal of Abnormal Child Psychology, 18*, 335–345.

Dawson, G., & McKissick, F. (1984). Self recognition in autistic children. *Journal of Autism and Developmental Disorders, 14*, 383–394.

Dawson, G., Toth, K., Abbott, R., Osterling, J., Munson, J., Estes, A., et al. (2004). Early social attention impairments in autism: Social orienting, joint attention and attention to distress. *Developmental Psychology, 40*(2), 271–283.

Day, J., & Cordon, L. (1993). Static and dynamic measures of ability: An experimental comparison. *Journal of Educational Psychology, 85*, 75–82.

Downs, A., & Smith, T. (2004). Emotional understanding, cooperation, and social behavior in high-functioning children with autism. *Journal of Autism & Developmental Disorders, 34*, 625–635.

Emerich, D., Creaghead, N., Grether, S., Murray, D., & Grasha, C. (2003). The comprehension of humorous materials by adolescents with high-functioning autism and Asperger's syndrome. *Journal of Autism and Developmental Disorders, 33*(3), 253–257.

Fogel, A. (1993). *Developing through relationships: Origins of communication, self, and culture.* Chicago: University of Chicago Press.

Gaussen, T. (2001). Dynamic systems theory: Revolutionising developmental psychology. *Irish Journal of Psychology, 22*(3–4), 160–175.

Geller, E. (1998). An investigation of communication breakdowns and repairs in verbal autistic children. *British Journal of Developmental Disabilities, 87*, 71–85.

Gipps, R. (2004). Autism and intersubjectivity: Beyond cognitivism and the theory of mind. *Philosophy, Psychiatry, & Psychology, 11*, 195–198.

Goldstein, G., Johnson, C., & Minshew, N. (2001). Attentional processes in autism. *Journal of Autism & Developmental Disorders, 31*, 433–440.

Gomez, C., & Baird, S. (2005). Identifying early indicators for autism in self-regulation difficulties. *Focus on Autism & Other Developmental Disabilities, 20*, 106–116.

Granic, I., & Hollenstein, T. (2003). Dynamic systems methods for models of developmental psychopathology. *Development & Psychopathology. 15*, 641–669.

Grigorenko, L., & Sternberg, R. (1998). Dynamic Testing. *Psychological Bulletin, 124*, 75–111.

Gutstein, S. (2000). *Solving the Relationship Puzzle.* Arlington, TX: Future Horizons.

Gutstein, S. (2005). Relationship Development Intervention: Developing a treatment program to address the unique social and emotional deficits of autism spectrum disorders. *Autism Spectrum Quarterly*, (winter), 2005.

Gutstein, S. (in press). The effectiveness of Relationship Development Intervention to remediate experience-sharing deficits of autism-spectrum children. *Journal of Autism & Developmental Disorders.*

Gutstein, S., Burgess, A., & Montfort, K. (in press). Evaluation of the Relationship Development Intervention program. *Autism.*

Gutstein, S., Gutstein, H., & Baird, C. (Eds.). (2006). *My baby can dance: Stories of autism, Asperger's and success through the Relationship Development Intervention Program.* Houston, TX: Connections Center Publications.

Gutstein, S., & Whitney, T. (2002). The development of social competence in Asperger syndrome. *Focus on Autism, 17,* 161–171.

Harding, C. G., Weissmann, L., Kromelow, S., & Stilson, S. R. (1997). Shared minds: How mothers and infants co-construct early patterns of choice within intentional communication partnerships. *Infant Mental Health Journal, 18,* 24–39.

Hill, E., & Russell, J. (2002). Action memory and self-monitoring in children with autism: Self versus other. *Infant & Child Development, 11,* 159–170.

Hobson, P. (1989). On sharing experiences. *Development and Psychopathology, 1,* 197–203.

Hobson, P. (2002). *The cradle of thought: Exploring the origins of thinking.* London: Macmillan.

Hobson, R., & Lee, A. (1998). Hello and goodbye: A study of social engagement in autism. *Journal of Autism and Developmental Disorders, 28,* 1998.

Hodapp, R., Goldfield, E., & Boyatzis, C. (1984). The use and effectiveness of maternal scaffolding in mother-infant games. *Child Development, 55,* 772–781.

Hoeksma, M. Kemner, C., Verbaten, M., & Van Engeland, H. (2004). Processing capacity in children and adolescents with pervasive developmental disorders. *Journal of Autism and Developmental Disorders, 34,* 341–354.

Howlin, P. (2003). Outcome in high-functioning adults with autism with and without early language delays: Implications for the differentiation between autism and Asperger syndrome. *Journal of Autism & Developmental Disorders, 33,* 3–13.

Howlin, P., & Goode, S. (2000). Outcome in adult life for people with autism and Asperger's syndrome. *Autism, 4*(1), 63–83.

Hughes, C., & Russell, J. (1993). Autistic children's difficulty with mental disengagement from an object: Its implications for theories of autism. *Developmental Psychology, 29,* 498–510.

Jarrold, C. (2003). A review of research into pretend play in autism. *Autism, 7,* 379–390.

Just, M., Cherkassky, V., Keller, T., & Minshew, N. (2004). Cortical activation and synchronization during sentence comprehension in high-functioning autism: Evidence of underconnectivity. *Brain, 127,* 1811–1821.

Kaye, K. (1982). *The mental and social life of babies: How parents create persons.* Chicago: The Harvester Press.

Keen, D. (2003). Communicative repair strategies and problem behaviors of children with autism. *International Journal of Disability, Development & Education, 50*(1), 53–64.

Klein, S., Chan, R., & Loftus, J. (1999). Independence of episodic and semantic self-knowledge: The case from autism. *Social Cognition, 17,* 413–436.

Klin, A., Jones, W., Schultz, R., & Volkmar, F. (2003). The enactive mind, or from actions to cognition: Lessons from autism. *Philosophical Transactions of the Royal Society of London B, 358,* 345–360.

Landry, R., & Bryson, S. (2004). Impaired disengagement of attention in young children with autism. *Journal of Child Psychology & Psychiatry, 45,* 1115–1122.

Lee, A., Hobson, R., & Chiat, S. (1994). I, you, me and autism: An experimental study. *Journal of Autism and Developmental Disorders, 24,* 155–176.

Lewis, M. (2000). The promise of dynamic systems approaches for an integrated account of human development. *Child Development, 71,* 36–43.

Lopez, B., & Leekam, S. R. (2003). Do children with autism fail to process information in context? *Journal of Child Psychology & Psychiatry, 44,* 285–300.

Mann, T. A., & Walker, P. (2003). Autism and a deficit in broadening the spread of visual attention. *Journal of Child Psychology & Psychiatry, 44,* 272–284.

Mayes, S., & Calhoun, S. (2001). Non-significance of early speech delay in children with autism and normal intelligence and implications for DSM-IV Asperger's disorder. *Autism, 5*(1), 81–94.

McGovern, C., & Sigman, M. (2005). Continuity and change from early childhood to adolescence in autism. *Journal of Child Psychology & Psychiatry, 46,* 401–408.

Millward, C., Powell, S., Messer, D., & Jordan, R. (2000). Recall for self and other in autism: Children's memory for events experienced by themselves and others. *Journal of Autism & Developmental Disorders, 30,* 15–27.

Minshew, N., Goldstein, G., & Siegel, D. (1997). Neuropsychologic functioning in autism: Profile of a complex information processing disorder. *Journal of the International Neuropsychological Society, 3,* 303–316.

Minshew, N., Johnson, C., & Luna, B. (2001). The cognitive and neural basis of autism: A disorder of complex information processing and dysfunction of neocortical systems. In L. Glidden (Ed.), *International review of research in mental retardation: Autism* (Vol. 23; pp. 111–138). San Diego, CA: Academic Press.

Minshew, N., Williams, D., & Goldstein, G. (2004). *A further characterization of complex cognitive abilities in high functioning autism.* Paper presented at the International Meeting for Autism Research, Sacramento, CA, 2004.

Mundy, P. (1995). Joint attention and social-emotional approach behavior in children with autism. *Development and Psychopathology, 7,* 63–82.

Mundy, P., Kasari, C., & Sigman, M. (1992). Nonverbal communication, affective sharing and intersubjectivity. *Infant Behavioral Development, 15,* 377–381.

Mundy, P., & Sigman, M. (1989). The theoretical implications of joint-attention deficits in autism. *Development and Psychopathologies, 1*(3), 173–183.

Nair, J. (2004). Knowing me, knowing you: Self-awareness in Asperger's and autism. In B. Beitman & J. Nair (Eds.), *Self-awareness deficits in psychiatric patients: Neurobiology, assessment, and treatment.* New York: W. W. Norton & Co.

Powell, S., & Jordan, R. (1993). Being subjective about autistic thinking and learning to learn. *Educational Psychology, 13,* 359–370.

Robertson, J., Tanguay, P., L'Ecuyer, S., Sims, A., & Waltrip, C. (1999). Domains of social communication handicap in autism spectrum disorder. *Journal of the American Academy of Child & Adolescent Psychiatry, 38*(6), 738–745.

Rogoff, B. (1990). *Apprenticeship in learning: Cognitive development in social context.* Oxford: Oxford University Press.

Rogoff, B. (1991). Social interaction as apprenticeship in thinking: Guided participation in spatial planning. In L. Resnick & J. Levine (Eds.), *Perspectives on socially shared cognition.* Washington, DC: American Psychological Association.

Rogoff, B. (1993). Children's guided participation and participatory appropriation in sociocultural activity. In R. Wozniak & K. Fischer (Eds.), *Development in context: Acting and thinking in specific environments.* Hillsdale, NJ: Lawrence Erlbaum Associates.

Russell, J., & Hill, E. (2001). Action-monitoring and intention reporting in children with autism. *Journal of Child Psychology & Psychiatry & Allied Disciplines, 42,* 317–328.

Shalom, D. (2003). Memory in autism: Review and synthesis. *Cortex, 39,* 1129–1138.

Sigman, M. (1998). Change and continuity in the development of children with autism. *Journal of Child Psychology and Psychiatry, 39,* 817–827.

Sigman, M., & McGovern, C. (2005). Improvement in cognitive and language skills from preschool to adolescence in autism. *Journal of Autism & Developmental Disorders, 35,* 15–23.

Sroufe, A. (1996). *Emotional development: The organization of emotional life in the early years.* Cambridge: Cambridge University Press.

Sternberg, R. J, Forsythe, G. B., Hedlund, J., & Horvath, J. (2000). *Practical intelligence in everyday life.* New York: Cambridge University Press.

Toichi, M., Kamio, Y., Okada, T., Sakihama, M., Youngstrom, E. A., Findling, R. L., et al. (2002). A lack of self-consciousness in autism. *American Journal of Psychiatry, 159,* 1422–1424.

Tomasello, M. (1999). *The cultural origins of human cognition.* Cambridge: Harvard University Press.

Trevarthen, C., & Aitken, K. J. (2001). Infant intersubjectivity: Research, theory, and clinical applications. *Journal of Child Psychology and Psychiatry, 42,* 3–48.

Trevarthen, C., Aitken, K., Papoudi, D., & Robarts, J. (1996). Where development of the communicating mind goes astray. *Children with autism.* London: Jessica Kingsley Publishers, Ltd.

Tronick, E., & Gianino, A. (1986). Interactive mismatch and repair: Challenges to the coping infant. *Zero to Three, 6,* 1–6.

STEVE GUTSTEIN

# REACTIVE ATTACHMENT DISORDER OF INFANCY OR EARLY CHILDHOOD

The *Diagnostic and Statistical Manual of Mental Disorders* (DSM-IV-TR; APA, 2000) defines two types of reactive attachment disorder: disinhibited type and inhibited type. In the former (disinhibited), the child lacks selectivity in the people from whom comfort is sought, shows clinging behavior in infancy, or indiscriminately friendly behavior in early or middle childhood coupled with attention seeking and poorly modulated social interactions. In the latter (inhibited), the child may respond to caregivers with a mixture of approach, avoidance, and resistance to comfort. They lack emotional responsiveness and may act aggressively in response to distress—either their own or another person's.

It is clear from these descriptions that there could be some difficulty in distinguishing reactive attachment disorders from autism spectrum disorders as the behaviors described may be evident in both. Research has indicated that the only way to clearly distinguish between the two in terms of the social difficulties is that reactive attachment disorders tend to respond more positively to interventions and therapy leading to the child no longer showing the behaviors (e.g., when placed in stable and positive foster care the child becomes more reciprocal and shows rapid emergence of social responsiveness), or that there has been a clear history of neglect or abuse in early childhood in those who develop reactive attachment disorder.

According to the DSM-IV-TR (APA, 2000), the following criteria are relevant for diagnosis of reactive attachment disorder: (a) severity—there is no attachment in any meaningful sense and no enduring relationship with caregivers; (b) pervasiveness—attachment difficulties must be seen across several different contexts and with several different caregivers; (c) distress or disability—the disorder causes the child persistent social disability or persistent distress; (d) onset before age five years; (e) not autistic—the lack of other autism impairments such as repetitive or ritualistic behaviors or communication difficulties indicates that the child does not have an autism spectrum disorder that could explain the impaired social relationships; (f) mental age greater than 10–12 months; and (g) pathogenic care—an early abnormal care giving environment either due to several changes of primary caregiver or due to neglect of the child's emotional or physical needs.

Reactive attachment disorders are rare, and are differentiated from insecure attachments. Around 40 percent of children may be classified as insecurely attached (Goodman & Scott, 2005, p. 123), but in insecure attachment this can relate to only one caregiver with the child being appropriately and securely attached to other caregivers. The condition is therefore not pervasive. Insecure attachment also does not necessarily lead to difficulties with social responsiveness and relatedness, whereas this is a core characteristic of reactive attachment disorder.

REFERENCES

American Psychiatric Association. (2000). *Diagnostic and statistical manual of mental disorders* (4th ed., text rev.). Washington, DC: Author.

Goodman, R., & Scott, S. (2005). *Child psychiatry* (2nd ed.). Oxford: Blackwell Publishing.

FURTHER INFORMATION
O'Connor, T. G. (2002). Attachment disorder of infancy and childhood. In M. Rutter & E. Taylor (Eds.), *Child and adolescent psychiatry* (4th ed., pp. 776–792). Oxford: Blackwell Science.
Zeanah, C. H. (1996). Beyond insecurity: A reconceptualisation of attachment disorders of infancy. *Journal of Consulting and Clinical Psychology, 64*, 42–52.

FIONA J. SCOTT

## RECEPTIVE LANGUAGE

Receptive language is the ability to understand and process spoken and written language (listening and reading). Processing auditory information is difficult for some individuals with autism. It is important to remember that frequently information, directions, rules, corrections, and procedures are presented verbally. Consider incorporating pictures, icons, gestures and sign language.

*See also* American Sign Language; visual strategies.

RASCHELLE THEOHARRIS

## RECIPROCAL COMMUNICATION/INTERACTION

Reciprocal communication refers to a specific component of interaction involving appropriate communication based on the understanding of the conversational partner's message. Reciprocal communication tends to extend conversations as an individual's comment (i.e., "I am tired") is met by comments and questions (i.e., "Did you not get enough sleep last night?"). Challenges with reciprocity, often referred to as "give and take," are hallmarks of autism spectrum disorders (ASD). Comments that would serve as a starting point for reciprocal communication may fail to receive a response from individuals with ASD; consequently, communication with or between individuals with ASD can seem disjointed or one-sided. Individuals with ASD are often explicitly taught to engage in reciprocal communication.

*See also* American Sign Language; augmentative and alternative communication; Picture Exchange Communication System; social skills; visual strategies.

JEANNE HOLVERSTOTT

## RED FLAGS

A red flag is an alert or warning intended to draw attention to a problem or potential problem. Certain behaviors can be red flags that alert parents and professionals to a child's potential needs and/or delays. There are numerous red flags that differentiate those with autism spectrum disorder (ASD) from children with other developmental disabilities and from typically developing youngsters. These red flags include: (a) lack of appropriate eye gaze; (b) coordination of eye gaze; (c) facial expression, gestures, and sounds; (d) lack of warm expression to others with gaze; (e) unusual vocal **prosody**; (f) repetitive movements of the body, hands, etc.; (g) not responding to name; and (h) absence of showing interest, sharing interest, or enjoyment (Wetherby & Woods, 2002). The Centers for Disease Control and Prevention started a new campaign in 2005 that highlighted the need for parents of infants and toddlers to know the warning signs of autism.

REFERENCES

Centers for Disease Control and Prevention. (2005). *Learn the signs: Act early* [Brochure]. National Center on Birth Defects and Developmental Disabilities. Atlanta, GA: Author.

Wetherby, A. M., & Woods, J. (2002). *Systematic observation of red flags for autism spectrum disorders in young children (SORF)*. Unpublished manual. Florida State University, Tallahassee, FL.

FURTHER INFORMATION

Osterling, J. A., Dawson, G., & Munson, J. A. (2002). Early recognition of 1-year-old infants with autism spectrum disorder versus mental retardation. *Development and Psychopathology, 14,* 239–251.

Wetherby, A. M., Woods, J., Allen, L., Cleary, J., Dickinson, H., & Lord, C. (2004). Early indicators of autism spectrum disorders in the second year of life. *Journal of Autism and Developmental Disorders, 34,* 473–493.

PAUL G. LaCAVA

# REHABILITATION ACT OF 1973

The Rehabilitation Act of 1973 guarantees certain rights to individuals with disabilities. Most notably, Section 504 is internationally recognized as the foundational civil-rights legislation for persons with disabilities, paving the way for further legislation for individuals with disabilities.

*See also* Section 504 of the Rehabilitation Act of 1973.

REFERENCE

Pub. Law No. 93-112, 87 Stat. 394 (September 26, 1973), codified at 29 U.S.C. § 701 et seq.

TERRI COOPER SWANSON

# REINFORCER

Reinforcement is a procedure that increases the likelihood of a behavior occurring again. A reinforcer is what is used to bring about that increase in behavior. Reinforcers can also be divided into primary and secondary types. Primary reinforcers are those things that are biologically necessary: food, water, and sex. All other reinforcers are secondary; however, there is some debate as to whether sensory reinforcers serve as primary or secondary reinforcers. Secondary reinforcers may be a tangible item, such as specific foods, toys, and movies, or social interaction.

*See also* sensory integration; sensory processing.

KATIE BASSITY

# RESIDENTIAL FACILITY

Students receive special education and related services in a facility where the students receive care and services 24 hours a day. Residential facilities can be public or privately owned. Students with visual impairments and hearing impairments represent the largest percentage of students receiving educational services in residential facilities.

KATHERINE E. COOK

## RESIDENTIAL SUPPORTS

As children grow into adults, families are faced with the complexities of how to best meet their child's needs and provide support for an appropriate living arrangement. Given the complexity and heterogeneity of autism spectrum disorders (ASD), no single residential treatment approach is appropriate for everyone. Individuals with autism need to be assessed on their strengths and needs when planning for continuity of services. The initiative for most residential supports currently available came from parents and teachers concerned about the future of their children and students as they transitioned into adulthood.

During the 1970s and 1980s, a number of autism-specific, community-based, residential programs were developed across the United States. In an effort to promote maximum integration into the community, most programs consisted of group homes in urban or suburban settings, with up to six clients in each (LaVigna, 1983; Wall, 1990). Some residential programs preferred smaller ratios of four per home, or garden apartments and town homes with two or three residents (CSAAC, 1995). Community-based programs often focus on sharing common goals of residents (Sloan & Schopler, 1977), optimizing development though independence and competence in various areas (Lettick, 1983), and facilitating individual independence (LaVigna, 1983).

During the last two decades, larger residential group settings have proven beneficial as well. Larger facilities are able to provide increased opportunities for social interactions and allow for an increase of staff members to provide a variety of background skills including more flexible supervision of residents. Larger settings also provide natural subgroups for social and work participation around common interests and skills (Kay, 1990).

Many community-based models include self-contained programs offering vocational and residential components, where residents interact with nondisabled neighbors in the community. Some sites offer educational and behavioral programming with a range of school, work, and agricultural environments, as well as individualized life skills instruction. The general model of these programs focuses on residents and staff working together to contribute to all aspects of the community. On-site activities emphasize visual, fine-motor and gross-motor skills in order to maximize each individual's possibilities for success.

When considering residential support programs, it is important for the family and the individual with ASD to consider the following. First, what are the facility's mission and goals and do they match or meet your family's needs? Every facility is going to have their own unique philosophy and it is important that it matches your family's. Second, visit the residential site to determine if the program is the right fit. Taking a tour of the facility will help to learn what features the facility has to offer, will allow formal and informal conversations with staff, which will provide first-hand information as to how individuals are treated and cared for. Third, does the facility offer the type or level of support that is appropriate for your child? For individuals with ASD, having the appropriate environment, staff training, and understanding of the characteristics of each individual is extremely important. Finally, ask to talk with other families whose children live or work at the facility. This is a great way to find out about the quality of the facility and services that they provide.

REFERENCES

Community Services for Autistic Adults and Children (CSAAC). (1995). *Adult residential program, adult vocational program* [Brochure]. Rockville, MD: Author.

Kay, B. R. (1990). Bittersweet Farms. *Journal of Autism and Developmental Disorders, 20,* 309–322.

LaVigna, G. W. (1983). The Jay Nolen Center: A community-based program. In E. Schopler & G. B. Mesibov (Eds.), *Autism in adolescents and adults* (pp. 381–410). New York: Plenum Press.

Lettick, A. L. (1983). Benhaven. In E. Schopler & G. B. Mesibov (Eds.), *Autism in adolescents and adults* (pp. 355–379). New York: Plenum Press.

Sloan, J. L., & Schopler, E. (1977). Some thoughts about developing programs for autistic adolescents. *Journal of Pediatric Psychology, 2,* 187–190.

Wall, A. J. (1990). Group homes in North Carolina for children and adults with autism. *Journal of Autism and Other Developmental Disorders, 20,* 353–366.

STACEY L. BROOKENS

## RESOURCE ROOM

During a student's **Individualized Education Program** (IEP) meeting, the team determines the most appropriate placement for the student in the **least restrictive environment** (LRE). The resource room is one possible environment in which the student could spend part of the school day. The resource room can offer students extra instruction or support in deficit areas (such as homework help, organization, and test or homework modification). The amount of time a student spends in the resource room is determined by the IEP team according to the student's individual needs.

RASCHELLE THEOARRIS

## RESPITE CARE

The autism spectrum includes children and adults with a variable range of complex issues. What is common to all families whose children have an autism spectrum disorder (ASD) is a comprehensive need for a myriad of services and supports. Near the top of the list for many families is the need for a break from the constant demands of parenting. This is often referred to as a need for respite.

### DEFINITION OF RESPITE

The concept of *respite* first appeared in the late 1960s based on the belief that a child with special needs would be served best at home. Most often, respite is thought of as temporary, short-term care for an individual with special needs. According to United Cerebral Palsy (n.d.), "Respite … is a service in which temporary care is provided to children or adults with disabilities, or chronic or terminal illnesses, and to children at risk of abuse and neglect." For purposes of discussion, the definition of respite will be broadened to include providing both temporary and ongoing support for children or adults with ASD within the context of their own home.

### SAMPLE JOB RESPONSIBILITIES

The job responsibilities of a respite provider span a wide range of duties, dependent on the particular needs of the individual with ASD being supported. Duties change over time dependent on the developmental needs of a particular child or adult with ASD.

Following are examples of duties with a younger child with ASD: (a) personal care and/or teaching of personal hygiene (bathing, face and hand washing, tooth brushing, dressing, (b) dispensing of medication, (c) food preparation, (d) implementing intervention strategies (e.g., Developmental Individual-Difference Relation-Based Intervention, Applied Behavior Analysis, Relationship Development Intervention, etc.), (e) transportation to therapy appointments, (f) engaging in prescribed activities between therapy sessions (e.g., speech, physical, occupational, vision therapy, etc.), (g) preparation of visual calendars and schedules, (h) regular communication with early intervention or school personnel, and (i) facilitating social interaction with peers.

For an older school-aged child with ASD, although many of the just-mentioned duties are applicable, new responsibilities emerge as a child matures. Examples include: (a) facilitating self-care, (b) overseeing preparation for the school day (e.g., selecting clothes, preparing lunch, gathering necessary school materials together, etc.), (c) facilitating completion of daily homework, and (d) attendance at **Individualized Education Program** (IEP) meetings.

As a child with ASD approaches their high school years, the focus of respite responsibilities shifts in the direction of supporting transition to adult life and greater independence. Examples include: (a) community skills (e.g., bus training, shopping, banking, etc.), (b) food preparation (table setting, kitchen clean-up, grocery lists, etc.), (c) use of public transportation, (d) seeking needed information and resources (e.g., via Internet, phone book, etc.), and (e) aid in developing social and recreational outlets.

### JOB DESCRIPTIONS

A useful job description should include a statement that describes the philosophy underlying how a provider is expected to treat that person. For example, if supporting the person to learn self-advocacy is a high-priority goal, one would expect the worker to solicit input from the child or young adult whenever possible, and to show respect for whatever is communicated. Key job responsibilities and expectations need to be spelled out so that an applicant has a clear idea of what the job entails (Lieberman, 2005).

### QUALITIES TO SEEK IN A PROVIDER

Prior to hiring an in-home respite worker, one must do some advance preparation. This entails thinking through specific duties that will be required. It also requires identifying desired personality qualities in a provider that will allow for a better match with the culture of the child or young adult's home. For example, a spontaneous, right-brain type of person will not fit easily into a household that operates best with solid structure and routine. (For a more detailed explanation, see Lieberman. A *Stranger Among Us*, 2005, Ch. 2.)

### DETERMINING BOTTOM-LINE ISSUES FOR HIRING

When hiring a respite provider, each family must decide what the essential bottom-line issues are in order to rule out inappropriate applicants. Following is a sample list of bottom-line issues that might be used for screening:

- Comfort relating to people with ASD or other neurological differences
- Use of a reliable car, good driving record, and current driver's license
- Nonsmoker

- Current schedule fits with desired hours and days
- Able to make one-year commitment
- Pay requirements within family's ability to pay. (Lieberman, 2005, p. 64)

## SPECIFIC AREAS TO EXPLORE IN A FACE-TO-FACE INTERVIEW

It is helpful to find somebody who has been exposed to people with ASD or other kinds of disabilities. Beyond that, there are other important areas to explore in-depth in a face-to-face interview.

### Self-Care and Emotional Stability

Working with a child or young adult with ASD requires, at the very least, calmness, a great deal of patience, and personal maturity. One way to assess whether a candidate possesses these qualities is to ask questions that explore self-care and emotional stability. "The ideal candidate should 'have a life' outside of work ... you don't want someone who is looking to meet the bulk of her emotional needs in your household ... You are looking for answers that demonstrate the ability to maintain control when confronted with a child's challenging behaviors" (Lieberman, 2005, pp. 80–81).

A good candidate should have a regular and healthy routine for managing stress, whether a regular fitness activity, a recreational sport, yoga or dance, prayer, or meditation practice. People who practice healthy stress management in their own lives are better equipped to handle difficult behaviors exhibited by children or young adults under stress.

### Relationship to Drugs and Alcohol

It is definitely pertinent to explore an applicant's relationship with drugs or alcohol. Most people who are in active recovery from drugs and/or alcohol are likely to be forthcoming in sharing the amount of time in recovery. A good rule of thumb is for someone to be in active recovery from addiction for at least 1 year before considering that person as a viable candidate. On the other hand, don't automatically rule out someone with a history of addiction. Those who overcome this challenge in their lives can exhibit strength of character that serves them well in supporting a child or young adult with ASD.

A word of caution: If an applicant with a history of addiction claims to no longer use a certain drug but still has an occasional drink, be prepared to question that person in greater detail. Addicts in recovery must stay away from all drugs if they truly intend to live a clean and sober lifestyle.

### Comfort with Expressing Emotion

Be cautious of someone who claims never to get angry. Nobody can avoid some degree of internal agitation just from living in today's fast-paced society. Those feelings must be expressed periodically to avoid unpredictable "explosions." Working with a child or young adult with behavioral challenges can tax a provider's emotions. It would therefore be important to assess how comfortable that applicant is with experiencing a full range of emotions in a healthy way.

### Ability to Set Limits

A quality provider must be comfortable with setting limits. Someone who says "yes" to doing things she is not comfortable doing is at risk for burning out or building up resentment. It works best when that person has bottom lines about what she will or won't do. Setting limits is also important in providing support to a child or young adult with ASD. Behaviors may arise that require a calm, but firm response that helps that child or young adult to learn appropriate boundaries. Examples of behaviors might include such things as invading someone's private space, grabbing something out of another person's hand, monopolizing a conversation without noticing a lack of interest on the part of the listener, etc.

### Attitudes Toward Discipline

How a candidate was disciplined as a child would have a direct effect on how he handles challenging situations with the child or young adults he is supporting. If someone has been physically abused, it is essential that a candidate can demonstrate emotional work that has been done to counteract the negative effects of being abused. Explore the candidate's ideas about what discipline is and how it should be implemented.

Discipline is teaching desired behavior, that is, helping a child or young adult to understand what is expected. It is distinctly different from punishment, which is defined as reacting, based on what that person has done wrong. It often takes the form of venting anger in response to challenging behavior. Punishment does not teach desired behavior. In short, look for candidates who clearly understand the difference between discipline and punishment.

Closely aligned with investigating attitudes toward discipline is how an applicant interprets the challenging behaviors exhibited by children and young adults with ASD. One way this can be accomplished is to pose a challenging situation and ask that person how she would handle it. How an applicant answers is a good indicator of whether she grasps the neurological basis of behavior in this population. Avoid candidates who automatically assign negative intent to difficult behaviors. This kind of attitude is rarely helpful when supporting people with ASD, and in fact, can be harmful.

### Positive Behavioral Support

Positive behavioral support is a more appropriate response to challenging behaviors. This involves seeking to understand what a child or young adult may be trying to say through their behavior. Howard and Pitonyak (2005), in an article entitled "All Behavior Is Meaningful," say:

> Difficult behaviors result from unmet needs . . . Supporting a person with difficult behaviors requires us to get to know the person as a human being influenced by a complex personal history. While it is tempting to look for a quick fix, which usually means attacking the person's behavior to make it go away, intervening in a person's life without understanding something about the life he or she is living is disrespectful and counterproductive. (p. 3)

Listen for indications that the candidate is able to avoid taking challenging behavior personally and screen out candidates who seem concerned with enforcing compliance. The best applicant will demonstrate an understanding of the many factors to take into consideration when trying to positively address difficult behavior, including the person's health, the sensory environment, changes in circumstances, and so forth.

Utilizing respite providers in the home is often overlooked as an option. Hiring a provider is a complex and time-consuming process fraught with uncertainty. But with careful preparation, a clear job description, upholding bottom lines, and a thoughtful in-depth interview, a quality provider can enhance the life of a child or young adult with ASD, while providing much needed respite to family members.

## REFERENCES
Howard, E., & Pitonyak, D. (2005). All behavior is meaningful—magic can happen! *ASP Cares* (June), 3.
Lieberman, L. (2005). *A stranger among us: Hiring in-home support for child with autism spectrum disorder or other neurological differences.* Shawnee Mission, KS: Autism Asperger Publishing Company.
United Cerebral Palsy. (n.d.). *What is respite care?* Retrieved December 14, 2006, from www.ucp.org/ucp_channeldoc.cfm/1/11/51/51-51/2106.

LISA ACKERSON LIEBERMAN

## RESPONDENT CONDITIONING

Respondent conditioning, also referred to as classical conditioning, is a type of learning within the behavioral school of thought. It is the process of pairing a neutral stimulus, something that inspires no response from the individual, with something that instigates an automatic reaction from the individual, an unconditioned stimulus. This pairing takes place until the neutral stimulus causes the same reaction as the unconditioned stimulus, without the presence of the unconditioned stimulus. The formerly neutral stimulus is then referred to as a conditioned stimulus. This process was originally referred to as classical conditioning by Ivan Pavlov, in his famous study with dogs.

*See also* antecedent-behavior-consequence analysis; applied behavior analysis; behavior modification.

KATIE BASSITY

## RESPONSE COST

Response cost falls into the category of **punishment**. In a response-cost system, a person is denied a certain piece of or the whole reinforcement for each behavior they perform that is deemed inappropriate. As in the definition of punishment, a procedure is not a response cost if after the reinforcement is taken away, the behavior does not decrease (Cooper, Heron, & Heward, 1987; Azrin & Holz, 1966). Response cost has been successful in token-based treatment programs in a variety of settings, including clinics, homes, hospitals, and schools (Kazdin, 1972). Because response cost utilizes the removal of positive reinforcement, positive reinforcement must be available and the **reinforcers** must be effective (Alberto & Troutman, 1999). Additionally, reinforcers must have the ability to be withdrawn (which is why edible reinforcers do not typically work). Fines for speeding and loss of tokens for talking out of turn are examples of response-cost procedures.

*See also* applied behavior analysis; token economy.

## REFERENCES
Alberto, P. A., & Troutman, A. C. (1999). *Applied behavior analysis for teachers.* Upper Saddle River, NJ: Merrill.

Azrin, N. H., & Holz, W. C. (1966). Punishment. In W. A. Honig (Ed.), *Operant behavior: Areas of research and application.* New York: Appleton-Century-Crofts.
Cooper, J. O., Heron, T. E., & Heward, W. L. (1987). *Applied behavior analysis.* Upper Saddle River, NJ: Prentice-Hall.
Kazdin, A. E. (1972). Response cost: The removal of conditioned reinforcers for therapeutic change. *Behavior Therapy, 3,* 533–546.

TARA MIHOK AND JESSICA KATE PETERS

## RESPONSE LATENCY

Response latency is the amount of time between a given command and the student's response. This measure may be used for a variety of purposes, including as a check for mastery and/or **fluency.** For example, a teacher asks a student to name an animal and immediately begins to count silently. If the student responds when the teacher reaches the count of five, the response latency for this situation would be 5 seconds.

KATIE BASSITY

## RESTRICTED INTEREST

These topical interests can become all consuming to the exclusion of others. Often, individuals on the autism spectrum will only talk or read about their interest, not participate in it. Restricted interests is one of the characteristics that defines **Asperger's disorder** as "restricted patterns of interest that is abnormal in intensity or focus" (APA, 2000). A survey by Online Asperger Syndrome Information and Support (OASIS) found the top five specialized interest topics to be: peer-appropriate fads or interests; video or computer games; works of art, movies, fictional books, or television programs; and computers (Bashe & Kirby, 2001, p. 39). Sometimes, the restricted interests lean toward the strange or odd. These have included interest in: bleach bottles, alarms and alarm systems, lawn mowers, organs and organ music, road signs, maps, clocks, time, directions (north, south, east, west), telephone books, game shows, and insects (Bashe & Kirby, 2001, p. 40).

### REFERENCES
American Psychiatric Association. (2000). *Diagnostic and statistical manual of mental disorders* (4th ed., text rev.). Washington, DC: Author.
Bashe, P. R., & Kirby, B. L. (2001). *The OASIS guide to Asperger syndrome, advice, support, insights and inspiration.* New York: Crown Publishers.

ANN PILEWSKIE

## RETROSPECTIVE VIDEO ANALYSIS (RVA)

Retrospective video analysis (RVA) uses home videos for documentation of a child's development. RVA has been used as an option for assessing very early periods in development. RVA can help identify behaviors that distinguish between autism and other developmental disabilities in children as young as 8 months of age.

JAN L. KLEIN

# RETT'S DISORDER

Rett's disorder is currently included within *Diagnostic and Statistical Manual of Mental Disorders* (DSM-IV-TR; APA, 2000) classifications of mental disorders and listed as a **pervasive developmental disorder**. However there is some controversy around whether it should be classified instead as a neurological disorder (e.g., Tsai, 1992). Rett's disorder is characterized according to DSM-IV-TR (APA, 2000) as follows: There must be the presence of normal prenatal and perinatal development, normal psychomotor development through the first 5 months after birth, and normal head circumference at birth. Then, after a period of normal development there should be onset of all of the following: (a) deceleration of head growth between ages 5 and 48 months, (b) loss of previously acquired purposeful hand skills between ages 5 and 50 months with the subsequent development of stereotyped hand movements (e.g., hand wringing or hand washing), (c) loss of social engagement early in the course (although social interaction often develops later), (d) appearance of poorly coordinated gait or trunk movements, and (e) severely impaired expressive and receptive language development with severe psychomotor retardation.

Other criteria not required for diagnosis but commonly observed include breathing dysfunctions including hyperventilation or apnea, **electroencephalogram** (EEG) abnormalities including slowing of normal electrical patterns, appearance of epileptiform patterns, and reduction in REM sleep, seizures, muscle rigidity or spasticity, scoliosis, teeth grinding, and small feet (Schilling, 1997).

Diagnosis of Rett's disorder is usually made between 6 and 24 months of age, and is believed to be present primarily in girls, with few confirmed male cases recorded (Hagberg, 1985), although the possibility remains of undiagnosed male cases. Recent research has indicated the possibility of a gene for Rett's disorder, MECP2 (Amir et al., 1999), with one reported male with the gene mutation who only survived to 1 year of age (Meloni et al., 2000). It is possible that the fatality of the gene mutation in males is what accounts for no known male cases of Rett's disorder. Although there is now a known genetic mutation, diagnosis is still predominantly based on the presence or absence of behavioral and clinical criteria.

Rett's disorder is a rare condition thought to occur in about 1 in every 10,000–15,000 live births (Glasson, Thomson, Fyfe, Leonard, Bower, et al., 1998; Deb, 1998). Following a relatively short period of normal development, there is a sudden regression with irreversible effects leading to a severe developmental disorder affecting cognitive, motor, communication, and social functioning (Perry, Sarlo-McGarvey, & Factor, 1992). Many of the early characteristics present similarly to autism, and Witt-Engerstrom and Gillberg (1987) report that around 78 percent of girls with Rett's disorder have been previously misdiagnosed as having infantile autism. In fact, the inclusion of Rett's disorder in the pervasive developmental disorders in DSM-IV-TR (2000) was in part to try and reduce the number of incorrect autism diagnoses (Volkmar & Lord, 1998). Van Acker (1997) argues that there are certain characteristics that distinguish between Rett's disorder and autism in young girls, and that assessing motor development could be an important means for making accurate differential diagnosis. Specifically, in Rett's disorder both communication and motor skills regress simultaneously, whereas in autism regression, if it occurs, tends to be in communication alone. Van Acker (1997) goes on to suggest that assessment in other areas should include:

(a) respiratory patterns, (b) ability and speed of movements, (c) purposeful hand movements, (d) degree and type of stereotypical movements, (e) ability to acquire new skills, (f) physical development, and (g) overall developmental milestones. However, he also contends that due to the developmental nature of the disorder any diagnosis of Rett's disorder should be tentative until between ages 3 and 5 years.

**REFERENCES**

American Psychiatric Association. (2000). *Diagnostic and statistical manual of mental disorders* (4th ed., text rev.). Washington, DC: Author.

Amir, R. E., Van der Veyver, I. B., Wan, M., Tran, C. Q., Franke, U., & Zoghbi, H. Y. (1999). Rett syndrome is caused by mutations in X-linked MECP2, encoding methyl-CpG binding protein 2. *Nature Genetics, 32*, 185–188.

Deb, S. (1998). Self injurious behaviour as part of the genetic syndromes. *British Journal of Psychiatry, 172*, 385–388.

Glasson, E. J., Thomson, M. R., Fyfe, S., Leonard, S., Bower, C., Rousham, E., et al. (1998). Diagnosis of Rett syndrome: Can a radiograph help? *Developmental Medicine and Child Neurology, 40*, 737–742.

Hagberg, B. (1985). Rett's syndrome: Prevalence and impact on progressive severe mental retardation in girls. *Acta Pediatrica Scandanavica, 74*, 405–408.

Meloni, I., Bruttini, M., Longon, I., Mari, F., Rizzolio, F., D'Adamo, P., et al. (2000). A mutation in the Rett syndrome gene, MECP2, causes X-linked mental retardation and progressive spasticity in males. *American Journal of Human Genetics, 67*, 982–985.

Perry, A., Sarlo-McGarvey, N., & Factor, D.C. (1992). Stress and family functioning in parents of girls with Rett syndrome. *Journal of Autism and Developmental Disorders, 22*, 235–248.

Schilling, D. (1997). Our Rett syndrome page. Retrieved August 17, 2005, from http://pages.prodigy.com/DebbieSchilling.

Tsai, L. Y. (1992). Is Rett syndrome a subtype of pervasive developmental disorders? *Journal of Autism and Developmental Disorders, 22*, 551–561.

Van Acker, R. (1997). Rett syndrome: A pervasive developmental disorder. In D. J. Cohen & F. R. Volkmar (Eds.), *Handbook of autism and pervasive developmental disorders* (2nd ed.) (pp. 60–93). New York: Wiley & Sons.

Volkmar, F. R., & Lord, C. (1998). Diagnosis and definition of autism and other pervasive developmental disorders (pp. 1–31). In F. R. Volkmar (Ed.), *Autism and pervasive developmental disorders*. Cambridge: Cambridge University Press.

Witt-Engerstrom, I., & Gillberg, C. (1987). Rett syndrome in Sweden. *Journal of Autism and Developmental Disorders, 17*, 149–150.

FIONA J. SCOTT

## RETT'S DISORDER–DIAGNOSTIC CRITERIA FOR 299.80 RETT'S DISORDER

According to the **Diagnostic and Statistical Manual of Mental Disorders** (DSM-IV-TR; APA, 2000), the diagnostic criteria for Rett's disorder include all of the following: (a) apparent normal prenatal and perinatal development, (b) apparent normal psychomotor development through the first 5 months after birth, and (c) normal head circumference at birth. Additional criteria include all of the following with onset following the period of normal development: (a) deceleration of head growth between ages 5 months and 48 months, (b) loss of previously acquired purposeful hand skills between ages 5 months and 30 months with the subsequent development of stereotyped hand movements (e.g., hand-wringing or hand washing), (c) loss of social engagement early in the course (although often social interaction develops later), (d) appearance of poorly coordinated gait or trunk movements, and (e) severely impaired expressive and receptive language development with severe psychomotor retardation.

**REFERENCE**

American Psychiatric Association. (2000). *Diagnostic and statistical manual of mental disorders* (4th ed., text rev.). Washington, DC: Author.

JEANNE HOLVERSTOTT

## RIMLAND, BERNARD

Bernard Rimland (1928–2006) received his PhD in experimental psychology and research design from Pennsylvania State University in 1953. A few years later, his son Mark was born. It was Mark, who was diagnosed with early infantile autism, who sparked his father's interest in better understanding the rare disorder. Much of Dr. Rimland's work has been controversial. Specifically, Dr. Rimland was one of the first professionals in the field to speak out against the "refrigerator mother" theory. In the 1990s, he was one of the first to call attention to the rise in autism and the use of **vaccinations** containing thimerosol. Dr. Rimland founded the Autism Society of America in 1965 and the Autism Research Institute in 1967, where he carried out his work until his death.

TERRI COOPER SWANSON

## RUMINATION SYNDROME

Rumination is the chewing of food. In rumination syndrome, a person chews and swallows food and then regurgitates it back to the mouth to chew and swallow again. Rumination may be voluntary or involuntary. In infants, rumination may begin at the age of 3–6 months and usually resolves on its own. In adults, the disorder may accompany physical and/or psychological disorders.

Contrary to thought, the regurgitated material does not taste bitter or sour. Severe health consequences can develop if the disorder is not treated. These include bad breath, tooth enamel damage, dehydration, weight loss, pneumonia, and even death.

LYNN DUDEK

# S

## SCALES OF INDEPENDENT BEHAVIOR–REVISED (SIB-R)

The Scales of Independent Behavior–Revised (SIB-R; Bruininks, Woodcock, Weatherman, & Hill, 1996) is a standardized measure of **adaptive behavior** across 7 skill clusters (e.g., Personal Living Skills) and 22 subscales (e.g., eating and meal preparation) and includes a measure of the impact of problematic behavior on adaptive functioning. Adaptive behavior generally refers to those skills or skill sets associated with personal, vocational, and social self-sufficiency in real-life situations (Klin, Saulnier, Tsatsanis, & Volkmar, 2005). The SIB-R was normed on 2,100 individuals across 15 states with these norms extending beyond adolescence (from 3 months to 80+ years of age). The SIB-R is generally regarded as a valid and reliable assessment of adaptive functioning and, when properly administered, can be very useful in individual evaluation, **Individual Education Plan** development, and functional transition planning.

*See also* individualized transition plan; standardization; transition planning.

### REFERENCES

Bruininks, R. H., Woodcock, R. W., Weatherman, R. F., & Hill, B. K. (1996). *The scales of independent behavior–revised.* Chicago: Riverside Publishing Company.

Klin, A., Saulnier, C., Tsatsanis, K., & Volkmar, F. (2005). Clinical evaluation in autism spectrum disorders: Psychological assessment within a transdisciplinary framework. In F. R. Volkmar, R. Paul, A. Klin, & D. Cohen (Eds.), *Handbook of autism and pervasive developmental disorders* (3rd ed., pp. 772–798). New York: Wiley & Sons.

PETER GERHARDT

## SCERTS MODEL

The Social Communication, Emotional Regulation, and Transactional Support or the SCERTS Model is a comprehensive educational approach and multidisciplinary framework designed to enhance the core challenges, communication, and social-emotional abilities faced by children with autism spectrum disorders (ASD) and related disabilities (Prizant, Wetherby, Rubin, & Laurent, 2003). The SCERTS Model was collaborated and developed by a group of interdisciplinary professionals. This model was derived from a theoretical- as well as a research-based foundation on communication and social-emotional development in children with ASD. It was developed to address the critical need identified by professionals and parents for a comprehensive **multidisciplinary team** model for children with ASD (Prizant, Wetherby, Rubin, Laurent, & Rydell, 2006). In addition, the model was designed to have broad application in educational settings, clinical settings, and in everyday activities at home and in the community (Prizant, Wetherby, Rubin, Laurent, & Rydell, 2002). Thus far, the model is not a treatment approach or methodology; instead, it is a framework that provides guidelines for implementing a comprehensive therapeutic and educational plan. Furthermore, although the model was designed for children with ASD, many other children with challenges in social communication and emotional regulation would potentially benefit from the SCERTS Model (The SCERTS Model, 2006).

## CORE VALUES OF THE SCERTS MODEL

The SCERTS Model is grounded in explicitly stated core values and principles that guide educational and treatment efforts (Prizant et al., 2006). Following are the statements of core values and guiding principles (The SCERTS Model, 2006, p. 18):

1. The development of spontaneous, functional communication abilities and emotional regulatory capacities are of the highest priority in educational and treatment efforts.
2. Principles and research on child development frame assessment and educational efforts. Goals and activities are developmentally appropriate and functional, relative to a child's adaptive abilities and the necessary skills for maximizing enjoyment, success, and independence in daily experiences.
3. All domains of a child's development (e.g., communicative, social-emotional, cognitive, and motor) are interrelated and interdependent. Assessment and educational efforts must address these relationships.
4. All behavior is viewed as purposeful. Functions of behavior may include communication, emotional regulation, and engagement in adaptive skills. For children who display unconventional or problem behaviors, there is an emphasis on determining the function of the behavior and supporting the development of more appropriate ways to accomplish those functions.
5. A child's unique learning profile of strengths and weaknesses plays a critical role in determining appropriate accommodations for facilitating competence in the domains of social-communication and emotional regulation.
6. Natural routines across home, school, and community environments provide the educational and treatment contexts for learning, and for the development of positive relationships. Progress is measured in reference to increasing competence and active participation in daily experiences and routines.
7. It is the primary responsibility of professionals to establish positive relationships with children and with family members. All children and family members are treated with dignity and respect.
8. Family members are considered experts about their child. Assessment and educational efforts are viewed as collaborative processes with family members, and principles of family-centered practice are advocated to build consensus with the family and enhance the collaborative process.

## ESSENTIAL CHARACTERISTICS OF THE SCERTS MODEL

There are three essential characteristics underlying the SCERTS Model identified by the model collaborators (Prizant et al., 2006). First, the model is systematic and semistructured but also flexible. In contrast to either adult-directed instructions or facilitative approaches, the model attempts to find the balance and work in the middle

**Table 6.** An Overview of Ultimate Goals of the SCERTS Model

| Social Communication | Emotional Regulation | Transactional Support |
|---|---|---|
| Enhance capacities for joint attention | Enhance capacities for self-regulation | Educational and learning support |
| Enhance capacities for symbolic behavior | Enhance capacities for mutual regulation | Interpersonal supports |
| | Enhance capacity to recover from dysregulation | Family support |
| | | Support among professionals |

ground. Second, instead of solely focusing on training skills, the model addresses underlying capacities as well as supports the development of functional skills. The primary goals in the model are to develop educational, self-help and independent living skills. Last, the model is flexible enough to incorporate practices from a variety of approaches and teaching strategies, such as augmentative communication, relaxation techniques, and sensory supports. However, it should be noted that only those that support social communication and emotional regulation, and that are philosophically consistent with the core values and guiding principles of the model are considered compatible with practice in the model (Prizant et al., 2006).

## CORE COMPONENTS OF THE SCERTS MODEL

The acronym *SCERTS* refers to Social Communication (SC), Emotional Regulation (ER), and Transactional Support (TS). These are the core components of the SCERTS Model as well as the primary developmental dimensions that Prizant and his colleagues (2002) believe should be prioritized in a program designed to support the development of children with ASD and their families (see Table 6).

## SOCIAL COMMUNICATION (SC)

The Social Communication (SC) component of the SCERTS Model addresses the over-riding goals of helping a child to be a confident, increasingly proficient, successful, and active communicator and participant in social activities (Prizant et al., 2006). In addressing this goal, the model collaborators believed that children must acquire capacities in two major areas of functioning: **joint attention** and symbolic behavior (Prizant et al., 2006). They further identified those two areas as foundations of social communication based on the following two reasons. First, children become more capable in sharing attention and emotion as well as expressing intentions in reciprocal interactions when their capacities of joint attention increase. Second, children develop more sophisticated and abstract means to communicate and play with others when their capacities of symbolic behavior increase. The ultimate goal targeted in the SC component of the SCERTS Model is to support a child in developing his or her foundational capacities in joint attention and symbolic behavior that support communicative and social competence and emotional well-being. It is believed that with these capacities, children are more likely to find satisfaction and even great joy in being with, relating to, and learning from others (Prizant et al., 2006).

## Emotional Regulation (ER)

The Emotional Regulation (ER) component of the SCERTS Model focuses on supporting a child's ability to regulate emotional arousal (Prizant et al., 2006). The model collaborators believed that emotional regulatory capacities enable a child (a) to seek assistance and/or respond to others' attempts to provide support for emotional regulation (referred to as *mutual regulation*), (b) to independently remain organized (referred to as *self-regulation*), and (c) to recover from states of emotional meltdown (referred to as *recovery from dysregulation*). Furthermore, they believed the child will be optimally available for learning once he or she has those emotional regulatory capacities and skills. Therefore, the ultimate goal of the ER component of the SCERTS Model is to support a child in adapting to and coping with the daily challenges he or she will face in maintaining optimal states of arousal most conducive to learning, relating to others, and experiencing positive emotions (Prizant et al., 2006).

## Transactional Support (TS)

Transactional Support (TS) is the third and concluding core component of the SCERTS Model. Transactional support includes: (a) interpersonal supports, (b) learning and educational supports, (c) support to families, and (d) support among professionals and other service providers. Furthermore, the model collaborators emphasized that transactional support needs to be infused across different activities and social partners since meaningful learning occurs only within the social context of everyday activities (Prizant et al., 2006). Thus far, the ultimate goals of the TS component of the SCERTS Model are: (a) to develop and provide the necessary learning and educational supports for a child, (b) to coordinate efforts among all partners in using interpersonal supports most conducive to social communication and emotional regulation, (c) to provide learning experiences with other children leading to the development of meaningful peer relationships, and (d) to support families with educational resources, direct strategies, and emotional support (Prizant et al., 2006).

## The Meanful Activities (MA) & Purposal Activities (PA) Approach

In light of designing individualized learning activities and modification of everyday activities to be both motivating and functional for a child, the SCERTS Model applies the Meanful Activities (MA) & Purposal Activities (PA) approach, which refers to the use of meaningful activities and purposeful activities (Prizant et al., 2006).

## Types of Activities

In the MA & PA approach, three types of activities are included: (a) goal-directed activities, (b) cooperative turn-taking games, and (c) theme-oriented activities (Prizant et al., 2006).

### Goal-Directed Activities

Goal-directed activities are the activities that have a sequence of steps with a clear and easily perceived end goal, such as making a sandwich, doing puzzles, and so on. They typically follow a logical sequence to conclusion. The primary function of engaging in such activities is to reach the end goal.

316

### Cooperative Turn-Taking Games

The primary goal of cooperative turn-taking games is in the success of social reciprocity, turn-taking, and mutual enjoyment derived from such shared activities. Such activities do not necessarily have clear end goals in the same sense as goal-directed activities. Rather, the success is measured by qualities like shared emotional experience, cooperation, and social reciprocity.

### Theme-Oriented Activities

Theme-oriented activities are organized around and may have multiple embedded components. Those components may be related to functional skills in daily routine such as going to school or visiting a doctor that involve sequences of smaller events that are organized in a logical manner. Such activities may be most appropriate for children at the more advanced language level.

#### GUIDELINES FOR IMPLEMENTING ACTIVITIES

In the training manual of the SCERTS Model (pp. 18–19), the model collaborators provided guidelines for (a) implementing activities within natural settings and routines according to the MA & PA approach, (b) individualizing educational programming to meet the unique needs of each child with ASD, and (c) providing the transactional supports necessary to best support a child with ASD while implementing the program. They are as follows:

1. Identify developmentally appropriate goals and outcomes.
2. Identify at least three activities that are meaningful, purposeful, and motivational.
3. Infuse goals across at least three activities across settings.
4. Identify/select optimal levels of social complexity in activities based on the child's learning need and strengths.
5. Within Steps 2–4, identify the sequential skills that are embedded into each activity.
6. Identify appropriate transactional supports for social communication and emotional regulation.
7. One-to-one or small-group planned activity routines may be provided as opportunities for increased practice or rehearsal of skills that require more instructional opportunities.

In summary, the MA & PA approach of the SCERTS Model is defined by the following six criteria made by the model collaborators. First of all, activities should make sense relative to a child's daily life activities and routines. That is, activities that occur across settings or that can readily be scheduled to occur are designed and/or modified to support the learning of functional skills. Second, activities should be selected on the basis of a child's interests, motivations, and strengths. If an activity is not inherently motivating, efforts should be made to infuse the activity with supports, topics, information, or qualities that support the child's learning and emotional regulation. Third, activities should be designed and/or transactional supports should be used to provide a child with a clear sense of the goal of the activity, the logical sequence of the activity, the steps within the activity, and clear indicators of when the activity is completed. Fourth, activities should provide a child with multiple and frequent opportunities for initiating communication, making choices, repairing breakdowns, and responding to the communication of partners. Fifth, activities should have an understandable structure for social participation and turn-ranking. Last but not least, whenever possible, activities should involve the participation of children who provide good language and social models as well as to support the development of positive relationships.

*See also* augmentative and alternative communication; play-oriented therapies; social skills training; symbolic thought.

REFERENCES

Prizant, B. M., Wetherby, A. M., Rubin, E., & Laurent, A. C. (2003). The SCERTS Model: A transactional, family-centered approach to enhancing communication and socioemotional abilities of children with autism spectrum disorder. *Infants and Young Children, 16*, 296–316.

Prizant, B. M., Wetherby, A. M., Rubin, E., Laurent, A. C., & Rydell, P. J. (2002). The SCERTS Model: Enhancing communication and socioemotional abilities of children with autism spectrum disorder. *Jenison Autism Journal, 14*, 2–19.

Prizant, B. M., Wetherby, A. M., Rubin, E., Laurent, A. C., & Rydell, P. J. (2006). *The SCERTS Model: A comprehensive educational approach for children with autism spectrum disorders.* Baltimore: Brookes Publishing Co.

The SCERTS Model (2006). Introduction to the SCERTS Model. Retrieved December 10, 2006, from http://www.scerts.com/frequently_asked_questions.htm.

KAI-CHIEN TIEN

## SCHEDULE OF REINFORCEMENT

Many different schedules of reinforcement may be applied to a person's behavior. Schedules of reinforcement are rules used to provide reinforcement for a target behavior (Skinner, 1953). Continuous schedules of reinforcement provide reinforcement for each instance of the behavior. Interval schedules of reinforcement require a minimum amount of time that must pass between reinforced responses (Ferster & Skinner, 1957). Interval schedules may have a consistent time period (fixed interval schedule) or a variable time period between **reinforcers** (variable interval schedule). Ratio schedules require a specific number of responses before a reinforced response (Ferster & Skinner, 1957). The number of responses may be fixed from one reinforcer to the next (fixed ratio schedule) or it may vary between reinforcers (variable ratio schedule). In extinction, reinforcement of a response is stopped, leading to a decline in the response (Zeiler, 1977). Finally, an intermittent schedule of reinforcement means that reinforcement follows at any rate that is lower than a continuous rate (Cooper, Heron, & Heward, 1996). Different schedules of reinforcement lead to different patterns of response.

REFERENCES

Cooper, J. O., Heron, T. E., & Heward, W. L. (1987). *Applied behavior analysis.* Upper Saddle River, NJ: Prentice Hall.

Ferster, C. B., & Skinner, B. F. (1957). *Schedules of reinforcement.* New York: Appleton-Century-Crofts.

Skinner, B. F. (1953). *Science and human behavior.* New York: Macmillan.

Zeiler, M. (1977). Schedules of reinforcement: The controlling variables. In W. K. Honig & J. E. R. Staddon (Eds.), *Handbook of operant behavior.* Englewood Cliffs, NJ: Prentice Hall.

JESSICA KATE PETERS AND TARA MIHOK

## SCHIZOPHRENIA

According to the ***Diagnostic and Statistical Manual of Mental Disorders*** (DSM-IV-TR; APA, 2000), schizophrenia is a mental disorder that lasts for at least 6 months and includes at least 1 month of active symptoms.

## SYMPTOMS

Active symptoms include:

- *Delusions*, which are disturbances of thinking involving misinterpretation of perceptions or experiences. Their content include a variety of topics, such as persecutory (e.g., the person believes that he or she is being spied on or followed), religious, referential (e.g., the person believes that passages from books, song lyrics, or certain gestures or comments from people are specifically directed to him or her), or somatic or grandiose (e.g., the person believes that he possess a special ability, beauty, or is an important person).
- *Hallucinations*, which are sensory perceptions but without the external stimulus that triggers them. They can be auditory, which are the most frequent, (e.g., hearing voices external to themselves), visual (e.g., seeing people, lights, animals that others can't see), olfactory, gustatory, and tactile.
- *Disorganized speech*, whereby the person switches from one topic to another, gives answers that are only minimally or not at all related to the question. In some cases the speech is so unorganized that it is nearly incomprehensible.
- *Disorganized or catatonic motor behavior,* which can be manifested in many ways, from decreased reactions to the environment to unpredictable agitation. Difficulties involve doing daily activities such as maintaining proper hygiene or dressing in unusual ways.
- *Negative symptoms*, which include poor eye contact, reduced body language, and an unexpressive face. Also, speech is brief and laconic, and the person is unable to initiate and persist in goal-directed activities.

## SUBTYPES OF SCHIZOPHRENIA

There are five subtypes of schizophrenia:

- *Paranoid.* Characterized by frequent preoccupation with one or more delusions or frequent auditory hallucinations.
- *Disorganized.* Characterized by disorganized speech and behavior and inappropriate or flat affect.
- *Catatonic.* Characterized by motoric immobility, trance or excessive motor activity, extreme negativism, mutism or **echolalia**, and stereotyped movements.
- *Undifferentiated.* This type of schizophrenia presents the core symptoms but does not meet the criteria for paranoid, disorganized, or catatonic types.
- *Residual.* Refers to instances when there has been at least one episode of schizophrenia but the actual clinical picture is without the core symptoms. Characterized by the presence of flat affect, poor speech, and attenuated symptoms of odd beliefs or unusual perceptual experiences.

This disorder involves dysfunction in one or more major areas of functioning such as interpersonal relations, work, education, or self-care. The dysfunction is clearly below the level that the person had achieved before the onset of the disorder.

## ONSET AND COURSE

The onset of schizophrenia typically occurs between the late teens and mid-30s; it is rare prior to adolescence. The age of onset for men is between 18 and 25 years and for women is between 25 and the mid-30s. The outbreak may be sudden; however, the majority of individuals manifest some early signs that develop slowly and gradually such as deterioration in hygiene, outbursts of anger, loss of interest in work or school, or social detachment. First-degree biological relatives of individuals with schizophrenia are 10 times more at risk for developing schizophrenia than the general population.

The course and outcome of schizophrenia are variable. Some patients will exhibit remissions, whereas others chronically show the symptoms. Complete remission is uncommon.

### PREVALENCE

Schizophrenia has been identified all around the world, and prevalence among adults is often reported to be 0.5–1.5 percent. Annual incidences range from 0.5 to 5.0 per 10,000.

### REFERENCE

American Psychiatric Association. (2000). *Diagnostic and statistical manual of mental disorders* (4th ed., text rev.). Washington, DC: Author.

### FURTHER INFORMATION

American Academy of Child and Adolescent Psychiatry. (1997). Practice parameters for the assessment and treatment of children and adolescents with schizophrenia. *Journal of the American Academy of Child and Adolescent Psychiatry, 36,* 177–193.

Mueser, K. T., & McGurk, S. R. (2004). Schizophrenia. *The Lancet, 363,* 2063–2072.

National Alliance for the Mentally Ill (NAMI): www.nami.org.

National Alliance for Research on Schizophrenia and Depression: www.narsad.org.

National Institute of Mental Health: www.nimh.nih.gov.

SUSANA BERNAD-RIPOLL

## SCHOOL FUNCTION ASSESSMENT

The School Function Assessment (SFA; Costerl, Deeney, Haltiwanger, & Haley, 1998) looks at functional tasks throughout a school day (kindergarten through grade 6) and the level of supported participation needed by the student. This questionnaire can be utilized to assist with collaborative program planning by school teams. The SFA is a tool that examines how much support is needed by the student so they can participate to the fullest extent possible and includes the adaptations will be needed to ensure that participation can happen.

### REFERENCE

Costerl, W., Deeney, T., Haltiwanger, J., & Haley, S. (1998). *School function assessment.* Austin, TX: Pro-Ed.

BROOKE YOUNG

## SCHOPLER, ERIC

Eric Schopler (1927–2006) received his PhD from the University of Chicago in Clinical Psychology and then joined the faculty at the University of North Carolina at Chapel Hill (UNC). It was at UNC in 1966 that Dr. Schopler furthered his dissertation research into what is now known as the TEACCH program (Treatment and Education of Autistic and Related Communication-Handicapped Children). Dr. Schopler wrote over 400 books and articles and received numerous awards for his work. The TEACCH program is recognized throughout the world. Dr. Schopler carried out his work at Division TEACCH until his death.

*See also* structured teaching.

TERRI COOPER SWANSON

# SCREENING

According to Ireton (1992), "the term screening technically refers to the process of selecting out for further study those high-risk individuals whose apparent problems might require special attention or intervention" (p. 487). Hooper and Umansky (2004) also stated that screening is a procedure used to identify infants and preschoolers who may be in need of a more comprehensive evaluation. To be more specific, screening is a quick process to identify young children who may be at risk for a **disability** or developmental problem or who may need further assessments for diagnosis. Screening is usually conducted through tests, checklists, or observations. In the process of screening, the professionals often depend on parents or others who know the child well to provide information on the child (e.g., sleeping patterns, eating behaviors, and so on).

*See also* Autism Screening Questionnaire; Checklist for Autism in Toddlers; Child Behavior Checklist for Ages 1½–5; Childhood Autism Rating Scale; Modified Checklist for Autism in Toddlers.

**REFERENCES**

Hooper, S. R., & Umansky, W. (2004). *Young children with special needs.* Upper Saddle River, NJ: Pearson Education.

Ireton, H. (1992). *Child development inventories.* Minneapolis, MN: Behavior Science Systems.

KAI-CHIEN TIEN

# SCREENING TOOL FOR AUTISM IN TWO-YEAR-OLDS (STAT)

The Screening Tool for Autism in Two-Year-Olds (STAT; Stone & Ousley, 1997) uses 12 interactive questions to assess an array of domains including play, communication, and imitation. The purpose of the STAT is to assist in the early identification and intervention of children with autism. To complete administration of the STAT, evaluators need a 20–30 minute semistructured play situation. The STAT is currently only given out at training workshops, as Vanderbilt University continues to study the validity of the administration.

*See also* screening.

**REFERENCE**

Stone, W. L., & Ousley, O. Y. (1997). *STAT Manual Screening Tool for Autism in Two-Year-Olds.* Unpublished manuscript, Vanderbilt University, Nashville, TN.

BROOKE YOUNG

# SECRETIN

Secretin is a **peptide** hormone that is found in the small intestine, brain, liver, and pancreas. Secretin is a controversial treatment for autism. At this printing, the U.S. Food and Drug Administration does not approve the use of secretin as a treatment for autism as there have been no **clinical trials** conducted. In 2004, Sturmey conducted a double-blind review of 15 articles related to the use of secretin to treat autism. The review found that none of the research articles reported that secretin showed significant effects, nor was it effective.

REFERENCE

Sturmey, P. (2005). Secretin is an ineffective treatment for pervasive developmental disabilities: A review of 15 double-blind randomized controlled trials. *Research in Developmental Disabilities, 26*, 87–97.

TERRI COOPER SWANSON

## SECTION 504 OF THE REHABILITATION ACT OF 1973

The **Rehabilitation Act of 1973** contains a variety of provisions focused on rights, advocacy, and protections for individuals with disabilities (U.S. Department of Health and Human Services, n.d.). Specifically, Section 504 of the Rehabilitation Act of 1973 is, in a sense, civil rights legislation for persons with disabilities by prohibiting discrimination on the basis of disabling conditions by programs and activities receiving or benefiting from federal financial assistance (deBettencourt, 2002; Smith, 2001, 2002).

According to the U.S. Department of Education (as cited by the U.S. Department of Health and Human Services, 2006), under Section 504 of the Rehabilitation Act, a recipient of federal financial assistance may not, on the basis of disability:

- Deny qualified individuals the opportunity to participate in or benefit from federally funded programs, services, or other benefits.
- Deny access to programs, services, benefits, or opportunities to participate as a result of physical barriers.
- Deny employment opportunities, including hiring, promotion, training, and fringe benefits, for which they are otherwise entitled or qualified.

Unlike the **Individuals with Disabilities Education Act** (IDEA), Section 504 protects individuals, birth through adulthood. Whereas IDEA is federally funded, school districts receive money based upon compliance with the law. Since Section 504 is a civil rights statute, the federal government does not provide additional funding for students identified under Section 504 (deBettencourt, 2002).

### DEFINING TERMS

Section 504 protects *otherwise qualified* individuals from discrimination based on their disability. This means that a person with a disability must be qualified to do something before the presence of the disability can be a factor in discrimination. For example, an individual with **attention deficit hyperactivity disorder** (ADHD) tries out for a baseball team and does not have the skills to throw, catch, hit the ball, or run the bases and, therefore, is not picked for the team. Discrimination under Section 504 in this case would not be an issue because the individual is not *otherwise qualified* to be on the team (Smith, 2001, 2002).

Section 504 states:

> No otherwise qualified individual with a disability ... shall solely by reason of her or his disability be excluded from the participation in, be denied the benefits of, or be subjected to discrimination under any program or activity receiving Federal financial assistance. (29 U.S.C.A. § 794)

To be eligible for services under Section 504, then, a person must satisfy this definition for disability. A person is considered to have a disability if he or she (Rehabilitation Act, § 706[8]):

- has a physical or mental impairment that substantially limits one or more of such person's major life activities,
- has a record of such an impairment, or
- is regarded as having such an impairment.

The Rehabilitation Act of 1973 defines a physical or mental impairment as: (a) any physiological disorder or condition, cosmetic disfigurement, or anatomical loss affecting one or more of the following body systems: neurological, musculoskeletal, special sense organs, respiratory, speech organs, cardiovascular, reproductive, digestive, genito-urinary, hemic and lymphatic, skin, and endocrine; or (b) any mental or psychological disorder such as emotional or mental illness (Smith, 2002, p. 260). The burden of providing proof of this disability falls on the individual (Madaus & Shaw, 2004).

Major life activities include a wide variety of daily activities such as caring for oneself, performing manual tasks, walking, stooping, seeing, hearing, speaking, eating, breathing, learning, and working. Basically, any function that is performed routinely by individuals is considered a major life activity. (Smith, 2002)

## QUALIFYING FOR SERVICES

To qualify for services under Section 504, a student must be identified through evaluation procedures that gather information from a variety of sources. A team of knowledgeable personnel is charged with the task of determining whether a disability *substantially limits* a major life activity. This is a very subjective process. According to Smith (2001), "substantially limits" may be defined as:

- unable to perform a major life activity that the average person in the general population can perform, or
- significantly restricted as to the condition, manner, or duration for which an individual can perform a particular major life activity as compared to the condition, manner, or duration for which the average person in the general population can perform that same major life activity. (p. 337)

Smith (2001, 2002) recommends that when teams are defining limits they make comparisons to the average child or person. Specifically, decisions should be based upon: the nature and severity of the disability, the duration of the disability, and any long-term impact of the disability. As with the requirements of IDEA, parent notification is required, but contrary to IDEA, for the 504 determination, assessment decisions do not require written parental consent. However, good professional practice would suggest that parental consent be obtained.

Section 504 requires "periodic" reevaluation, and a reevaluation is required before a "significant" change in placement takes place. Unlike IDEA, there is no provision that allows for independent evaluation at the school district's expense (deBettencourt, 2002).

It is important to note that children who qualify for protection and services under IDEA also qualify for protection under Section 504. Thus, they are entitled to all the rights and privileges of this act as well (Turnbull, Brennan, & Stowe, 2002).

## SERVICES

Under Section 504, an "appropriate" education means an education that is comparable to that provided to students without disabilities (deBettencourt, 2002). Blazer (1999) outlines a structured, collaborative approach to program planning that includes parents, the student, and school personnel. Although a written document is not mandated, it is recommended. The **Individualized Education Program** (IEP) form may be used, but many schools use a different form for the Section 504 plan. There are no specific requirements for parent participation, nor is a time period specified for review of the 504 plan, but best practice suggests reviewing the document annually.

For many school-aged children, the major life activity affected by their disability is learning. Accommodations are one way that schools provide services for individuals that qualify for a 504 plan. The vast majority of accommodations will occur in the general education setting.

Section 504 is not limited to individuals within the school. For purposes of employment, qualified individuals with disabilities are persons who, with *reasonable accommodation*, can perform the essential functions of the job for which they have applied or have been hired to perform (Smith, 2002). "Reasonable accommodation" means that employers must take reasonable steps to accommodate the disability unless it would cause them undue hardship. Again, it is important to keep in mind that a person must be otherwise qualified for the job in order for the employer to be required to make reasonable accommodations.

In summary, Section 504 is the civil rights legislation that protects persons, birth through death, who qualify for services under IDEA. In addition, it protects all other individuals who meet the definition for having a disability outlined within the Rehabilitation Act of 1973.

## REFERENCES

Blazer, B. (1999). Developing 504 classroom accommodation plans: A collaborative, systematic, parent-student-teacher approach. *Teaching Exceptional Children, 32*(2), 28–33.

deBettencourt, L. U. (2002). Understanding the differences between IDEA and Section 504. *Teaching Exceptional Children, 34*(3), 16–23.

Madaus, J. W., & Shaw, S. F. (2004). Section 504: Differences in the regulations for secondary and postsecondary education. *Intervention in School and Clinic, 40*(2), 81–87.

Rehabilitation Act of 1973, 29 U.S.C. § 701 *et seq.*

Smith, T. E. C. (2001). Section 504, the ADA, and public schools: What educators need to know. *Remedial and Special Education, 22*(6), 335–343.

Smith, T. E. C. (2002). Section 504: What teachers need to know. *Intervention in School and Clinic, 37*(5), 259–266.

Turnbull, H. R., III, Brennan, L. W., & Stowe, M. J. (2002). A brief overview of special education law with focus on autism. *Journal of Autism and Developmental Disorders, 32*(5), 479–493.

United States Department of Education, Office of Special Education and Rehabilitative Services. (2004). *The rehabilitation act.* Retrieved September 15, 2006, from http://www.ed.gov/policy/speced/reg/narrative.html.

United States Department of Health and Human Services, Office of Civil Rights, (n.d.). *Your rights under Section 504 of the rehabilitation act.* Retrieved September 15, 2006, from http://www.hhs.gov/ocr/504.html.

SHEILA M. SMITH

# SEIZURE DISORDER

Seizure disorder (or epilepsy) is a neurological disorder in which abnormal electrical signals occur in the brain. There are different kinds of seizure disorders, and people are affected differently by them. Some people experience seizures frequently and others experience them quite infrequently.

## COMMON TERMINOLOGY

### Aura

Many people experience a "warning feeling" right before a seizure occurs. These warning feelings may include a change in body temperature, a strange taste or smell, or a particular sound.

### Febrile Seizures

These seizures result from a child experiencing a rapidly increasing fever. Although they look like tonic-clonic seizures, these are not epileptic seizures.

### Partial Seizures

In these seizures, the excessive electrical signals occur in only one part of the brain and are many times unnoticeable. In fact, the child may look like he or she is simply daydreaming for a few seconds. These seizures used to be referred to as petit mal seizures.

### Status Seizures

These seizures occur so rapidly that the child does not regain consciousness between seizures. If this occurs, it is considered a medical emergency.

### Tonic-Clonic Seizures

In these seizures, a child undergoes two phases. In the tonic phase, the child loses consciousness and becomes rigid. In the clonic phase, the child's extremities jerk. After the seizure, the child slowly begins to regain consciousness.

## SEIZURE DISORDER AND AUTISM

There are many causes for a person to develop seizures, although, in some cases, there are no known causes for the seizures. Some known causes include head injury, meningitis, brain tumors, stroke, poisoning, or birth defects that affect the brain. Additionally, several studies have reported that individuals with autism are at a greater risk for developing a seizure disorder. These studies have found that seizure disorders are more common in individuals with autism who have a lower IQ.

## FURTHER INFORMATION

Jurasek, G. (2001). Options in seizure management: The vagus nerve stimulator—experiences to date. Part 1: An introduction to seizure disorders and existing therapies. *The Exceptional Parent, 31*(8), 107–112.

Tuchman, R. (2003). Brain waves, seizures, and the child with autism. *The Exceptional Parent, 33*(3), 104–107.

MAYA ISRAEL

## SELECTIVE MUTISM

Selective mutism is a childhood disorder, characterized by the persistent failure to speak in at least one social environment. It usually occurs before a child is 5 years old and in most cases the child will speak to their parents and/or select others. The *Diagnostic and Statistical Manual of Mental Disorders* (DSM-IV-TR; APA, 2000, pp. 125–127) defines selective mutism as:

- Consistent failure to speak in specific social situations (in which there is an expectation for speaking, e.g., at school) despite speaking in other situations.
- The disturbance interferes with educational or occupational achievement or with social communication.
- The duration of the disturbance is at least one month (not limited to the first month of school).
- The failure to speak is not due to a lack of knowledge of, or comfort with, the spoken language required in the social situation.
- The disturbance is not better accounted for by a communication disorder (e.g., stuttering) and does not occur exclusively during the course of a **pervasive developmental disorder**, **schizophrenia**, or other psychotic disorder.

Features and severity of selective mutism vary from child to child. Individual children with the disorder sometimes display excessive shyness, fear, anxiety, and embarrassment. They usually do not display other speech or language problems, although there can be associated articulation or phonological difficulty or receptive or expressive language disorder, but these are not implicit in the mutism disorder.

Children with selective mutism often will respond by head nodding or gestures. They may "wait out" a person trying to guess what the child wants or needs to communicate. Children with selective mutism have a real fear of speaking and often will stand motionless when requested to speak.

Many children from bilingual families, or who have lived in a foreign country, make up a proportion of children who are selectively mute. There is no correlation or association between children who are selectively mute and those who are on the autism spectrum. The differences are distinct in that children who are selectively mute have the ability to speak and process language normally, whereas children with autistic disorders do not process language in the same way as typically developing children, and they display atypical social interactions and repetitive behaviors.

Due to the rarity of selective mutism, few professionals are familiar with the disorder, and sometimes misinterpret the child's behavior as "just shy," oppositional, or defiant. Often selective mutism is misdiagnosed, and therefore children with the disorder do not receive appropriate treatment. The child with suspected selective mutism should be evaluated by a knowledgeable **psychologist** and a **speech language pathologist** should conduct a thorough language evaluation. The evaluation process should include a comprehensive interview with the parent and observations in different settings where the child is expected to speak, such as the home and school.

There are several approaches to treatment for selective mutism. Behavioral approaches include the use of positive reinforcement and desensitization techniques. Slowly introducing the child to social environments in nonthreatening ways can help reduce the child's anxiety of speaking. Play or interaction with one other child in the classroom setting when no one else is there, can be slowly extended into two children, and then a small group when the child with selective mutism becomes more comfortable and begins to speak. The child should be positively reinforced when he or she is comfortable receiving praise or encouragement.

Psychological approaches to treatment, such as play therapy and psychotherapy, can be used effectively when the child does not feel threatened to speak and can help a child lessen his or her anxiety. Cognitive behavior therapy is used to redirect fears and highlight the child's positive characteristics.

Certain medications such as selective serotonin reuptake inhibitors that help reduce anxiety and/or depression have been found to be effective for treating selective mutism, especially when paired with behavioral treatments. Other treatment approaches include self-esteem boosters, frequent socialization, school involvement, and family involvement and acceptance.

REFERENCE

American Psychiatric Association. (2000). *Diagnostic and statistical manual of mental disorders* (4th ed., text rev.). Washington, DC: Author.

FURTHER INFORMATION

Anstendig, K. (1998). Selective mutism: A review of the treatment literature by modality from 1980–1996. *Psychotherapy, 35,* 381–391.
Anstendig, K. D. (1999). Is selective mutism an anxiety disorder? *Journal of Anxiety Disorders, 13,* 417–434.
Bergman, R. L., Piacentini, J., & McCracken, J. T. (2002). Prevalence and description of selective mutism in a school-based sample. *Journal of the American Academy of Child and Adolescent Psychiatry, 41,* 938–946.
Dow, S. P., Sonies, B. C., Scheib, D., Moss, S. E., & Leonard, H. L. (1995). Practical guidelines for the assessment and treatment of selective mutism. *Journal of the American Academy of Child and Adolescent Psychiatry, 34*(7), 836–846.

ANN PILEWSKIE

## SELF-ADVOCACY

Self-advocacy is the practice of knowing of and controlling one's own rights, responsibilities, and resources without undue influence from others.

*See also* advocate; self-determination.

JEANNE HOLVERSTOTT

## SELF-CONTAINED CLASSROOM

A self-contained classroom is an educational setting outside of the general education classroom where students with disabilities receive educational and related services for the majority of their school day. Students with mental retardation represent the largest disability category represented in self-contained classrooms.

KATHERINE E. COOK

## SELF-DETERMINATION

Promoting self-determination has become an increasingly important topic in disability advocacy and supports. This is, in large measure, because people with disabilities have identified enhanced self-determination as being important to and because research has shown that adolescents and young adults who are more self-determined achieve more positive adult outcomes and a more positive quality of life.

The meaning of the term has its roots in the philosophical doctrine of *determinism*. Determinism refers to the idea or proposition that all events, including human behavior and thought, are caused by events that occurred before the event. Self-determined behavior refers to human behavior that is *caused* (e.g., determined) by the person as opposed to being caused by someone or something else.

People who are self-determined, then, make or cause things to happen in their own lives. They act volitionally (based on their own will, preferences, choices, and interests) instead of being coerced or forced to act in certain ways by others or by circumstances.

Just as important, self-determined behavior is intentional and goal oriented. That is, self-determined people intentionally and purposefully act to achieve goals in their lives. Particularly with regard to individuals with more significant intellectual impairments, it is important to note that what constitutes "self-determined" behavior is not independently performing all the steps in achieving a goal, but that it is the person who is causing this to happen.

During the twentieth century, the self-determination construct began to be used with reference to the right or rights of people to self-governance. The right to self-determination, as applied to citizens of a country or to members of a minority group such as people with disabilities, implies that individuals have the right to a voice in decisions that impact their lives—to have a say in governing themselves. Again, however, even in this group context, self-determination implies that it is the people themselves (self-) who have the right to cause things to happen to and for them—the essence of governing.

People with disabilities express the desire both to have greater opportunities to become more self-determined as individuals and to the right to self-determination as a group.

## SELF-DETERMINATION IN DISABILITY ADVOCACY AND SUPPORTS

Efforts to promote self-determination in disability advocacy and services have taken several forms. Among the first such initiatives were programmatic efforts to provide instruction and opportunities to promote the self-determination of transition-age youth with disabilities. Research with adolescents with disabilities has shown that students who leave high school more self-determined achieve more positive adult outcomes, including better employment, community inclusion, and independent living outcomes. Educational efforts focus on teaching students the skills and knowledge they will need to act in a self-determined manner. Curricular areas include teaching decision making, problem solving, goal setting, **self-advocacy**, and self-management skills. In addition, providing opportunities for students to express preferences and make choices has also been recognized as important. Thus, a frequent practice involves instructional efforts and supports to enable students to play a meaningful role in their own transition planning meeting, including, in some circumstances, having the student be the chairperson for the meeting.

A second application of the self-determination construct to disability advocacy and supports has involved initiatives that enable people with disabilities (and, when necessary or appropriate, their family members) to make decisions about how money and other resources that are intended to provide supports are allocated and used. Historically, funding for services was given to agencies that created these supports. However, many people with disabilities found that available services did not fit their needs well. As an alternative, model programs began to be developed in which the funding went to the person with the disability and/or his or her family, who then made decisions about what services to purchase. These models often involved person-centered planning, individualized budgeting, and the use of service brokers, who act on behalf of the person with the disability or his or her family to identify what options exist to provide the types of supports identified by the person and his or her family.

What is central to both of these initiatives and similar efforts is that they enable people with disabilities to act in a self-determined manner—that is, to act volitionally, without coercion, and to make or cause things to happen in their lives.

Writing in 2000, Jean Paul Bovee, a man with autism, stated that "people with autism should be treated with the same dignity, respect, and equality as people without autism" (pp. 250–251). Recognizing the importance of promoting self-determination is an important way to ensure that people are treated with dignity and respect and to enable people to attain true equality.

## REFERENCE

Bovee, J. P. (2000). A right to our own life, our own way. *Focus on Autism and Other Developmental Disabilities, 15*(4), 250–252.

## FURTHER INFORMATION

Algozzine, B., Browder, D., Karvonen, M., Test, D. W., & Wood, W. M. (2001). Effects of intervention to promote self-determination for individuals with disabilities. *Review of Educational Research, 71*, 219–277.

Field, S., Martin, J., Miller, R., Ward, M., & Wehmeyer, M. (1998). *A practical guide to teaching self-determination.* Reston, VA: Council for Exceptional Children.

Palmer, S., & Wehmeyer, M. L. (2003). Promoting self-determination in early elementary school: Teaching self-regulated problem-solving and goal setting skills. *Remedial and Special Education, 24*, 115–126.

Sowers, J., & Powers, L. (1995). Enhancing the participation and independence of students with severe physical and multiple disabilities in performing community activities. *Mental Retardation, 33*, 209–220.

Test, D. W., Karvonen, M., Wood, W. M., Browder, D., & Algozzine, B. (2000). Choosing a self-determination curriculum: Plan for the future. *Teaching Exceptional Children, 33*(2), 48–54.

Wehmeyer, M. L. (1998). Self-determination and individuals with significant disabilities: Examining meanings and misinterpretations. *Journal of the Association for Persons with Severe Handicaps, 23*, 5–16.

Wehmeyer, M. L. (1999). A functional model of self-determination: Describing development and implementing instruction. *Focus on Autism and Other Developmental Disabilities, 14*, 53–61.

Wehmeyer, M. L., Abery, B., Mithaug, D. E., & Stancliffe, R. J. (2003). *Theory in self-determination: Foundations for educational practice.* Springfield, IL: Charles C Thomas, Publisher.

Wehmeyer, M. L., Agran, M., & Hughes, C. (1998). *Teaching self-determination to students with disabilities: Basic skills for successful transition.* Baltimore: Brookes Publishing Co.

Wehmeyer, M. L., & Palmer, S. B. (2003). Adult outcomes for students with cognitive disabilities three years after high school: The impact of self-determination. *Education and Training in Developmental Disabilities, 38*, 131–144.

Wehmeyer, M. L., Palmer, S. B., Agran, M., Mithaug, D. E., & Martin, J. (2000). Teaching students to become causal agents in their lives: The self-determining learning model of instruction. *Exceptional Children, 66,* 439–453.

Wehmeyer, M. L., & Schwartz, M. (1997). Self-determination and positive adult outcomes: A follow-up study of youth with mental retardation or learning disabilities. *Exceptional Children, 63,* 245–255.

MICHAEL L. WEHMEYER

## SELF-HELP SKILLS

Self-help skills generally focus on necessary skills for an individual to perform independently the routine activities of daily living. At the most basic level, these include dressing oneself, demonstrating knowledge of personal hygiene (bathing, brushing teeth, grooming), feeding oneself, and caring for one's possessions. At a more advanced level, these skills can include knowing how and who to ask for assistance, exercising judgment in terms of interacting with others and decision making, using money to make purchases, traveling in the community independently, maintaining a job, living successfully in semi-independent or independent circumstances, socializing appropriately with peers and coworkers, and other necessary skills expected for independence.

*See also* adaptive behavior; self-advocacy.

ANDREA M. BABKIE

## SELF-INJURIOUS BEHAVIOR

Self-injurious behavior (SIB) is any self-inflicted physical behavior that causes bruises, open wounds, tissue damage, redness, bleeding, and welts. These behaviors are most commonly inflicted by biting the hand, wrist, or arm, head-banging, and scratching or rubbing the skin. Sometimes seen in individuals with autism or severe developmental disabilities, self-injurious behavior may have many reasons for its manifestation. These include possible biochemical problems (release of beta-endorphins from the injury); seizure activity; masking of pain from competing infections, headaches, or gastrointestinal problems; sensory stimulation to increase arousal levels; frustration due to communication difficulties; and social attention. A thorough functional behavioral/medical analysis is needed to determine causes and interventions for self-injurious behavior.

*See also* functional behavior assessment; seizures; sensory integration.

### FURTHER INFORMATION
Durand, V. M., & Crimmins, D. B. (1988). Identifying the variables maintaining self-injurious behavior. *Journal of Autism and Developmental Disorders, 18,* 99–117.

Dyer, K., & Larsson, E. V. (1997). Developing functional communication skills: Alternatives to severe behavior problems. In N. Singh (Ed.), *Prevention and treatment of severe problems: Models and methods in developmental disabilities* (pp. 121–148). Pacific Grove, CA: Brooks Cole Publishing Company.

Edelson, S. M. (1984). Implications of sensory stimulation in self-destructive behavior. *American Journal of Mental Deficiency, 89,* 140–145.

Edelson, S. M., Taubman, M. T., & Lovaas, O. I. (1983). Some social contexts to self-destructive behavior. *Journal of Abnormal Child Psychology, 11,* 299–312.

ANN PILEWSKIE

## SELF-REGULATION

Self-regulation is the ability of an individual to recognize her own sensory needs and adjust her actions and behaviors as needed to meet the demands of the activity or situation in which she is engaged.

KELLY M. PRESTIA

## SENSATION AVOIDING

Sensation avoiding is a neurological characteristic of individuals who have a low sensory threshold, or tolerance, for sensory stimuli in which they withdraw or avoid certain environments or activities that are overwhelming or unpleasant for them. For example, an individual with a low threshold for tactile stimulation may refuse to wear loose or scratchy clothing.

KELLY M. PRESTIA

## SENSATION SEEKING

Sensation seeking is a neurological characteristic of individuals who have a high threshold, or tolerance, for sensory stimuli. Sensory seekers are constantly looking for sensory stimuli in their environment in an attempt to fulfill their sensory need. The child who runs his hand along the wall as he walks down the hall may be seeking sensory input from the changes in textures on the wall.

KELLY M. PRESTIA

## SENSORIMOTOR

Sensorimotor refers to the connection between movement and sensation. The brain receives sensory information via one or more of the sensory systems, the nervous system processes that information, and the body turns that information into a meaningful, appropriate motor response.

KELLY M. PRESTIA

## SENSORIMOTOR EARLY CHILDHOOD ACTIVITIES

Young children with poor **sensory processing** abilities, especially those with autism spectrum disorder (ASD), benefit from specific **sensorimotor** input in order to modulate their nervous systems so that they can participate in **activities of daily living**. Such activities are most beneficial in early childhood, the period of time when their sensory systems are at the most crucial neurological development. There are many ways to introduce these sensory-rich experiences to children with sensory processing disorder (SPD), for example including sensory strategies incorporated into a child's daily routine along with sensorimotor activities can help a child maintain a "just right" alertness for participation and focusing.

Early childhood sensorimotor activities involve integration on multiple levels. The activities are integrated within the context of a child's educational curriculum, an integrative team of therapists and teachers work together, and the activities themselves integrate each child's nervous system in an organized manner. These activities are based on four principles: (a) they are created around the **sensory integration** (Ayers, 1979), so that sequenced activities follow sensorimotor development for each lesson plan; (b) they are theme based, as activities are developed around thematic educational curriculum, and literature based, as a storybook is included in every lesson plan, allowing children to develop early emergent literacy skills; (c) they use a trans-disciplinary approach to treatment in which an integrated team crosses the disciplinary lines collaborating and modeling for one another utilizing best practice for services; and (d) the children engage in the sensorimotor activities within classroom settings for inclusion with peer models.

There can be many different themes included with these early childhood sensori-motor activities, anything from apples to zoo. As outlined by Brack (2004), the structure of the early childhood sensorimotor activities always follows a prescribed sequence:

1. A warm-up activity cues children that group time is ready to begin and introduces them to the theme.
2. A movement activity involving the vestibular system helps to alert the nervous system for engagement.
3. A "heavy work" activity involving the proprioceptive system helps to modulate the nervous system allowing the children to focus.
4. A balance activity is a higher level of sensory integration and balance skills are necessary for large motor skills development.
5. An eye-hand coordination activity helps children develop skills necessary for school readiness, such as handwriting, coloring, and cutting.
6. A cool-down activity helps children attain a "just right" alertness level so that they are prepared to focus on the fine-motor activity.
7. A fine-motor activity completes the routine as the children engage in functional activities. The children work on refined fine-motor coordination skills so that they can hold a pencil, use crayons and scissors, and manipulate fasteners such as buttons and zippers.

Transitions can be difficult for children with SPD and especially children who are on the autism spectrum. Therefore a transition sequence is included in every lesson plan. This involves the children giving themselves a hug, pushing on their heads, (proprioceptive input), blowing a feather (for deep diaphragmatic breathing for sensory modulation), "kissing their brains" for self-affirmation, finally saying, "You're so smart, you're ready to start!"

While the children are engaged in the sensorimotor activities, they are developing essential school readiness skills for cognitive development, language skills for communication, social skills for cooperative and imaginative play, and emotional development to give courage and hope for children with sensory processing difficulties.

*See also* imagination; proprioception; sensory processing; sensory processing dysfunction; social skills training; vestibular.

**REFERENCES**
Ayres, A. J. (1979). *Sensory integration and the child.* Los Angeles: Western Psychological Services.
Brack, J. C. (2004). *Learn to move, move to learn: Sensorimotor early childhood activity themes.* Shawnee Mission, KS: Autism Asperger Publishing Company.

JENNY CLARK BRACK

## SENSORY HISTORY

Sensory history is documented information from a primary caregiver regarding an individual's sensory preferences and patterns of behavior. This information is important in developing appropriate interventions and setting up the individual's environment for optimal performance.

KELLY M. PRESTIA

## SENSORY INTEGRATION

Sensory integration is often used interchangeably to describe three different, but related, areas. The term *sensory integration* can describe a theory, a neurological process, and a form of therapy. First, sensory integration is often used to describe a theory developed in the 1970s by Dr. A. Jean Ayres, an **occupational therapist** who researched sensory functioning in individuals with learning disabilities. Ayres proposed that maladaptive, inappropriate behaviors result from a dysfunction in the nervous system between the sensory receptors: the brain and the motor responses (Ayres, 1979). Sensory integration is a model that describes, as well as anticipates, behavior from a neurological perspective. Ayres also described sensory information as "food for the brain" (Ayres, 1979). Similar to the way our bodies process food for nourishment and physical activity, our brains must process sensory information for optimal physical, cognitive, and neurological development. Fisher and Murray (1991) describe five assumptions of sensory integration as a theory. First, the central nervous system is "plastic"—that is, its structure and processes can be modified or changed. Second, sensory integration within the nervous system occurs in a developmental sequence. This means that behaviors can change as the nervous system matures. Third, the brain functions as a whole but the individual sensory systems are organized in a hierarchy. The brain is composed of low and high areas. The lower areas are where the sensory information is received and organized. The higher areas are where more complex, cognitive functioning takes place, such as language, learning, and complex behavior. The emergence of the higher levels is dependent upon the ability of the lower levels to receive, organize, and integrate information properly. Fourth, eliciting **adaptive behaviors** facilitates a nervous system that functions in an organized, integrated manner. Conversely, an accurately and appropriately functioning sensory and nervous system is reflected through adaptive responses. Sensory integration theory believes that the development of behaviors is circular, in that each behavior gives feedback to the nervous system, which in turn, promotes further maturation of the nervous system. Finally, there is an inner drive within people to develop integration between their sensory systems and nervous system through **sensorimotor** activities. Simply "being" or "seeing" is not enough for people. Individuals have a strong desire to explore and learn about their environment and its contents for themselves.

Sensory integration also describes the neurological process between the sensory receptors, the brain, and the muscles and nerves that produce behaviors and responses. It is the ability of the brain to receive input from various receptors in the body, organize and prioritize that input, and produce an appropriate behavior or response, known as an adaptive behavior or adaptive response. The sensory receptors have two main functions. First, sensory receptors respond to a sensation to alert or arouse the brain to generate awareness. This is important for detecting harmful situations. Second, the receptors respond to gather information about the environment to create a sort of "map" of the body and the environment. These "maps" help the brain to organize a response and take appropriate action. It also helps us to differentiate objects in the environment, and know where our bodies end and where the world begins. In typical sensory integration, these two functions of the sensory receptors work together and balance one another so that we may be alerted to harmful situations, as well as learn from our environment. When an imbalance of these two systems occurs, a dysfunction of sensory integration occurs. Typical sensory integration is important for the development of self-control, self-esteem, motor skills, and higher-level cognitive functions (Kranowitz, 2003). When sensory integration within the body is disrupted or dysfunctional, atypical or inappropriate behaviors and responses can be seen.

Third, sensory integration can also refer to a specific therapeutic intervention, often provided by an occupational therapist. Sensory integration therapy is a direct intervention, which provides controlled sensory input, often combined with physical activity, to produce an adaptive response. Interventions that combine increasing challenges with activities in which the individual is already successful often have the most successful results for changing behaviors. The behaviors and responses of the individual receiving sensory integration therapy must be carefully monitored by the intervening therapist to determine if the sensory input is appropriate in intensity and length, and is meaningful to the individual. If sensory stimulation is too intense or not meaningful for the individual, then no change in response or an adverse change in responses may occur. The overall goal of sensory integration therapy is to rewire the nervous system to process and organize sensory information more efficiently and effectively to produce adaptive responses. Before an intervention begins, the intervening therapist may use specific assessment tools to gather important information about how the individual is functioning. For example, *The Sensory Profile* (Dunn, 1999) or *The Sensory Integration and Praxis Test* (Ayres, 1989) are tools used by professionals to gather information regarding the individual's ability to process sensory information, and how they respond to typical sensory stimuli. Specialized certifications and training programs in sensory integration therapy are available for professionals.

*See also* maladaptive behavior; self-injurious behavior.

## REFERENCES

Ayres, A. J. (1979). *Sensory integration and the child*. Los Angeles: Western Psychological Services.

Ayres, A. J. (1989). *The sensory integration and praxis test*. Los Angeles: Western Psychological Services.

Dunn, W. (1999). *The sensory profile*. San Antonio, TX: Harcourt Assessment.

Fisher, A. G., & Murray, E. A. (1991). Introduction to sensory integration theory. In A. G. Fisher, E. A. Murray, & A. C. Bundy (Eds.), *Sensory Integration Theory and Practice* (pp. 3, 15–17). Philadelphia: F. A. Davis Company.

Kranowitz, C. S. (2003). *The out of sync child has fun*. New York: Berkley Publishing Group.

KELLY M. PRESTIA

## SENSORY INTEGRATION AND PRAXIS TEST (SIPT)

The Sensory Integration and Praxis Test (SIPT; Ayres, 1989) is a standardized battery consisting of 17 subtests designed to identify patterns of function and dysfunction in **sensory integration** and motor planning (**praxis**). Administration of this assessment is time-consuming (2–3 hours) and scoring is tedious (computer scoring programs can help cut down on scoring time). It is appropriate for use with children ages 4 through 8 years, 11 months of age. Competent administration and interpretation of this assessment require specific training and certification provided by Sensory Integration International or Western Psychological Services.

### REFERENCE

Ayres, J. (1989). *The Sensory Integration and Praxis Test*. Los Angeles: Western Psychological Services.

LISA ROBBINS

## SENSORY INTEGRATION DYSFUNCTION

Individuals on the autism spectrum are often called lazy, overactive, stubborn, or even accident prone. These descriptions often misrepresent individuals when it comes to the child with an autism spectrum disorder (ASD). Many individuals with ASD have difficulty regulating their sensory systems. This is known as sensory integration dysfunction (SID).

A. Jean Ayres (1973) wrote *Sensory Integration and Learning Disorders*. It was in this first book that she described the first six sensory modalities: (a) the **vestibular** system, (b) the tactile system, (c) **proprioception**, (d) the auditory system, (e) olfaction, and (f) vision. Today professionals in the area of sensory systems have added the gustatory system to the sensory systems to make the total seven. These seven sensory systems work together to interpret the sensory input coming in from the environment, changing the input into information that the body can use. For further descriptions of each sensory system and where they are found, see Table 7.

SID is the inability of the sensory system to interpret input from the environment in a manner that is usable. Individuals with SID do not effectively utilize sensory information coming through the sensory systems in a manner that is functional. As a result, individuals with SID appear to be clumsy, unoriented, or lazy (Miller & Lane, 2000). In response, an individual may avoid confusing or distressing sensations or seek out more of the sensation to find out more about it (Biel & Peske, 2005).

A variety of sensory assessments are available to provide the necessary information for professionals, such as **occupational therapists**, to provide the correct form of sensory integration therapy. Commonly used assessments include: (a) the Sensory Profile (Dunn, 1999), (b) the Short Sensory Profile (McIntosh, Miller, Schyu, & Dunn, 1999), and (c) Sensory Integration and Praxis Test (SIPT; Ayres, 1989). Administration and interpretation of these assessments are typically the first steps in determining the type(s) of sensory integration therapy necessary for an individual. These interventions aid the sensory systems of individuals with SID to organize themselves, thus allowing the child to function appropriately.

**Table 7. Location and Functions of the Sensory Systems**

| System | Location | Function |
|---|---|---|
| Tactile (touch) | Skin—density of cell distribution varies throughout the body. Areas of greatest density include mouth, hands, and genitals. | Provides information about the environment and object qualities (touch, pressure, texture, hard, soft, sharp, dull, heat, cold, pain). |
| Vestibular (balance) | Inner ear—stimulated by head movements and input from other senses, especially visual. | Provides information about where our body is in space, and whether or not we or our surroundings are moving. Tells about speed and direction of movement. |
| Proprioception (body awareness) | Muscles and joints—activated by muscle contractions and movement. | Provides information about where a certain body part is and how it is moving. |
| Visual (sight) | Retina of the eye—stimulated by light. | Provides information about objects and persons. Helps us define boundaries as we move through time and space. |
| Auditory (hearing) | Inner ear—stimulated by air/sound waves. | Provides information about sounds in the environment (loud, soft, high, low, near far). |
| Gustatory (taste) | Chemical receptors in the tongue—closely entwined with the olfactory (smell) system. | Provides information about different types of taste (sweet, sour, bitter, salty, spicy). |
| Olfactory (smell) | Chemical receptors in the nasal structure—closely associated with the gustatory system. | Provides information about different types of smell (musty, acrid, putrid, flowery, pungent). |

*Source:* From *Asperger Syndrome and Sensory Issues: Practical Solutions for Making Sense of the World* (p. 5), by B. S. Myles, K. T. Cook, N. E. Miller, L. Rinner, & L. A. Robbins, 2000, Shawnee Mission, KS: AAPC.

**REFERENCES**

Ayres, A. J. (1973). *Sensory integration and learning disorders*. Los Angeles: Western Psychological Services.

Ayres, A. J. (1989). *Sensory integration and praxis test*. Los Angeles: Western Psychological Services.

Biel, L., & Peske, N. (2005). *Raising a sensory smart child*. New York: Penguin Books.

Dunn, W. (1999). *The Sensory Profile: A contextual measure of children's responses to sensory experiences in daily life*. San Antonio, TX: The Psychological Corporation.

McIntosh, D. N., Miller, L. J., Schyu, V., & Dunn, W. (1999). *Short sensory profile*. San Antonio, TX: The Psychological Corporation.

Miller, L. J., & Lane, S. J. (2000). Toward a consensus in terminology in sensory integration theory and practice: Part 1: Taxonomy of neurophysiological processes. *Sensory Integration Special Interest Section Quarterly, 23*(1), 1–4.

Myles, B. S., Cook, K. T., Miller, N., Rinner, L., & Robbins, L. (2000). *Asperger syndrome and sensory issues: Practical solutions for making sense of the world*. Shawnee Mission, KS: Autism Asperger Publishing Company.

**FURTHER INFORMATION**

Brack, J. C. (2004). *Learn to move; move to learn: Sensorimotor early childhood themes*. Shawnee Mission, KS: Autism Asperger Publishing Company.

Brack, J. C. (2005). *Sensory processing disorder: Simulations and solutions for parents, teachers and therapists.* Shawnee Mission, KS: Autism Asperger Publishing Company.

Emmons, P. G., & Anderson, L. M. (2005). *Understanding sensory dysfunction: learning, development and sensory dysfunction in autism spectrum disorders, ADHD, learning disabilities and bipolar disorder.* London: Jessica Kingsley.

Kranowitz, C. (1998). *The out of sync child: Recognizing and coping with sensory integration dysfunction.* New York: Skylight Press.

Williams, M. W., & Shellenberger, S. (1996). *How does your engine run? A leader's guide to the Alert Program for Self-Regulation.* Albuquerque, NM: Therapy Works.

Yack, E., Aquilla, P., & Sutton, S. (2003). *Building bridges through sensory integration* (2nd ed.). Las Vegas: Sensory Resources.

JENNIE LONG

## SENSORY INTEGRATION INVENTORY–REVISED (SII-R)

The Sensory Integration Inventory–Revised (SII-R; Reisman & Hanschu, 1992) is a screening tool can be used in two ways: (a) it can be completed by therapists, staff, or teachers familiar with a child in approximately 30 minutes; or (b) it can be used by an **occupational therapist** as a semistructured interview for parents, teachers, caregivers, and others. Respondents mark whether or not a described behavioral response is typical, not typical, or unsure if the behavior is typical or not. Items are organized into four sections: tactile, **vestibular**, proprioceptive, and general reactions. Items are considered to reflect possible patterns of **sensory processing** difficulties.

*See also* proprioception.

**REFERENCE**

Reisman, J., & Hanschu, B. (1992). *Sensory integration inventory–revised.* Farmington, MA: Therapro, Inc.

LISA ROBBINS

## SENSORY PROCESSING

Sensory processing is the process of receiving sensory information from the environment through one or more of the senses and transmitting that information to the brain.

*See also* sensory integration; sensory integration disorder; sensory processing dysfunction.

KELLY M. PRESTIA

## SENSORY PROCESSING DYSFUNCTION

Sensory processing dysfunction is the inability to accurately perceive sensory information from the environment through one or more of the sensory systems.

*See also* sensorimotor early childhood activities; sensory integration disorder.

KELLY M. PRESTIA

## SENSORY PROFILE

The Sensory Profile (Dunn, 1999) is a norm-referenced questionnaire completed by someone who is very familiar with the child. The items on the profile describe children's behavioral responses to different sensory experiences, and their ability to modulate/adjust their reactions efficiently. It provides a description of emotional and behavioral responses associated with sensory processing difficulties. The Sensory Profile can be given in an interview format or to the respondent for independent completion. The person completing the profile reads each description and determines how often the child engages in a certain behavior (always, frequently, occasionally, seldom, or never). Scoring and interpretation takes approximately 20 to 30 minutes.

*See also* norm-referenced assessment; sensory integration disorder.

**REFERENCE**
Dunn, W. (1999). *Sensory profile*. San Antonio, TX: Harcourt Assessment.

LISA ROBBINS

## SENSORY SENSITIVITY

Sensory sensitivity is a neurological characteristic of individuals who have a low threshold, or tolerance, for sensory stimuli. Accordingly, these individuals are easily overwhelmed or disorganized by sensory information. Individuals with sensory sensitivity may be easily distracted or hyperactive, as they attend to all new stimuli in their environment.

KELLY M. PRESTIA

## SENSORY STIMULI

*Sensory stimuli* is a general term that refers to any occurrence within an environment that evokes a response.

KELLY M. PRESTIA

## SENSORY THRESHOLD

Sensory threshold refers to the amount of a stimulus needed to evoke a response from an individual. Thresholds are neurological points within the nervous system at which an action may result when enough of a stimulus is provided.

KELLY M. PRESTIA

## SEROTONIN

Serotonin is a chemical that serves as a neurotransmitter in the brain but also is found in other parts of the body with other functions. It is found in gastrointestinal mucosa, platelets (for blood clotting), and mast cells (related to allergies and inflammation).

BRUCE BASSITY

## SETTING EVENTS

A setting event is something happening in the environment that controls or influences behavior. This control usually takes the form of temporarily changing the way an individual responds to an interaction that follows the setting event. For example, a student is being bullied on the bus ride home. This is a setting event for the interactions that he will have at home that evening, and possibly even into the next day.

The setting events for a behavior may not always happen immediately before the behavior; there may be a delayed impact.

*See also* applied behavior analysis.

FURTHER INFORMATION

Cooper, J. O., Heron, T. E., & Heward, W. L. (1987). *Applied behavior analysis.* Upper Saddle River, NJ: Pearson Education.

KATIE BASSITY

## SHAPING

Shaping is a behavioral strategy used to teach an individual a new behavior. Shaping a new behavior involves providing reinforcement for successive approximations of the target behavior. Reinforcement is provided each time a behavior is exhibited that approximates the target behavior. Once that particular behavior is firmly established in the individual's repertoire of behaviors, then reinforcement is reserved only for a new behavior that more closely approximates the target behavior. This process is continued to help guide the individual towards the acquisition of a goal behavior in a step-by-step manner.

*See also* applied behavior analysis.

FURTHER INFORMATION

Anderson, S. R., Taras, M., & Cannon, B. O. (1996). Teaching new skills to young children with autism. In C. Maurice, G. Green, & S. L. Luce (Eds.), *Behavioral intervention for young children with autism* (pp. 181–194). Austin, TX: Pro-Ed.

ANDREA HOPF AND TARA MIHOK

## SHORT SENSORY PROFILE

The *Short Sensory Profile* (Dunn, 2001) is a 38-item abbreviated form of the *Sensory Profile* (1999) and is appropriate for children ages 3 to 17. It can be used as a screening tool to determine whether or not more in-depth assessment is needed in the area of sensory processing. It can be completed in about 10 minutes by someone who knows the child, and scored and interpreted in 10 to 20 minutes by someone with knowledge in the area of sensory integration.

REFERENCES

Dunn, W. (1999). *Sensory profile.* San Antonio, TX: Harcourt Assessment.
Dunn, W. (2001). *Short sensory profile.* San Antonio, TX: Harcourt Assessment.

LISA ROBBINS

## SIBLING SUPPORT PROJECT

Sibling Support Project is a national program devoted to providing information and creating peer support programs for siblings of individuals with disabilities, illnesses, and mental health issues. This project provides workshops, listservs, children's books, publications, and Web sites to assist siblings of all ages gain a better understanding of their brother or sister and cope with the unique issues surrounding having a sibling with a disability. Additionally, the Sibling Support Project has developed curricula to assist agencies or schools in developing **Sibshops**.

FURTHER INFORMATION
6512 23rd Ave NW, #213
Seattle, WA 98117
Phone: 206.297.6368
Fax: 509.752.6789
Web site: www.thearc.org/siblingsupport/.

KATHERINE E. COOK

## SIBSHOPS

In families that include children with disabilities, siblings of exceptional children are often lost in the shuffle. Siblings should be included in planning for meeting the needs of families with children with disabilities. Often siblings may assume roles not required in the typical family such as taking on care-giving roles similar to a parent. Research shows that meeting the needs of typical siblings is critical in the big family picture (Winter, n.d.).

Donald Meyer, the director of **The Sibling Support Project**, created Sibshops in 1994 as a way to support typical siblings and help them deal with their personal situations involving their families in a healthy manner. Typical siblings deal with a variety of concerns that need to be addressed in an appropriate manner. These include isolation, feeling guilt about or resentment toward their sibling and/or family, being a caregiver to their sibling, feeling pressured to perform well in school, and other activities and future concerns regarding their sibling (Harakas, 2005a). Sibling concerns should be addressed as part of the whole family's health and well-being.

Often Sibshops are described as parties or celebrations for these brothers and sisters who bring so much to their exceptional families. They were created specifically for child siblings of individuals with health and developmental needs but have been modified successfully for similar concerns. Currently the Sibshop model is used in 160 specific gatherings including 10 countries worldwide. These countries include: Argentina, Canada, Croatia, England, Guatemala, Iceland, Japan, Mexico, New Zealand, and the United States (Harakas, 2005b).

The Sibshop model has five specific goals for each session. First, Sibshops will provide typical siblings the opportunity to meet with other brothers and sisters in a fun and recreational event. Second, the activity will allow opportunities to share common joys and difficulties with other typical siblings. Third, siblings will have an opportunity to see how other siblings handle similar situations they have encountered in their own lives. Fourth, siblings will have a chance to learn more about the needs of their exceptional sibling. Finally, Sibshops will gain information about the needs and concerns experienced by typical siblings of individuals with disabilities, which will, in turn, be shared with parents and professionals in the hopes of better meeting the needs of the whole family (Meyer & Vadasy, 2000). By having these goals, Sibshops are easily run by organizations that have received the proper training and keep these goals in mind with planning.

Sibshops were originally created for children ages 8 to 13, but with a little modification they can meet the needs of older and younger siblings. They have been adapted to meet the needs of specific populations as well. Sibshops are recreational in theme, with fun games and activities, as well as time for discussions. They are designed to be unique and appeal to a wide variety of children. Sibshops can be held on a weekly, monthly, or yearly schedule (Meyer & Vadasy, 2000). Sometimes they are offered in conjunction with conferences for parents.

Sibshops run from 2 to 6 hours and include a variety of activities and discussions that are similar during each meeting. Sibshops generally start with a "trickle-in activity" that allows latecomers to arrive and time for participants to transition into the activities. This is followed with an introductory activity. The rest of the time is filled with fun recreational games, crafts, peer discussion groups, informational activities, and guest speakers (Meyer & Vadasy, 2000).

One favorite activity that is a standard for Sibshops is "Dear Aunt Blabby." During this activity, Aunt Blabby, a fictional advice columnist, requires expert help in answering letters written by typical siblings with an exceptional brother or sister. Aunt Blabby does not have a sibling with a disability and requires expert help in answering her letters. Participants are asked to read a letter to Aunt Blabby and then answer it using their own expertise and experiences. This is an easy activity to involve siblings, as they are often interested in sharing their own ideas and experiences (Meyer & Vadasy, 2000).

Successful Sibshops require forethought and preparation. Depending on the expected attendance there should be at least two facilitators. In general, it is best to have an adult sibling as a facilitator to share their perspectives. Other appropriate facilitators are often service providers and could include teachers, nurses, doctors, therapists, social workers, and psychologists. Parents of exceptional children may volunteer their services but should not facilitate a Sibshop in which their child participates (Meyer & Vadasy, 2000).

Sibshops are not a therapy, although a therapeutic effect may be seen in some participants. They offer similar support that an adult group would offer to parents in a parent support group (Harakas, 2005b). They focus on the idea that most families are functioning acceptably with concerns and issues and offer a safe place to share and learn. Facilitators of Sibshops may refer siblings for further interventions if concerns are noted (Meyer & Vadasy, 2000). One study showed that there was no significant increase in self-esteem in siblings (D'Arcy, Flynn, McCarthy, O'Connor, & Tierney 2005). However, most reported they liked the activities and thought they had learned from the event. Parents also reported positively regarding the program and felt their typical children received benefits from attending.

Sibshops are a valuable tool for families with exceptional and typical siblings. They offer a fun, safe environment for typical siblings to share their experiences and learn from other typical siblings as they engage in activities. While Sibshops are not considered therapy, they offer a supportive place for siblings to interact with other typical peers with similar families. Sibshops are similar to a support group setting for adults, just geared to meet the needs of children.

## REFERENCES

D'Arcy, F., Flynn, J., McCarthy, Y., O'Connor, C., & Tierney, E. (2005). Sibshops: An evaluation of an interagency model. *Journal of Intellectual Disabilities, 9*(1), 43–57.

Harakas, M. (2005a, January 2). The invisible ones. *South Florida Sun-Sentinel*. Retrieved December 10, 2006, from http://www.sun-sentinel.com/features/lifestyle/sfl-lisiblingsjan02,0,4197092.story?coll=sfla-features-headlines.

Harakas, M. (2005b, January 2). Sibshops is about fun, friendship. *South Florida Sun-Sentinel*. Retrieved June 10, 2005, from www.sun-sentinel.com/features/lifestyle/sfl-lisiblings-sidejan02,0,6947269.story?coll=sfla-features-headlines.

Meyer, D. J., & Vadasy, P. F. (2000). *Sibshops: Workshops for siblings of children with special needs.* Baltimore: Brooks Publishing Co.

Winter, J. (n.d.) *Sibshops*. Retrieved June 10, 2005, from www.enabledonline.com/BackIssues/Jan-Feb2002/text/kids1.html.

**FURTHER INFORMATION**

Meyer, D. J. (Ed.). (2005). *The sibling slam book: What it is really like to have a brother or sister with special needs.* Bethesda, MD: Woodbine House.

The Sibling Support Project: www.siblingsupport.org.

VALERIE JANKE REXIN

**SINGLE PHOTON EMISSION COMPUTED TOMOGRAPHY.** *See* Positron Emission Tomography

## SINGLE-SUBJECT DESIGN

Single-subject design is often considered the design of choice when measuring behavioral change or when performing behavioral modification. Rather than comparing groups of subjects, this design relies on the comparison of treatment effects on a single participant or on a small group of individuals.

*See also* behavior modification.

JAN L. KLEIN

## SITUATION-OPTIONS-CONSEQUENCES-CHOICES-STRATEGIES-SIMULATION (SOCCSS)

SOCCSS, the Situation-Options-Consequences-Choices-Strategies-Simulation strategy, was developed by Jan Roosa (Myles & Adreon, 2001) to help students with social disabilities process social situations and develop problem-solving skills by putting social and behavioral issues in a sequential form. SOCCSS is commonly used after a social situation to help students process and interpret the situation and their choices. This strategy may also be used to preteach social skills or social situations that the students may encounter. This may be done in a small group or a one-on-one situation.

The steps in the SOCCSS strategy are as follows:

1. Situation: Following a social problem, students report to a teacher the *who, what, when, where,* and *why* of the conflict. Who was involved in the situation? What actually happened? When did it happen? Where did the problem occur? Why did it happen? As the students become familiar with the SOCCSS strategy, the goal is for them to independently report these variables without prompting.

2. Options: The students and adult brainstorm behavioral options that the student could have chosen. The adult should accept all answers and record them on the SOCCSS form.

At the beginning of the process, adults may need to encourage the students to brainstorm multiple options that they could have chosen.

3. Consequences: For each behavioral option generated, a consequence is listed. To do so, the adult asks the student, "So what would happen if you..." and names the first option from the list. As the adult goes down the list of created options, some of the options may have one or more consequences. Students may have difficulty generating consequences; thus role-playing at this stage may be beneficial.

4. Choices: Options and consequences are prioritized using 1 through 5 or a yes/no response. Once prioritized, the student should be prompted to pick the choice that she thinks (a) she will be able to carry out, and (b) the one that most likely gets her what she wants.

5. Strategies: Next, the student develops a plan to carry out the choice that she made if the situation occurs again. It is crucial for the student to develop the plan so she feels like she has ownership over the plan.

6. Simulation: Practice is the last stage in the SOCCSS strategy. Simulation can occur by visually imagining, talking with another person about the plan, writing down the plan, or role-playing. Regardless of the method selected, the student ends up evaluating his impressions of the simulation.

SOCCSS allows students to learn cause and effect, that choices exist in all situations, and that, through choice making, they can impact the result of the situation.

REFERENCE

Myles, B. S., & Adreon, D. (2001). *Asperger syndrome and adolescence: Practical solutions for school success.* Shawnee Mission, KS: Autism Asperger Publishing Company.

MELISSA L. TRAUTMAN

**SOCIAL ARTICLES.** *See* Social Stories

## SOCIAL AUTOPSIES

Developed by Richard LaVoie (cited in Bieber, 1994), social autopsies are designed to help students with autism spectrum disorders (ASD) understand social situations and mistakes made during those situations. A social skills autopsy is guided by an adult who asks a series of questions to identify the error and possible solutions. These questions and their answers can be documented in a worksheet, filled out either by the student or the teacher. This visual format capitalizes on the favored mode of processing for many students with ASDs, and serves as a record to reference in future situations. For an example of what a social autopsy worksheet may look like, see Figure 17.

The autopsy begins with an adult asking, "What happened?" to the student. This prompt allows the student to start the process of "dissecting" the social situation. As the student describes the social situation, the adult asks clarifying questions designed to help the student identify the error, determine who was harmed by the error, decide how to correct the error, and finally develop a plan so that the error does not happen again.

Social autopsies help students learn the cause-and-effect relationship between a social behavior and its consequences. Adults in all of the students' environments should be knowledgeable on how to complete a social autopsy to help foster generalization and skill acquisition.

*See also* social skills training; theory of mind.

Figure 17  Worksheet for Social Autopsies

## Social Autopsies Worksheet

**What happened?**_____

_____

_____

_____

_____

| What was the social error? | Who was hurt by the social error? |
|---|---|
| | |
| | |
| | |
| | |

**What should be done to correct the error?**_____

_____

_____

_____

**What could be done to next time?**_____

_____

_____

_____

_____

_____

_____

_____

_____

_____

_____

*Source:* Myles, B. S., & Adreon, D. A. (2001). *Asperger syndrome and adolescence: Practical solutions for school success* (p. 109). Shawnee Mission, KS: Autism Asperger Publishing Company.

REFERENCES

Bieber, J. (1994). *Learning disabilities and social skills with Richard LaVoie: Last one picked ... first one picked on.* Washington, DC: Public Broadcasting Service.

Myles, B. S., & Adreon, D. A. (2001). *Asperger syndrome and adolescence: Practical solutions for school success.* Shawnee Mission, KS: Autism Asperger Publishing Company.

MELISSA L. TRAUTMAN

## SOCIAL BEHAVIOR MAPPING

Social behavior mapping is a practical strategy that helps us explore how our own behavior causes people to have emotional reactions that impact how others react to us (the consequences, positive or negative), which then impacts how we feel about ourselves. The map is a cognitive behavioral strategy to help students explore how all behavior, when produced in the presence of others, impacts others as well as one's self. Another important feature of the social behavior map is that it explores the notion that behavioral expectations vary by environment, or context within a specific environment. (For example: at dinnertime, or while working in the classroom, eating in the cafeteria, etc.) Within each environment or context there is a set or sets of "hidden curriculum" (hidden rules) that we are expected to follow and adjust our behavior to in order to keep those around us calm and responding to us in a neutral or positive (versus negative) way.

The social behavior maps (SBM) are usually printed on two sides of one piece of paper: on one side of the paper are the "expected behaviors" and on the other side are the "unexpected behaviors." See Tables 8 and 9 for examples of expected and unexpected social behavior maps. To use the map well, those working with a student need to catch the child in the "act of doing what is expected," and then demonstrate the resulting behavioral chain by circling the words or concepts that best represent the student's expected behavior, how it makes someone feel, the natural consequences the communicative partner produced in response to the behavior, and then how the student feels about himself on the "expected side of the SBM." Draw lines to connect one circle to the next; this provides a graphic organizer of social behavioral responses. On less frequent occasions, the maps can be turned over to the "unexpected side" and the unexpected behavior, related emotional responses, and resultant consequences should also be circled with lines drawn to connect the circles and demonstrate the overall effect a behavior has on the interaction pattern with

### Table 8. Social Behavior Mapping: Expected Behaviors

| *Expected Behaviors | Feelings of Other People | Consequences | How You Feel about the Consequences |
|---|---|---|---|
| 1. Listen with body and eyes | 1. Happy | 1. People talk to you with a calm faces and voice | 1. Happy |
| 2. Use a 2 ft. voice | 2. Proud | 2. The teacher may praise you | 2. Proud of myself |
| 3. Use friendly words | 3. Pleased that you are learning as part of the group | 3. You may earn rewards for working as part of the group | 3. Confident that I can be a good student |
| 4. Talk about what the group is talking about | 4. Calm | 4. Other students want to include you in their work and or play | 4. You stay calm |
| 5. Don't let words bump into others | 5. Group members feel good because they can learn too | | |
| 6. Follow directions | | | |
| 7. Do the work, even if it is boring or you think you already know how to do it | | | |

*Behaviors/feeling/consequences are listed in categories in arbitrary order. There is not a 1:1 correlation between the information listed in each column. For example: whatever behavior is listed first does not have to match to the first emotional reaction or the first consequence, etc.

**Table 9. Social Behavior Mapping: Unexpected Behaviors**

| *Unexpected Behaviors | Feelings of Other People | Consequences | How You Feel about the Consequences |
|---|---|---|---|
| 1. Distracted as body and eyes are not focused on the teacher | 1. Unhappy | 1. People talk to you with an unhappy faces and voice | 1. Mad |
| 2. Use a loud voice | 2. Frustrated | 2. The teacher may nag you to do what is expected | 2. Sad |
| 3. Use unfriendly words | 3. Worried you are not working as part of the group | 3. You may lose privileges | 3. Stressed out |
| 4. NOT talking about what the group is talking about | 4. Stressed | 4. Other students may not want to work or play with you | |
| 5. Words bump into others | 5. Group members feel frustrated because you are not working with the group | | |
| 6. Do NOT follow directions | | | |
| 7. Avoid doing the classwork | | | |

*Behaviors/feeling/consequences are listed in categories in arbitrary order. There is not a 1:1 correlation between the information listed in each column. For example: whatever behavior is listed first does not have to match to the first emotional reaction or the first consequence, etc.

others. This side should be used far less frequently since our job as parents and educators is to illuminate when our students are doing what is expected (typically this set of behaviors is ignored by others) and then contrast that cycle of behavior and emotional responses with what happens when the unexpected does occur. Students always do more expected than unexpected behaviors; we have to learn to positively acknowledge this! An example of information gleaned from social behavior maps is demonstrated below. SBMs can be written for any situation and individualized to what a child needs to focus on.

*See also* cognitive learning strategies; social cognition; social skills training.

FURTHER INFORMATION

Attwood, T. (2006). *The complete guide to Asperger syndrome*. London: Jessica Kingsley Publishers.

Buron, K. D., & Curtis, M. (2003). *The incredible 5-point scale*. Shawnee Mission, KS: Autism Asperger Publishing Company.

Gray, C. (1994). *Comic strip conversations*. Arlington, TX: Future Horizons.

Winner, M. (2000). *Inside out: What makes the person with social cognitive deficits tick?* San Jose, CA: Michelle Garcia Winner.

Winner, M. (2002). *Thinking about you thinking about me*. San Jose, CA: Michelle Garcia Winner.

Winner, M. (2003). Social thinking across the home and school day (DVD). Grand Rapids, MI: The Gray Center Publishers.

Winner, M. (2005). *Think social! A social thinking curriculum for school aged students.* San Jose, CA: Michelle Garcia Winner.

Winner, M. (2005). *Worksheets! For teaching social thinking and related skills.* San Jose, CA: Michelle Garcia Winner.

MICHELLE GARCIA WINNER AND JAMIE RIVETTS

## SOCIAL COGNITION. *See* Social Thinking

## SOCIAL COMMUNICATION

Generally, social communication refers to a field of study that primarily explores the ways information can be perceived. It could also be used to assess severity of symptoms in individuals with autism spectrum disorder. It refers to the communication of cognitive and emotional information through facial expression, gestures, and prosody, and through implicit understanding of **pragmatics**. Moreover, it implies knowledge of the social rules of human communication and the implicit ability to deduce the thoughts and motives of others, a phenomenon that has been called **theory of mind** (Baron-Cohen, 1995).

### REFERENCE
Baron-Cohen, S. (1995). *Mind blindness.* Cambridge, MA: MIT Press.

### FURTHER INFORMATION
Tanguay, P., Robertson, J., & Derrick, A. (1998). A dimensional classification of autism spectrum disorder by social communication domains. *Journal of the American Academy of Child and Adolescent Psychiatry, 37,* 271–277.

JOUNG MIN KIM

## SOCIAL COMMUNICATION QUESTIONNAIRE (SCQ)

The Social Communication Questionnaire (SCQ), formerly published as the *Autism Screening Questionnaire*, is a parent report questionnaire designed by Berument, Rutter, Lord, Pickles, & Bailey (1999) to screen for autism spectrum disorder in clinical populations. The SCQ is based on DSM-IV-TR criteria for autism, and closely follows the **Autism Diagnostic Interview–Revised** (ADI-R; Lord, Rutter, & LeCouteur, 1994) algorithm for autism. There are two versions of the SCQ: one for children younger than age 6, and one for individuals 6 years and older. The SCQ is designed to differentiate children with **pervasive developmental disorders** from those who do not have pervasive developmental disorders in a clinic-based sample (i.e., those who are already referred to medical services with possible developmental disorder). The SCQ does not differentiate between subgroups on the autism spectrum. The authors point out that the questionnaire is not recommended for use at a population level (Bailey, 2001).

### REFERENCES
Bailey, A. (2001). *The social communication questionnaire.* Presentation at NIASA working group meeting on screening and surveillance for autism spectrum disorders for pre-school and school-age children. London: National Autistic Society.

347

Berument, S. K., Rutter, M., Lord, C., Pickles, A., & Bailey, A. (1999). Autism screening questionnaire: Diagnostic validity. *British Journal of Psychiatry, 174*, 444–451.

Lord, C., Rutter, M., & LeCouteur, A. (1994). Autism diagnostic interview–revised: A revised version of a diagnostic interview for careers of individuals with possible pervasive developmental disorders. *Journal of Autism and Developmental Disorders, 24*, 659–685.

FIONA J. SCOTT

## SOCIAL COMPETENCE

Social competence indicates the abilities to establish meaningful, emotional-based relationships; to work collaboratively with classmates, coworkers, or other teammates; and to participate in various social settings, including schools, workplaces, or communities (Gutstein & Whitney, 2002). Three essential elements of social competence include secure attachment, instrumental social learning, and experience-sharing relationships (Bruner, 1983; Emde, 1989; Fogel, 1993; Gottman, 1983). *Attachment* refers to the bond and secure relationship between children and caregivers; *instrumental social learning* helps individuals understand the relationships between specific social behaviors and the desired consequences; *experience-sharing relationships* are the fundamental principles of establishing friendships. Children with autism spectrum disorders demonstrate limited social competence, such as lacking eye contact, facial expression, social play, **joint attention, reciprocal communication/interaction**, and so on.

*See also* social skills training.

### REFERENCES

Bruner, J. S. (1983). *Child's talk*. Oxford, UK: Oxford University Press.

Emde, R. N. (1989). The infant's relationship experience: Developmental and affective patterns. In A. Sameroff & R. Emde (Eds.), *Relationship disturbances in early childhood: A developmental approach* (pp. 33–51). New York: Basic Books.

Fogel, A. (1993). *Developing through relationships*. Chicago: The University of Chicago Press.

Gottman, J. M. (1983). How children become friends. *Monographs of the Society for Research in Child Development, 48*(3), 1–82.

Gutstein, S. E., & Whitney, T. (2002). Asperger syndrome and the development of social competence. *Focus on Autism and Other Developmental Disabilities, 17*(3), 161–171.

YU-CHI CHOU

## SOCIAL FAUX PAS

The ability to detect a social faux pas is an "advanced" theory of mind ability. Typically the ability to detect social faux pas develops around age 8 (Baron-Cohen, O'Riordan, Stone, Jones, & Plaisted, 1999). Individuals with an autism spectrum disorder have challenges with theory of mind; that is, they have difficulty with perspective taking. In a test to detect advanced theory of mind, Happe (1994) uses sarcasm, bluff, irony, and the double bluff to assess a person's ability to detect a social faux pas.

*See also* false-belief paradigm; theory of mind.

### REFERENCES

Baron-Cohen, S., O'Riordan, M., Stone, V., Jones, R., & Plaisted, K. (1999). A new test of social sensitivity: Detection of faux pas in normal children and children and Asperger syndrome. *Journal of Autism and Developmental Disorders, 29*, 407–418.

Happe, F. (1994). An advanced test of theory of mind: Understanding of story characters' thoughts and feelings by able autistic, mentally handicapped, and normal children and adults. *Journal of Autism and Developmental Disorders, 24,* 129–154.

TERRI COOPER SWANSON

## SOCIAL GAZE

Social gaze is the movement of one's eyes for a communicative purpose. This movement can involve "eye-to-eye" contact, for the purposes of reading body language and facial expression, or "eye-to-object" contact, also referred to as *joint attention*. Joint attention involves making eye contact with a person and then shifting the focus of the eyes to a third party (object or person). Abnormalities in social gaze are among the earliest pronounced symptoms of autism, with 1-year-old infants with autism tending to make less eye-to-face contact than typically developing infants.

JEANNE HOLVERSTOTT

## SOCIAL PLAY

Children with autism spectrum disorders present distinct problems in developing social play with both adults and other children (APA, 2000). Social play reflects the ability to coordinate mutually enjoyed activities with another person. Building on early capacities for **joint attention** (e.g., following another's gaze to share the experience of observing an object or event), imitation, and emotional responsiveness, social play increases in frequency, duration, and complexity with growing exposure to peers. Examples of social play include: onlooker (e.g., watching peers at play), parallel play (e.g., playing independently beside peers), common focus (e.g., reciprocal play with one or more peers), and common goal (e.g., cooperative play with one or more peers; for reviews, see Jordan, 2003; Wolfberg, 1999, 2003).

*See also* integrated play groups; play-oriented therapies; social skills training.

**REFERENCES**

American Psychiatric Association. (2000). *Diagnostic and statistical manual for mental disorders* (4th ed., text rev.). Washington, DC: Author.

Jordan, R. (2003). Social play and autistic spectrum disorders. *Autism: The International Journal of Research and Practice, 7*(4) 347–360.

Wolfberg, P. J. (1999). *Play and imagination in children with autism.* New York: Teachers College Press, Columbia University.

Wolfberg, P. J. (2003) *Peer play and the autism spectrum: The art of guiding children's socialization and imagination.* Shawnee Mission, KS: Autism Asperger Publishing Company.

PAMELA WOLFBERG

## SOCIAL SCRIPTS

A social script is an intervention used with children with autism spectrum disorders (ASD) to improve their social and communication skills (Simpson, Myles, & Ganz, in press). Such scripts are designed to give children with ASD the words or phrases they should use in a variety of contexts. This intervention is appropriate for children with autism as an intervention that accommodates for memory and social skills deficits common in autism. Social scripts have been used to improve imitation (Pierce &

Schreibman, 1995) and social (Johnston, Nelson, Evans, & Palazolo, 2003; Krantz & McClannahan, 1998) and communication (Krantz & McClannahan, 1993; Sarokoff, Taylor, & Poulson, 2001) skills in individuals with ASD. Social scripts have also resulted in reduced problem behaviors (Sasso, Melloy, & Kavale, 1990).

### Steps in Implementing Social Scripts

Ganz, Cook, and Earles-Vollrath (in press) recommend the following steps when implementing social scripts. First, a sociocommunicative skill or skills should be chosen (e.g., asking questions for information), as well as settings and scenarios in which the skills should be demonstrated. These should be skills and scenarios that cause the individual with ASD difficulty. Then, a script or scripts should be written including specific phrases the student should learn. Drawings may be included or used in place of the written words if the student is unable to read or unable to read fluently. Prior to implementing the script in the difficult setting, the script or scripts should be taught to the student until he or she can read it aloud fluently and without prompts. At this time, the script may need to be adjusted for ease of reading. Next, the script or scripts should be implemented during the difficult activity or setting. The script may be given to the student to check off or an adult (e.g., teacher, parent) may hold phrases up periodically to be read aloud. Finally, the script should be faded (e.g., remove portions of the script from the end to the beginning).

### Example of a Social Script

The following is an example of a social script intervention with Sarah, a 10-year-old fifth-grader with high-functioning autism. Sarah infrequently used spontaneous social speech and preferred to draw alone. Her teacher decided to implement social scripts to increase her social initiations. Specifically, they decided to work on increasing positive comments and offers to share during art class, which took place once a week. Sarah's teacher wrote a script including a variety of phrases she could use during art, such as, "I like your drawing of a ____," and, "Do you want the purple paint?" These phrases were put on note cards on a ring for Sarah to carry with her. Because Sarah could read, the script did not include pictures. Sarah's teacher then spent three 15-minute sessions practicing the script with her until she was able to read the phrases independently, fluently, and with affect. Then, the script was given to Sarah to use during art class. The first few classes during which the script was used, her teacher reminded her beforehand and periodically pointed to the cards to remind Sarah to read them aloud. Finally, once Sarah used the scripts independently in art class, they were faded by cutting the note cards starting at the end of the sentence, and gradually removing more of each sentence until no words were visible. At that point the script was removed and a new skill and scenario was targeted.

*See also* social skills training; visual strategies.

### References

Ganz, J. B., Cook, K. E., & Earles-Vollrath, T. L. (in press). *How to write and implement social script interventions with learners with autism spectrum disorders.* Austin, TX: Pro-Ed.

Johnston, S., Nelson, C., Evans, J., & Palazolo, K. (2003). The use of visual supports in teaching young children with autism spectrum disorder to initiate interactions. *Augmentative and Alternative Communication, 19*(2), 86–103.

Krantz, P., & McClannahan, L. (1993). Teaching children with autism to initiate to peers: Effects of a script-fading procedure. *Journal of Applied Behavior Analysis, 26*(1), 121–132.

Krantz, P., & McClannahan, L. (1998). Social interaction skills for children with autism: A script-fading procedure for beginning readers. *Journal of Applied Behavior Analysis, 31*(2), 191–202.

Pierce, K., & Schreibman, L. (1995). Increasing complex social behaviors in children with autism: Effects of peer-implemented pivotal response training. *Journal of Applied Behavior Analysis, 28*(3), 285–295.

Sarokoff, R. A., Taylor, B. A., & Poulson, C. L. (2001). Teaching children with autism to engage in conversational exchanges: Script fading with embedded textual stimuli. *Journal of Applied Behavior Analysis, 34*(1), 81–84.

Sasso, G. M., Melloy, K. J., & Kavale, K. (1990). Generalization, maintenance, and behavioral co-variation associated with social skills training through structured learning. *Behavioral Disorders, 16*(1), 9–22.

Simpson, R. L., Myles, B. S., & Ganz, J. B. (in press). Efficacious interventions and treatments for learners with autism spectrum disorders. In R. L. Simpson & B. S. Myles (Eds.), *Educating children and youth with autism: Strategies for effective practice* (2nd ed.). Austin, TX: Pro-Ed.

JENNIFER B. GANZ

## SOCIAL SKILLS DEFINED AS SHARING SPACE EFFECTIVELY WITH OTHERS

While we use our social skills to share, play with others, interact in discussion and conversation, it is important to realize that we even use our social skills at all the times that we are just sharing space with others. When we enter into a space shared by another person(s), all people(s) should be having a little thought about those around them. The thoughts usually stay "small" and "routine" if people are sharing space effectively and not making people have "weird thoughts." However, if when sharing space we produce an unexpected social behavior, people can become less comfortable with the person who is doing the "unexpected" social behavior even if no one is speaking to each other in that environment. To consider this more fully, think about how aware each person is of the other when just sharing space on an elevator. If one does it well, then this is one example of using "good social skills."

### FURTHER INFORMATION

Winner, M. (2002). *Thinking about you thinking about me.* San Jose, CA: Michelle Garcia Winner.

Winner, M. (2005). *Think social! A social thinking curriculum for school aged students.* San Jose, CA: Michelle Garcia Winner.

MICHELLE GARCIA WINNER AND JAMIE RIVETTS

## SOCIAL SKILLS TRAINING

Social skills training refers to instruction or support designed to improve or facilitate the acquisition and/or performance of social skills. Social skills are critical to successful social, emotional, and cognitive development. Social skills have been defined as "socially acceptable learned behaviors that enable a person to interact with others in ways that elicit positive responses and assist in avoiding negative responses" (Elliot, Racine, & Busse, 1995, p. 1009). Effective social skills allow us to elicit positive reactions and evaluations from peers as we perform socially approved behaviors (Ladd & Mize, 1983).

Impairment in social functioning is a central feature of autism spectrum disorder (ASD) and is well documented in the literature (Attwood, 1998; Rogers, 2000). Typical social skill deficits include difficulties with reciprocity, initiating interactions, maintaining eye contact, sharing enjoyment, empathy, and inferring the interests of others. The cause of these skill deficits varies, ranging from inherent neurological impairment (e.g., limbic system dysfunction) to lack of opportunity to acquire skills (e.g., social withdrawal). Regardless of origin, social skill deficits make it difficult for the individual to develop, and keep, meaningful and fulfilling personal relationships.

Although social skill deficits are a central feature of ASD, few children receive adequate social skills programming (Hume, Bellini, & Pratt, 2005). This is a troubling reality, especially considering that the presence of social impairment may portend the development of detrimental outcomes, such as social failure and peer rejection, possibly leading to anxiety, depression, substance abuse, and other forms of psychopathology (Bellini, 2004; La Greca & Lopez, 1998; Tantam, 2000). Most important, social skill deficits impede the ability to establish meaningful social relationships, which often leads to withdrawal and a life of social isolation. Social skills training should be an integral part of a child's overall programming.

Social skills are primarily acquired through learning that involves observation, modeling, coaching, social problem solving, behavior rehearsal, feedback, and reinforcement-based strategies (Gresham & Elliot, 1990). Two underlying assumptions of all social skills training programs are that individuals can be taught to behave differently, and that they will elicit more positive reactions and evaluations from peers as they acquire and perform more socially approved behaviors (Ladd & Mize, 1983). Gresham and Elliot discuss five factors that contribute to social skills deficits: (a) lack of knowledge, (b) lack of practice or feedback, (c) lack of cues or opportunities, (d) lack of reinforcement, and (e) the presence of interfering problem behaviors. Social skills training programs should identify which factors are contributing to the social skill deficits of the target child and attempt to ameliorate these deficits through programming.

## SOCIAL SKILLS ASSESSMENT

The first step in any social skill training program should consist of a thorough evaluation of the child's current level of social functioning, including both strengths and weaknesses. The purpose of such assessment is to answer one very basic, yet complicated, question: What is precluding the child from establishing and maintaining social relationships? For most children, the answer takes the form of specific social skill deficits. For others, the answer takes the form of cruel and rejecting peers. And for yet other children, the answer is both.

The assessment should involve a combination of observation (both naturalistic and structured), interview (e.g., parents, teachers, playground supervisors), and standardized measures (e.g., behavioral checklists, social skills measures). The skills that are identified during the social skills assessment will be the direct target of the intervention. For more information on social skill checklists specifically designed for children with ASD, see *Do-Watch-Listen-Say* by Quill (2000), or *Building Social Relationships* by Bellini (2006).

## SOCIAL SKILLS TRAINING STRATEGIES

When teaching social skills to children with ASD, it is important to use a large repertoire of strategies. It is also important to teach social skills across a variety of settings, including home, community, classroom, **resource room**, playground, and therapeutic clinic, and with multiple persons. Thus, the success of a social skills program is dependent upon the cooperation and contribution of both parents (and other family members and caregivers) and professionals (teachers, counselors, **speech language pathologists**, social workers, **occupational** and **physical therapists**, **psychologists**, physicians, case managers, or many others).

A number of important questions must be considered when selecting social skill strategies. For instance, does the strategy target the skill deficits identified in the social assessment? Does the strategy enhance performance? Does the strategy promote skill acquisition? Is there research to support its use? If not, what is the plan to evaluate its effectiveness with the child? Is it developmentally appropriate for the child?

In his review of the research, McConnell (2002) concluded that indirect strategies such as arranging the environment to include structured, preferred activities and opportunities for interactions with more socially competent peers can help promote social interactions for young children with ASD. However, these strategies are rarely sufficient in themselves and should be part of comprehensive intervention plans that include more targeted, direct interventions.

One example of direct intervention is to specifically teach and reinforce social skills. The use of teacher prompts has also been shown to be an effective way to increase social initiations and duration of interactions in young children (Odom & Strain, 1986). Another well-studied strategy (McConnell, 2002), peer-mediated interventions, involves the use of trained peers to prompt the social interactions of young children with ASD. Furthermore, the use of multiple peer mentors has been found to increase the **generalization** of these skills to other settings or persons. Various social intervention programs have been designed to facilitate both adult-child and child-child interactions in children with ASD, including **pivotal response training**, visual cuing, peer-mediated instruction, **video modeling**, peer mentoring, social scripting, and **Social Stories** (Rogers, 2000). Social skills interventions should focus on positive behaviors and use methods that can be easily incorporated into the classroom curriculum.

Social skills training strategies can typically be separated into one of two categories: (a) strategies that teach new skills (skill acquisition) and (b) strategies that enhance the performance of existing skills (performance enhancement). Examples of skill acquisition strategies include social stories, video modeling, social problem solving, teaching social rules, and social scripting. Performance enhancement strategies include reinforcement strategies, environmental modifications, peer-mediated interventions, and social priming. Social skills training can focus on early social-communicative skills, play skills, initiations and responses, and other prosocial skills.

## RESEARCH ON SOCIAL SKILLS TRAINING

Research has shown that traditional social skills training programs are only minimally effective in teaching social skills to children and adolescents (Gresham, Sugai, & Horner, 2001; Quinn, Kavale, Mathur, Rutherford, & Forness, 1999). Quinn et al.

(1999) found that social skills programs that targeted specific social skills (turn taking, social initiations, etc.) were more effective than programs that focused on more global social functioning for larger groups of students, such as "friendship" skills, cooperation, and so on. The researchers concluded that effective social skill programs must be adapted to fit the needs of the child. Too often the opposite logic is used. We force children to "fit" into the social skill strategy or strategies that we have selected for them. After reviewing numerous studies on social skills training, Gresham et al. (2001) recommended that social skills training be implemented more frequently and more intensely than what is typically the case. They concluded that "thirty hours of instruction, spread over 10–12 weeks is not enough" (p. 341) and that the social skill instructional strategies should match the type skill deficits. Matching instructional strategies to the type of skill deficit exhibited by the child is a key component of successful social skills programs.

## PLAN FOR GENERALIZATION

A critical aspect of all social skills programs is a plan for generalization, or transfer of skills. Generalization refers to performance of skills across settings, persons, situations, and time. The ultimate goal of social skills training is to teach the child to interact successfully with peers in natural environments. From a behavioral perspective, the inability to generalize a skill or behavior is a result of too much stimulus control. That is, the child only performs the skill or behavior in the presence of a specific **stimulus** (person, prompt, directives, etc.). For instance, the child may respond to the social initiations of other children, but only if his mother is there to prompt him. If mom is not available, he does not respond. Therefore, the skill has not been generalized. Several strategies may be used to facilitate generalization of social skills, including (a) reinforcing the performance of social skills in the natural environment, (b) training with multiple persons and in multiple settings, (c) ensuring the presence and delivery of natural **reinforcers** for the performance of social skills, (d) practicing the skill in the natural environment, (e) fading prompts as quickly as feasible, (f) providing multiple exemplars for social rules and concepts, and (g) teaching self-monitoring strategies.

## SOCIAL ACCOMMODATION VERSUS SOCIAL ASSIMILATION

Prior to selecting intervention strategies, it is important to consider the concepts of social accommodation and social assimilation. **Accommodation**, as it relates to social skills instruction, refers to the act of modifying the physical or social environment to promote positive social interactions. Examples include training peer mentors to interact with the child throughout the school day, conducting autism awareness training or sensitivity training for classmates, and signing the child up for various group activities, such as Little League, Boy or Girl Scouts, and so on. Whereas accommodation addresses changes in the environment, *assimilation* focuses on changes in the child. Specifically, it refers to instruction that facilitates skill development that allows the child to be more successful in social interactions. By their nature, social accommodations enhance social performance, and social assimilation involves promoting skill acquisition.

The key to a successful social skills training program is to address both accommodation and assimilation. For example, providing ample opportunity for the child to interact with others without providing him/her with the skills necessary to be successful in those interactions may lead to failure and frustration. Similarly, providing skill instruction (assimilation) without modifying the environment to be more accepting of the child with ASD also sets the child up for failure. This happens the moment an eager child with ASD tries out a newly learned skill on a group of nonaccepting peers. Thus, the key is to teach skills *and* modify the environment.

*See also* social scripts.

## REFERENCES

Attwood, T. (1998). *Asperger's syndrome: A guide for parents and professionals.* Philadelphia: Jessica Kingsley Publishers.

Bellini, S. (2004). Social skill deficits and anxiety in high-functioning adolescents with autism spectrum disorders. *Focus on Autism and Other Developmental Disabilities, 19*(2), 78–86.

Bellini, S. (2006). *Building social relationships: A systematic approach to teaching social interaction skills to children and adolescents with autism spectrum disorders and other social difficulties.* Shawnee Mission, KS: Autism Asperger Publishing Company.

Elliott, S. N., Racine, C. N., & Busse, R. T. (1995). Best practices in preschool social skills training. In A. Thomas & J. Grimes (Eds.), *Best practices in school psychology* (3rd ed., pp. 1009–1020). Washington, DC: NASP.

Gresham, F. M., & Elliot, S. N. (1990). *Social skills rating system–manual.* Circle Pines, MN: American Guidance Service.

Gresham, F. M., Sugai, G., & Horner, R. H. (2001). Interpreting outcomes of social skills training for students with high-incidence disabilities. *Teaching Exceptional Children, 67,* 331–344.

Hume, K., Bellini, S., & Pratt, C. (2005). The usage and perceived outcomes of early intervention and early childhood programs for young children with autism spectrum disorder. *Topics in Early Childhood Special Education, 25*(4), 195–207.

Ladd, G. W., & Mize, J. (1983). A cognitive-social learning model of social skill training. *Psychological Review, 90,* 127–157.

La Greca, A. M., & Lopez, N. (1998). Social anxiety among adolescents: Linkages with peer relations and friendships. *Journal of Clinical Child Psychology, 26,* 83–94.

McConnell, S. R. (2002). Interventions to facilitate social interaction for young children with autism: Review of available research and recommendations for educational intervention and future research. *Journal of Autism and Developmental Disorders, 32,* 351–372.

Odom, S. L., & Strain, P. S. (1986). A comparison of peer-initiation and teacher-antecedent interventions for promoting reciprocal social interaction of autistic preschoolers. *Journal of Applied Behavior Analysis, 19,* 59–71.

Quill, K. (2000). *Do-watch-listen-say: Social and communication intervention for children with autism.* Baltimore: Brookes Publishing Co.

Quinn, M. M., Kavale, K. A., Mathur, S. R., Rutherford Jr., R. B., & Forness, S. R. (1999). A meta-analysis of social skills interventions for students with emotional and behavioral disorders. *Journal of Emotional and Behavioral Disorders, 7,* 54–64.

Rogers, S. (2000). Interventions that facilitate socialization in children with autism. *Journal of Autism and Developmental Disorders, 30,* 399–409.

Tantam, D. (2000). Psychological disorder in adolescents and adults with Asperger syndrome. *Autism, 4,* 47–62.

SCOTT BELLINI, ANDREA HOPF, AND JESSICA KATE PETERS

## SOCIAL STORIES

A Social Story describes a situation, skill, or concept in terms of relevant social cues, perspectives, and common responses in a specifically defined style and format. Social Stories were originally developed to share social information with children with autism spectrum disorders (ASD) that most people take for granted, with each Story patiently describing the details of an often unspoken social code. For example, a Social Story may outline the general routine of a birthday party, explain the thoughts, statements, and actions of children at the party, or the rationale behind expectations for the behavior of those attending the party.

Social Articles (Gray, 1999) are similar to Social Stories, but tailored for review and use by adolescents and young adults. Thus, Social Articles use (a) the third-person perspective instead of first-person, (b) advanced vocabulary, and (c) in many cases columns like a newspaper article, to share information. For many children and adults with ASD, Social Stories and Social Articles have resulted in improved responses to situations or understanding of concepts that were previously problematic for them. Most are written by parents and professionals, and people with ASD of all ages are their most frequent audience.

First described by Gray & Garand in 1993, Social Stories have been updated and expanded upon in subsequent articles and book chapters (Gray, 1995, 1998a, 1998b, 2000a; 2000b; Gray & White, 2000) The continually expanding use and popularity of the approach created a need for an updated, detailed delineation of what is—and is not—a Social Story. Thus, many stories were being developed for students with ASD, and referred to by their authors as Social Stories, though relatively few adhered to the defining criteria. Concern for students' social and emotional safety when exposed to unauthorized use of the approach, and concern for its overall quality and effectiveness, resulted in an expansion and reorganization of the 10 defining characteristics, referred to as Social Stories 10.0 (Gray, 2004). Currently, Social Stories 10.0 clearly distinguishes Social Stories from fiction and traditional nonfiction, task analyses, **social scripts**, or other **visual strategies**.

First gaining credibility in practice, numerous studies have been conducted on Social Stories, the majority of them reporting positive results. New studies are continually being launched to improve understanding of the approach and answer questions that emerge with continued practice. Though the original guidelines and the new defining criteria are based on the learning characteristics of people with ASD, experience indicates that Social Stories may also be helpful for individuals with other impairments, as well as for those who are developing normally.

### REFERENCES

Gray, C. (1995). Teaching children with autism to "read" social situations. In K. A. Quill (Ed.), *Teaching children with autism: Strategies to enhance communication and socialization* (pp. 219–241). New York: Delmar Publishers.

Gray, C. (1998a). Social Stories and comic strip conversations. In E. Schopler, G. Mesibov, & L. Kunce (Eds.), *Asperger Syndrome or high-functioning autism?* (pp. 167–198). New York: Plenum Press.

Gray, C. (1998b). The advanced social story workbook. *The Morning News, 10*(2), 1–24.

Gray, C. (1999). Gray's guide to compliments. *The Morning News, 11*(1), 1–20.

Gray, C. (2000a). *Writing social stories with Carol Gray* [Video]. Arlington, TX: Future Horizons.

Gray, C. (2000b). *Writing social stories with Carol Gray: Workbook to accompany video.* Arlington, TX: Future Horizons.

Gray, C. (2004). Social Stories 10.0: The new defining criteria and guidelines. *The Jenison Autism Journal, 16*(1), 2–21.

Gray, C. A., & Garand, J. (1993). Social Stories: Improving responses of individuals with autism with accurate social information. *Focus on Autistic Behavior, 8,* 1–10.

Gray, C. A., & White, A. L. (2000). My *social stories book.* London: Jessica Kingsley Publishers.

**FURTHER INFORMATION**
The Gray Center: www.TheGrayCenter.org.

CAROL GRAY

## SOCIAL THINKING

Social thinking is a user-friendly term for **social cognition**. Social cognition is one of many different forms of intelligence that each of us has to a greater or lesser extent that helps to define how we interpret, relate, and respond to the people and information around us (written, spoken, media, etc.). In relation to others, there are multiple and complex factors that combine synergistically to create communicative competence. Factors related to social thinking involve reading people's gestures, body language, tone of voice, facial expressions, breathing patterns, and intended language meaning in an environmental context to glean the overall communicative intention of the message. Social thinking is active in every situation where two people share (even outside of language-based communication); and it is actively present in the classroom environment. There is no single moment in a classroom when social thinking does not need to be actively considered.

An example of teaching by "social thinking methods" includes teaching "eye-contact" to students who lack this skill. If we are teaching a child eye contact by teaching him or her to use the "social skill," then we simply remind the child to "look at me." If we are teaching the child the concept of eye contact through "social thinking methods," then we help the child to learn that eye-gaze direction helps the "listener" to understand what others might be thinking about based on where they are looking. The student (i.e., "listener") is then taught to "think with his or her eyes" to consider what others might be looking at or thinking about. The listener can then be cued to think with his or her eyes to better understand why he or she should look to the face of another person.

**FURTHER INFORMATION**

Winner, M. (2002). *Thinking about you thinking about me.* San Jose, CA: Author.

Winner, M. (2005). *Think social! A social thinking curriculum for school aged students.* San Jose, CA: Michelle Garcia Winner.

Winner, M. (2005). *Worksheets! For teaching social thinking and related skills.* San Jose, CA: Michelle Garcia Winner.

Social Thinking: www.socialthinking.com.

MICHELLE GARCIA WINNER AND JAMIE RIVETTS

## SOCIAL VALIDITY

Social validity is the perceived worth of research and its results.

JAN L. KLEIN

## SOMATOSENSORY

Somatosensory refers to the sensory receptors on the skin's surface, which help to determine where the body ends and where the world begins. The somatosensory system is also referred to as the tactile system.

KELLY M. PRESTIA

## SPECIAL DAY SCHOOL OR ALTERNATIVE SCHOOL

Special day school/alternative school programs are settings where students receive educational and related services for more than 50 percent of their school day. Multiple disabilities represent the disability category most often represented within special day school or alternative school programs.

KATHERINE E. COOK

**SPECT.** *See* Positron Emission Tomography

## SPEECH DELAY

Speech delay refers to a delay in the development or use of the mechanisms that produce speech. Speech, which is distinct from language, refers to the actual process of making sounds, using such organs and structures as the lungs, vocal cords, mouth, tongue, teeth, etc. Because language and speech are two independent developmental stages, delays may present independently.

JEANNE HOLVERSTOTT

## SPEECH LANGUAGE PATHOLOGIST

Speech language pathologists (SLP) are trained professionals who work in hospitals, private clinics, and the school system diagnosing speech/language disorders, preparing for, and providing direct services. Speech language pathologists are trained to diagnose and provide services for students with speech impairments including: fluency disorders, articulation and phonological disorders, and voice disorders. Language disorders focused on by speech language pathologists include aphasia and language delays. These services can be provided in individual, small, or large group settings. Additionally, many SLPs focus on **pragmatics** and social skill instruction within individual, small, and group settings.

In order to practice as a speech pathologist, a minimum of a master's degree, passage of a national exam, a minimum of 400 (325 at the graduate level) supervised clinical hours, and the completion of a clinical fellowship year must be completed (American Speech-Language-Hearing Association, n.d.). The American Speech-Language Hearing Association (ASHA) is the organization that awards the Certificate of Clinical Competence (CCC) upon successful completion of these requirements. The addition of a state license to practice may be required depending on that specific state.

*See also* fluency; social skills training.

REFERENCE

American Speech-Language-Hearing Association. (n.d.). *Academic, Clinical, and Exam Standards for the Certificate of Clinical Competence (CCC)*. Retrieved September 22, 2006, from www.asha.org.

KATHERINE E. COOK AND LYNN DUDEK

## SPEECH THERAPY

Speech therapy, also known as speech pathology or speech-language pathology, is the diagnosis and treatment of communication and swallowing disorders. Speech pathologists (or speech therapists) diagnose, treat, and prevent communication disorders. In addition to diagnosing and treating disorders, speech pathologists are responsible for programs that stress the prevention of certain disorders—such as a vocal hygiene program to avoid the development of poor vocal behaviors (yelling, vocal abuse).

Communication encompasses many areas. Language skills refer to syntax (grammar), semantics (vocabulary), and **pragmatics** (language use and social skills). Speech skills mean articulation (pronunciation), voice (hoarseness, resonance), and **fluency** (stuttering). Swallowing ability refers to the intake, manipulation (chewing), movement, and swallowing of liquids and solids.

The need for services from a speech pathologist may be for a variety of reasons including:

- Developmental delays (not developing speech and language)
- Articulation errors
- Motor planning disorders (dyspraxia, apraxia)
- Accident or injury
- Stroke
- Traumatic brain injury
- Cancer
- Autism spectrum disorders
- Cerebral palsy
- Congenital disorders
- Birth injuries
- Trauma (car accident)
- Feeding/swallowing disorders

A speech pathologist may use many different methods to develop or redevelop the skills necessary for effective communication and swallowing. These may include:

- **Play-oriented therapy**
- Articulation practice
- Oral-motor therapy
- Articulation "drills"
- Reading readiness
- Memory activities
- **Augmentative and alternative communication** devices
- Sign language
- **Picture Exchange Communication System (PECS)**
- Homework

Speech pathologists work in a variety of settings including private practice, nursing homes, schools, rehabilitation centers, hospitals, and universities. Along with diagnosing and treating communication disorders, speech pathologists are responsible for diagnosing and treating disorders associated with feeding and swallowing.

Speech pathologists may see patients/clients in a variety of settings including individual and/or group treatment. In a school setting, group therapy is utilized to take advantage of peer modeling and generalization. In other settings, such as a hospital or clinic, they may utilize individual treatment. One of the growing areas of treatment for speech pathologists is in the area of pragmatics/social language and **social skills training**. As children with autism spectrum disorders grow on caseloads, so too do the number of social skills groups.

It is important to remember that the child, the family, and the speech pathologist are all partners in the therapy process. It is vitally important that the family be involved in creating goals and the speech pathologist helps the family learn how to practice at home. Only going to therapy once or twice a week will not be of benefit unless home programs are instituted as well.

FURTHER INFORMATION
Social Thinking: www.socialthinking.com.

LYNN DUDEK

## SPLINTER SKILLS

Splinter skills (also called islets of ability or islands of precocity) are abilities in one or several areas that a person is quite talented in relative to their overall cognitive ability. For example, an individual may be cognitively impaired, yet have a photographic memory or be able to play a song on a musical instrument perfectly after only hearing it once.

FURTHER INFORMATION
Frith, U. (1989). *Autism: Explaining the enigma.* Cambridge, MA: Blackwell Publishers.
Kanner, L. (1943). Autistic disturbances of affective contact. *Nervous Child, 2,* 217–250.
Scheuermann, B., & Webber, J. (2002). *Autism: Teaching does make a difference.* Belmont, CA: Wadsworth Group.

PAUL G. LaCAVA

## SPONTANEOUS PLAY

A lack of spontaneous play appropriate to developmental level is a defining feature of autism spectrum disorders (APA, 2000). Spontaneous play reflects the child's active engagement in intrinsically motivating activity that is self-generated and freely chosen. Spontaneous play manifests in both symbolic and social forms, which transform in form, function, and degree of complexity as children develop (Boucher & Wolfberg, 2003; Libby, Powell, Messer, & Jordan, 1998; Wolfberg, 1999, 2003).

Spontaneous forms of play within the symbolic dimension may include: sensory exploration of objects (e.g., spinning the wheels of a toy car), functional play with objects (e.g., rolling a toy car on a surface or placing a cup on a saucer), and pretending to do or be someone else (e.g., holding a tea party with dolls). Spontaneous forms of play within the social dimension may include: onlooker (e.g., watching peers at play), parallel play (e.g., playing independently beside peers), common focus (e.g., reciprocal play with one or more peers), and common goal (e.g., cooperative play with one or more peers; Wolfberg, 2003).

*See also* integrated play groups; play-oriented therapies.

REFERENCES

American Psychiatric Association. (2000). *Diagnostic and statistical manual of mental disorders* (4th ed., text rev.). Washington, DC: Author.

Boucher, J., & Wolfberg, P. J. (2003). Editorial: Special issue on play. *Autism: The International Journal of Research and Practice, 7*(4), 339–346.

Libby, S., Powell, S., Messer, D., & Jordan, R. (1998). Spontaneous play in children with autism: A reappraisal. *Journal of Autism and Developmental Disorders 28*, 487–497.

Wolfberg, P. J. (1999). *Play and imagination in children with autism.* New York: Teachers College Press, Columbia University.

Wolfberg, P. J. (2003). *Peer play and the autism spectrum: The art of guiding children's socialization and imagination.* Shawnee Mission, KS: Autism Asperger Publishing Company.

PAMELA WOLFBERG

# STANDARD DEVIATION

In statistics, standard deviation (SD) is a measure of variability. The SD is the average distance that each score, in a distribution of scores, deviates from the average of all scores (also known as the mean). The SD tells how far scores vary and how they disperse around the average score.

FURTHER INFORMATION

Kotz, S., & Johnson, N. L. (Eds.). (1988). *Encyclopedia of statistical sciences, Vol. 8.* New York: John Wiley & Sons.

Salkind, N. J. (2005). *Exploring research* (6th ed.). Upper Saddle River, NJ: Prentice Hall.

PAUL G. LaCAVA

# STANDARDIZATION

Standardization is the process of applying a consistent set of procedures for designing, administering, and scoring an assessment in order to ensure that all students are assessed under the same conditions and are not affected by different conditions. Standardization also ensures that optimal results are obtained.

FURTHER INFORMATION

Wrightslaw (n.d.). *Glossary of assessment terms.* Retrieved August 8, 2006, from http://www.wrightslaw.com/links/glossary.assessment.htm.

THERESA L. EARLES-VOLLRATH

# STANDARDIZATION SAMPLE

A standardization sample is a large group of test takers who represent the population for which the test is intended and to which comparisons can be made. Knowledge of the standardization sample, also referred to as the norm group, is important when using standardized or **norm-referenced assessment** measures.

FURTHER INFORMATION

Pierangelo, R., & Giuliani, G. (1998). *Special educators' complete guide to 109 diagnostic tests: How to select and interpret tests, use results in IEPs, and remediate specific difficulties.* West Nyack, NY: Center for Applied Research in Education.

Salvia, J., & Ysseldyke, J. E. (2007). *Assessment: In special and inclusive education* (10th ed.). Boston: Houghton Mifflin Company.

THERESA L. EARLES-VOLLRATH

## STANDARDIZED TESTS

Standardized tests are a form of measurement that has been normed against a specific population. These assessment measures are uniformly developed, administered, and scored according to very specific procedures. A variety of standardized scores are calculated for comparison against the performance of the norm group.

*See also* norm-referenced assessment.

FURTHER INFORMATION

Pierangelo, R., & Giuliani, G. (1998). *Special educators' complete guide to 109 diagnostic tests: How to select and interpret tests, use results in IEPs, and remediate specific difficulties.* West Nyack, NY: Center for Applied Research in Education.

THERESA L. EARLES-VOLLRATH

## STANDARD SCORE

Standard scores are raw test scores that have been converted to a scale with equal means and standard deviations. These scores allow "raw scores" on different assessments to be compared, allowing one to determine where a student's score falls in comparison to his/her overall ability, to another person, or to a group.

FURTHER INFORMATION

Salvia, J., & Ysseldyke, J. E. (2007). *Assessment: In special and inclusive education* (10th ed.). Boston: Houghton Mifflin Company.

Taylor, R. L. (2006). *Assessment of exceptional students: Educational and psychological procedures* (7th ed.). Needham Heights, MA: Allyn and Bacon.

THERESA L. EARLES-VOLLRATH

## STANFORD-BINET INTELLIGENCE SCALES–FIFTH EDITION

The Stanford-Binet Intelligence Scales–Fifth Edition (SB5; Roid, 2005) is individually administered to individuals ranging in ages from 2 to 90+ as an assessment of intelligence and cognitive abilities. The SB5 allows assessors to compare nonverbal and verbal performance, which is beneficial when evaluating for a learning disability. SB5 aids in determining special needs and assists with identifying and describing individuals who qualify as learning disabled, gifted and talented, mentally retarded, ADHD, speech and language delayed, traumatic brain injured, and/or autistic.

REFERENCE

Roid, G. H. (2005). *Stanford-Binet Intelligence Scales–Fifth Edition.* Rolling Meadows, IL: Riverside Publishing Company.

AMY BIXLER COFFIN

## STEREOTYPIC BEHAVIOR

Stereotypic behaviors may include hand waving, rocking, playing with hands, fiddling with fingers, twirling objects, head banging, self-biting, or hitting various parts of one's own body (APA, 2000). In addition, individuals may use an object in performing these behaviors.

### REFERENCE

American Psychiatric Association. (2000). *Diagnostic and statistical manual for mental disorders* (4th ed., text rev.). Washington, DC: Author.

HYO JUNG LEE

## STIMULANT MEDICATIONS

Stimulant medications are a very commonly used psychotropic medication. Ritalin, Adderall, and Concerta are examples of this class of drugs. Stimulants work by triggering the level of activity in the central nervous system. Stimulants are often prescribed to persons with autism spectrum disorders (ASD) to help improve attention, decrease hyperactivity, restlessness, and impulsivity, and for other behavioral concerns. Some common side effects include reduction in appetite and mild insomnia. Many stimulants are produced in regular and sustained-release forms. Individuals with ASD may benefit from stimulants, but research has shown that those without autism who take stimulants respond at a higher rate.

### FURTHER INFORMATION

Aman, M. G., Lam, K. S., & Collier-Crespin, A. (2003). Prevalence and patterns of use of psychoactive medicines among individuals with autism in the Autism Society of Ohio. *Journal of Autism and Developmental Disorders, 33,* 527–534.

Quintana, H., Birmaher, B., Stedge, D., Lennon, S., Freed, J., Bridge, J., et al. (1995). Use of methylphenidate in the treatment of children with autistic disorder. *Journal of Autism & Developmental Disorders, 25,* 283–294.

Tsai, L. (2000). Children with autism spectrum disorder: Medicine today and in the new millennium. *Focus on Autism and Other Developmental Disabilities, 15,* 138–145.

Tsai, L. (2002). *Taking the mystery out of medications in autism/Asperger syndromes: A guide for parents and non-medical professionals.* Arlington, TX: Future Horizons.

Werry, J. S. (2001). Pharmacological treatments of autism, attention deficit hyperactivity disorder, oppositional defiant disorder, and depression in children and youth: Commentary. *Journal of Clinical Child Psychology, 30,* 110–113.

PAUL G. LACAVA

## STIMULUS

Stimulus refers to a specific element in the environment that influences behavior. It is normally used to refer to something that is being changed or administered in order to impact behavior, or to find what its impact is on the behavior of an individual. Stimuli can be internal or external, although the focus within **applied behavior analysis** is the study and manipulation of external stimuli. However, some interventions for individuals with autism spectrum disorders also attempt to teach recognition of internal stimuli and self-control or **self-regulation**, in light of such stimuli.

FURTHER INFORMATION

Cooper, J. O, Heron, T. E, & Heward, W. L. (1987). *Applied behavior analysis*. Upper Saddle River, NJ: Pearson Education.

KATIE BASSITY

## STIMULUS CONTROL

A behavior is said to be under stimulus control when that behavior is more probable to occur after a particular stimulus than under other normal circumstances (Halle & Holt, 1991). The reason for this control is that the stimulus that produces higher rates of behavior also is followed by higher rates of reinforcement (Cooper, Heron, & Heward, 1996). Once it has been associated with the behavior, the **stimulus** or cue may then induce the response (Alberto & Troutman, 1999). For example, a child knows how to walk out of the classroom, but it would be under stimulus control if the child does this automatically during a fire drill. Likewise, if a parent or teacher often gives in to tantrums, it is likely that a child will throw more tantrums in his or her presence in the future.

REFERENCES

Alberto, P. A., & Troutman, A. C. (1999). *Applied behavior analysis for teachers* (p. 20). Upper Saddle River, NJ: Merrill.

Cooper, J. O., Heron, T. E., & Heward, W. L. (1987). *Applied behavior analysis*. Upper Saddle River, NJ: Prentice Hall.

Halle, J. W., & Holt, B. (1991). Assessing stimulus control in natural settings: An analysis of stimuli that acquire control during training. *Journal of Applied Behavior Analysis, 24*, 579–589.

JESSICA KATE PETERS AND TARA MIHOK

## STIMULUS OVERSELECTIVITY

Stimulus overselectivity, also called restricted stimulus control, is attention being given to a limited number of stimuli, or features of a stimulus, in a given situation. For example, an individual may identify any red fruit as an apple and not recognize a green apple as an apple. This is because they have learned to identify an apple based on one feature, ignoring the other components that make an apple an apple. This can also apply to only attending to one piece of visual information being presented or attending only to visual information when it is accompanied by oral directions.

*See also* stimulus control.

KATIE BASSITY

## STORYMOVIES

A Story*movie* (Gray & Shelley, 2006) is a **Social Story** (Gray & Garand, 1993) illustrated with a short (2–6 minutes), professionally developed movie shot on location, which merges descriptions of social concepts and skills with footage of live situations. Although developed specifically for individuals with autism spectrum disorders (ASD) to help them understand the interactions and situations that surround them, Story*movies* may be useful with other audiences as well. In all Story*movies*, a black-and-white freeze frame—that frequently stills an important social cue—appears with an announcer reading superimposed text. This is the Story that describes what is occurring and why. When the announcer finishes reading the segment, the action continues.

Story*movies* require no specialized training to implement and are equally user-friendly in the hands of parents or professionals. In a school or clinical setting, Story*movies* may complement a current social curriculum or initiative, and may be used to achieve existing classroom or individual objectives. At home, parents may use Story*movies* more informally to illustrate topics that arise in daily conversations or to help them explain important social concepts and skills.

Story*movies* utilize features that are impossible with other forms of illustration, such as instant replay, slow motion, and relaxing background music. Carefully placed where needed, instant replay and slow motion provide an immediate second opportunity to look for social cues that may occur too fast or elude identification altogether. Background music is optional; a simple click on the DVD menu turns the music on or off.

Many of the Story*movies* within a chapter use the same movie for illustration. There are two important reasons for this. Working from the same movie introduces new details on a familiar backdrop and focuses attention on the Story to emphasize related ideas within a chapter. To demonstrate the important ties between concepts, ideas covered in one chapter are mentioned and applied in subsequent chapters and DVDs, with new movies as a backdrop. This promotes the generalization of concepts to new contexts, and encourages the retrieval of previous experience and/or information relevant to the current topic.

Each Story*movie* DVD addresses a specific theme. Story*movies* are grouped into chapters that build one or more basic concepts related to that theme. Topics are listed from simpler to more advanced and are designed to be used in sequence. Any Story*movie* may also be used in isolation, making it possible to skip a review of topics that are already understood.

## REFERENCES

Gray, C. A., & Garand, J. (1993). Social Stories: Improving responses of individuals with autism with accurate social information. *Focus on Autistic Behavior, 8*, 1–10.

Gray, C.A., & Shelley, M. (2006). [DVD]. *Social concepts and skills at school*. Columbia, SC: Specialminds Foundation.

## FURTHER INFORMATION

The Gray Center: www.TheGrayCenter.org.

The Special Minds Foundation: www.specialminds.org.

CAROL GRAY AND MARK SHELLEY

## STRUCTURED TEACHING (TEACCH)

Structured Teaching is a primary component of the Treatment and Education of Autistic and related Communication-Handicapped Children (TEACCH) program's approach to working with individuals with autism spectrum disorders (ASD). TEACCH is a statewide program that offers support to individuals with ASD and their families in North Carolina. In addition, TEACCH is able to offer support to families and children with ASD around the country and throughout the world through a set of intervention strategies, referred to as Structured Teaching, that are used in classrooms, at home, and in community-based services to increase the independence and competence of individuals with ASD (Mesibov, Shea, & Shopler, 2005).

An underlying principle of Structured Teaching is to match educational practices and daily interventions to the specific way in which people with ASD think and learn (Mesibov & Howley, 2003, chap. 2). Specifically, individuals with ASD display neurological differences that can result in receptive and expressive language difficulties, problems with attending to relevant detail and switching attention, poor organizational skills, distractibility when faced with sensory stimulation, and difficulty with abstract thinking and perspective-taking. In addition, individuals with ASD tend to be visual, rather than auditory learners (Mesibov et al., 2005).

Incorporating the distinct learning pattern and thought processes of individuals with ASD, the elements of Structured Teaching include physical organization, the use of schedules, the use of work systems, and the use of visual structure and information.

### PHYSICAL ORGANIZATION

The physical layout of classrooms, homes, and job settings plays an important role in providing visual information that adds meaning to the environment for individuals with ASD (Mesibov & Howley, 2003, chap. 4). That is, the way the furniture, materials, and general surroundings are organized can help clarify expectations and activities and reduce distracting visual and auditory stimulation. Providing individuals with ASD with a neat and orderly environment can increase independence and alleviate anxiety often caused by ambiguity.

The degree of physical organization necessary in an environment varies, depending on the needs of the individual with ASD. For younger children or children with more severe needs, more physical structure may be required. This may be created through the strategic placement of furniture to provide natural boundaries and define specific areas within the classroom (Mesibov & Howley, 2003, chap. 2). For example, a teacher can arrange separate and distinctive areas for group work, independent work, play, one-to-one teaching, and snack by arranging the furniture in a clear manner (Mesibov & Howley, 2003, chap. 4). These boundaries convey to children with ASD what is expected of them within these particular areas, which can lead to greater independence. Another way to provide clear physical organization is visual cues. That is, different areas of the classroom can be clearly labeled, materials can be color-coded in a meaningful way, and visual prompts can be used to let a student know where to sit (Mesibov et al., 2005).

Students with ASD who are included in a general education classroom may require a lesser degree of physical organization. For example, it is often helpful to create a quiet, nonstimulating area within the classroom where the student can go when feeling stressed or frustrated. In addition, for these students, the independent work area should be located in the least stimulating part of the classroom to eliminate distractions, perhaps assigning them to the same seat each day. Finally, a clear place in which to put finished work is helpful for almost all individuals with ASD, as it provides closure on a task and prepares them for the next step.

### SCHEDULES

Schedules are visual cues that tell us what to expect during the day and in what order (Mesibov & Howley, 2003, chap. 5). Schedules are particularly helpful for individuals with ASD, as they reduce a reliance on language. Visual schedules can also remain accessible, eliminating the need to rely on memory for sequential information. Finally, schedules aid in transitions, which are often the most difficult times of the day for individuals with ASD.

### Types of Schedules

Visual schedules take many forms depending on the level of functioning of the intended user (Mesibov et al., 2005). For more capable individuals, the schedule may be written to match their reading level. For nonreaders, schedules should be in the form of pictures or icons, depending on what makes the most sense to the particular individual. For example, a picture of a paintbrush could symbolize art, a picture of a parent could indicate it is time to go home, or an icon of a table could represent independent work. Icon and picture schedules can be paired with a simple word or phrase for those with emerging reading skills for additional clarity. Finally, object schedules, which provide a one-step indication of what is next, may be used for individuals who require a high degree of concrete structure. Objects must be clear and meaningful, such as using a plate to symbolize lunchtime or a part of a task to symbolize work sessions.

The length of the schedule should also be determined based on individual needs. Whereas object schedules typically only present one item at a time, picture and written schedules can provide a sequence of activities in whatever length is most appropriate. Some individuals are most successful with just a few activities on their schedule, while others benefit from seeing a half day or full day of activities on their schedule.

The ways in which schedules are manipulated also vary depending on the individual. For example, some schedules require students to remove a picture card to carry with them and match to a corresponding picture card in an area, whereas others simply require the user to cross off or place check marks over completed activities (Mesibov & Howley, 2003, chap. 5). This manner of checking a schedule should be established as a routine to increase independent functioning.

It is helpful to not only provide individualized schedules for particular students, but also to provide a general classroom schedule, giving students the most information possible (Mesibov et al., 2005). General classroom schedules should remain similar from week to week, while the individual schedule provides an opportunity to vary activities. Such variation prevents students from becoming too accustomed to a particular routine, which might be difficult to break.

### Work Systems

Whereas physical organization and schedules tell an individual where to go and what to expect during the day, work systems explain how to approach particular activities (Mesibov & Howley, 2003, chap. 6). Thus, work systems offer the structure individuals with ASD need to understand what is expected of them when completing a task, remain focused on the task, and work independently. Specifically, work systems convey which tasks students are supposed to complete, how many tasks must be completed, how much progress they have made as they are working, and finally, what happens after they have completed the work.

Like physical organization and schedules, work systems are tailored to the level of understanding of the individual with ASD. A work system for the most capable students might be a written checklist embedded within a schedule (Mesibov & Howley, 2003, chap. 6). The schedule typically tells the individual to go to a particular area, where he will utilize a separate work system to complete the work or tasks within that area. For example, a student with high-functioning autism might benefit from a work system consisting of a written list of tasks, along with materials that correspond with each task. By using this list to cross off items as they are finished, the student has a clear sense of making progress and then finishing (Mesibov et al., 2005). The work system should include information at the end regarding what to do next; this may be as simple as a message reading, "Check Schedule."

For individuals with ASD who have limited language, work systems can use pictures, icons, objects, or colors to convey what is expected. For example, a nonreader might use a work system consisting of separate picture cards attached to a Velcro strip. These pictures cards correspond to a matching picture on a bin that contains the task. The number of bins containing tasks indicates how much work the student must complete. When no more cards remain, the student knows that she has completed the work session. The last card on the Velcro strip should indicate what the student should do next.

Such work systems can be used in one-to-one teaching areas until the tasks have been mastered. The work system can then be transferred to an independent work area. Work systems are not only useful in the classroom, but can be helpful in completing everyday activities, such as brushing teeth, preparing a sandwich, establishing a routine for riding the bus, or shopping in the community (Mesibov et al., 2005).

## VISUAL STRUCTURE AND INFORMATION

As mentioned before, individuals with ASD display visual strengths. Visual information provides clarity and meaning, which increases understanding, success, and independence. In contrast, tasks that rely solely on language-based information tend to be confusing for a person with ASD. Three components of visual structure will be discussed in this section: visual clarity, visual organization, and visual instructions.

### Visual Clarity

Visually clarifying important information for individuals with ASD can accommodate for their difficulty in recognizing relevant information. Rather than including an excessive number of materials, which can cause confusion regarding what needs to be done, work areas can be clarified by presenting tasks with a limited amount of materials (Mesibov et al., 2005). Further, information within tasks can be clarified by highlighting important instructions or putting a tab on an important reference page within a textbook (Mesibov & Howley, 2003, chap. 2). Similarly, a more basic sorting task could include two distinctly different colors that are to be sorted, such as red and green, to highlight the purpose of the task (Mesibov et al., 2005).

### Visual Organization

Individuals with ASD often prefer neat and orderly environments and are easily distracted by extraneous materials or disorganized work areas. Furthermore, they often lack the ability to organize materials themselves. Visual organization refers to the distribution and stabilization of materials, which provides an orderly environment and clarifies what is expected (Mesibov & Howley, 2003, chap. 2). For example, in a sorting task involving several materials, individuals with ASD have a greater under-standing of the task if the materials are distributed in containers rather than spread out across the table. Thus, a task consisting of separating red from blue fish could be presented with a container holding all the materials to be sorted, an additional empty container labeled "Red Fish," and another empty container labeled "Blue Fish." This level of organization provides the meaning and clarity needed for an individual with ASD to understand the task and complete it independently.

## Visual Instructions

Finally, visual instructions are essential in providing meaning for most individuals with ASD (Mesibov & Howley, 2003, chap. 2). Individuals with ASD often benefit from a *jig*, or visual representation, of where materials belong or how a task is to be completed. For example, a jig can provide a visual depiction of how to set a table. Visual instructions not only utilize the strong visual perceptual skills of individuals with ASD, but also support the development of flexibility. That is, visual instructions allow individuals with ASD to learn the routine of relying on instructions, rather than learning a rigid routine of how to perform a particular task, which will not generalize to other tasks and can be hard to break.

Overall, Structured Teaching incorporates the strengths of individuals with ASD, such as their visual perception skills, while accommodating for weaknesses, such as poor organization and receptive language, difficulty determining relevant information, and problems with transitions. Not only is Structured Teaching useful for teaching academic or functional daily living skills, it can be helpful in teaching communica-tion, social, and leisure activities. Used across many different settings such as the school, home, and community, these intervention strategies provide the organization and structure needed for individuals with ASD to understand their environments and our expectations more fully, and to function more independently and successfully.

### REFERENCES

Mesibov, G., & Howley, M. (2003). *Accessing the curriculum for pupils with autistic spectrum disor-ders*. London: David Fulton Publishers.
Mesibov, G. B., Shea, V., & Shopler, E. (2005). *The TEACCH approach to autism spectrum dis-orders*. New York: Kluwer Academic/Plenum Publishers.

SIGNE M. BOUCHER AND GARY B. MESIBOV

## STUDENT SOCIAL ATTRIBUTION SCALE (SSAS)

The Student Social Attribution Scale (SSAS; Bell & McCallum, 1995) measures a student's awareness of the reason(s) behind school-related success and failure. The questionnaire includes 30 written scenarios that illustrate examples of school success and failure that are followed by four possible causes including ability, chance, effort, and task difficulty. The participant is required to identify how often these causes apply to him or her. The most current version of the SSAS is made up of 16 subscales. A shorter 12-scenario version is also available.

### REFERENCE

Bell, S. M., & McCallum, R. S. (1995). Development of a scale measuring student attributions and its relationship to self-concept and social functioning. *School Psychology Review, 24,* 271–286.

FURTHER INFORMATION
Barnhill, G. (2001). Social attributions and depression in adolescents with Asperger syndrome. *Intervention in School and Clinic, 16*(1), 46–53.

AMY BIXLER COFFIN

## SUPPLEMENTAL SECURITY INCOME (SSI)

One program that individuals with autism spectrum disorders may access is Supplemental Security Income (SSI), which is a program of the federal government designed to provide enough personal income each month to subsidize basic needs of food, clothing, and shelter. Generally speaking, eligibility is reserved for the aged and disabled who have little or no income and less than $2,000.00 in assets. SSI is a means-tested program, which means that there are income guidelines that include the parents if the child is under age 18. The means-test is also a consideration when estate planning because if the disabled individual receives a sizeable inheritance, it is possible that would jeopardize their eligibility for further SSI payments. It is also possible to work while receiving SSI benefits, and your local Social Security Office should be able to guide you as to the amount of employment income you may have so that you do not accidentally forfeit your program eligibility. IQ and previous employment are also taken into consideration when determining eligibility; however, once you are deemed eligible for SSI it is also possible that you will qualify for food stamps, Medicaid or Medicare. Even though SSI is a federal program, there are specific rules for income or benefit caps that vary from state to state. The best way to get started with the application process is to use the Web site provided by the Social Security Administration, which is http://www.socialsecurity.gov/pubs/11000.html or the toll-free phone line at 1-800-772-1213.

SHERRY MOYER

## SUPPORTED EMPLOYMENT

The Division of Vocational Rehabilitation (VR) provides supported employment as a support for individuals with the most severe disabilities who are eligible for competitive employment with ongoing, continual job coach support. VR usually contracts this service with an agency that provides adult services for individuals with cognitive or emotional disabilities. This service allows individuals with cognitive disabilities, significant developmental delays, and severe emotional disturbances to attain and maintain community-based employment. The adult service agency provides ongoing job coach support to assist with the needs an individual may have that may prevent him or her from maintaining competitive employment independently or with minimal support. An example of a need for supported employment is an individual who is blind and has been diagnosed with autism. This individual completes daily tasks in order at work; however, he needs frequent reminders to move from one task to another or to continue a task and needs assistance with transitions from one place to another.

Supported employment provides an opportunity for individuals with more severe disabilities to receive employment in the community with their adult peers. It is a benefit for the individual as well as the community.

*See also* individualized transition plan; vocational rehabilitation.

BETH CLAVENNA-DEANE

## SURTHRIVAL

For many years, parents and professionals have witnessed sharp contrasts in the educational experiences of many students with autism spectrum disorders (ASD). Parents may report that their child thrives during first grade, only to struggle for social and emotional survival in second grade. Similarly, a teacher may have a wonderful year working with her first student with Asperger syndrome, only to watch sadly as he is repeatedly "in trouble" with his teacher the following year.

Attempts to explain these sharp contrasts, this *thrive* versus *struggle to survive* phenomenon, often center around the personality or attitude of the teacher and/or others on the student's educational team. However, attitude can explain only part of the difference. A student's social and emotional success does not rest solely in mastery of the goals and objectives in his or her educational plan. Instead, it is the result of effort and learning by a student *and all of those working on his behalf. Surthrival* is the shared social goal in ASD—a positive social process that yields benefits for all.

Created by merging the terms *survive* and *thrive*, Surthrival derives its meaning from both words (see Figure 18). Students have a responsibility to learn the concepts and skills to help them socially and emotionally survive, and those who surround them have an equal responsibility to learn the attitudes and practices that create contexts where students can thrive. Based on a belief that the social impairment in ASD is a shared challenge, Surthrival seeks to *discover* social solutions rather than *invent* predetermined, prescribed outcomes. For this reason, Surthrival often results in outcomes that take everyone pleasantly by surprise!

Formally defined in Figure 18, Surthrival is supported by a paradigm, *social curiosity,* and five practices. Social curiosity has strong roots in respect for other perspectives and social styles, and is fueled by the possibilities of a third social option that is not typical, and not ASD, but collaboration between the two. The five practices are represented by occupations used as metaphors to represent important skill sets. These include: (a) an *Investigative Reporter,* who seeks to understand the roots of unique responses; (b) a *Personal Trainer,* who has a great sense of humor and extends a "come as you are" welcome; (c) a *Travel Agent,* who provides support by structuring experience; (d) an *Air Traffic Controller,* who can foresee problem situations and "coach pilots" through challenging situations; and (e) a *Choir Director,* who leads "individual voices: learning to work effectively as a group. Sharing a strong foundation in social curiosity, these five practices are interdependent and work together to create opportunities for Surthrival.

**Figure 18 Definition of Surthrival**

Surthrival /sər thrīv' əl (noun). 1) the shared goal and solution to "the social impairment in autism spectrum disorders (ASD)," often with unanticipated benefits for all, 2) the social, emotional, and intellectual growth of a child, adolescent, or adult with an ASD in an environment governed by a philosophy and defined set of practices (possibly within an environment not otherwise conducive to such learning), 3) a state of inherent social health and balance between two or more parties with often distinct perceptions, perspectives, and responses to social contexts and communication. *To surthrive* (verb).

Returning to the reality of the "survive" versus "thrive" phenomenon of students with ASD described earlier, can the paradigm and practices of Surthrival be taught and learned? Or does it require inborn traits, delegating opportunities for students with ASD to thrive in learning environments to a random hit or miss luck of the draw? These authors believe that "if Surthrival can be identified, it can be measured. If Surthrival can be measured, it can be taught. If Surthrival can be taught, it can be learned" (Gray & Krusniak, 2006, p. 31).

REFERENCE
Gray, C., & Krusniak, W. M. (2006, Summer). Evidence of Surthrival. *Autism Spectrum Quarterly*, 30–32.

FURTHER INFORMATION
The Gray Center: www.TheGrayCenter.org.

CAROL GRAY AND WHITNEY MITCHELL KRUSNIAK

## SYMBOLIC PLAY

Children with ASD show delays or differences in the development of symbolic play (a.k.a. pretend, make-believe, imaginary play; APA, 2000). Symbolic play reflects the child's capacity to intentionally disengage from reality and act as if he is doing something or being someone else in a manner that is representational. This includes object substitutions, attribution of absent or false properties, and representing imaginary objects or events as present (Baron-Cohen, 1987; Leslie, 1987; Wolfberg, 1999, 2003).

*See also* integrated play groups; play-oriented therapies.

REFERENCES
American Psychiatric Association. (2000). *Diagnostic and statistical manual of mental disorders* (4th ed., text rev.). Washington, DC: Author.
Baron-Cohen, S. (1987). Autism and symbolic play. *British Journal of Developmental Psychology*, 5(2), 139–148.
Leslie, A. M. (1987). Pretense and representation: The origins of "theory of mind." *Psychological Review*, 94, 412–426.
Wolfberg, P. J. (1999). *Play and imagination in children with autism*. New York: Teachers College Press, Columbia University.
Wolfberg, P. J. (2003). *Peer play and the autism spectrum: The art of guiding children's socialization and imagination*. Shawnee Mission, KS: Autism Asperger Publishing Company.

FURTHER INFORMATION
Autism Institute on Peer Relations and Play: www.autisminstitute.com.

PAMELA WOLFBERG

## SYMBOLIC THOUGHT

Symbolic thought is the developmental stage when a child begins to use formal symbols such as words and pictures to create meanings and communicate ideas. This is typically manifested in spoken words. This stage develops between 18 and 30 months of age. A child will progress through several levels of symbolic thought: words and actions used together; action words used instead of the corresponding behavior; words used to convey feelings such as, "I'm happy"; words used to convey bodily states, "my stomach aches"; words used to communicate global feelings as, "I'm OK"; and words used to convey more specific feelings, such as, "I feel angry" (Greenspan & Shanker, 2004). Children also begin to use symbolic thought in play by using toys, props, and other people to direct their actions. Later, children will communicate symbolic thought by pretending in play using object substitution, role taking, and role-play. (Quill, 2000).

**REFERENCES**

Greenspan, S., & Shanker, S. (2004). *The first idea, how symbols, language, and intelligence evolved from our primate ancestors to modern humans.* Cambridge, MA: Da Capo Press.

Quill, K. A. (2000). *Do-watch-listen-say: Social and communication intervention for children with autism.* Baltimore: Brookes Publishing Co.

ANN PILEWSKIE

## SYMPTOM

A symptom is a change in health, such as having a raised temperature, being in pain, or being nauseous. When referring to an illness, a symptom is used in aiding in diagnosis. When discussing symptoms, one may talk about general symptoms or specific symptoms related to body systems or diseases.

TERRI COOPER SWANSON

## SYNDROME

The term *syndrome* refers to a disorder or abnormality that is diagnosed based upon a group of signs and symptoms that tend to occur together. When certain signs and symptoms co-occur frequently, it is suspected that they may have the same underlying cause, may run in certain families, may follow the same course, or may respond to the same treatments. All autism spectrum disorders are, in fact, syndromes, because they are diagnosed based on combinations of difficulties in social interaction, communication, and repetitive behaviors (APA, 2000).

**REFERENCE**

American Psychiatric Association. (2000). *Diagnostic and statistical manual of mental disorders* (4th ed., text rev.). Washington, DC: Author.

LISA BARRETT MANN

## SYSTEMATIC DESENSITIZATION

Systematic desensitization was first used by Wolpe in 1958. This technique is usually applied to situations in which people are experiencing anxiety and/or phobias. The person is asked by the therapist to rank a group of scenarios from least or most anxiety or fear producing. Then while the person is experiencing that situation or imagining it, he or she learns to replace their anxious feelings with feelings of relaxation. Once the least fearful situation becomes no longer anxiety producing, the person can move to more anxiety-producing situations (Cooper, Heron, & Heward, 1987).

*See also* anxiety disorders.

**REFERENCES**

Cooper, J. O., Heron, T. E., & Heward, W. L. (1987). *Applied behavior analysis.* Upper Saddle River, NJ: Prentice Hall.

Wolpe, J. (1958). *Psychotherapy by reciprocal inhibition.* Stanford: Stanford University Press.

TARA MIHOK

# T

## TACT

The term *tact* originated with writings on **verbal behavior** within the field of **applied behavior analysis**. A tact is the labeling of an item. An example would be a parent holding up a shoe and the child labeling the shoe. No requesting is involved in the tacting of an item; it is simply labeling an item in the environment (Lerman, Parten, Addison, et al., 2005).

### REFERENCE

Lerman, D. C., Parten, M., Addison, L. R., Vorndran, C. M., Volkert, V. M., & Kodak, T. (2005). A methodology for assessing the functions of emerging speech in children with developmental disabilities. *Journal of Applied Behavior Analysis, 38*(3), 303–316.

TARA MIHOK

## TACTILE

Located in the skin cells, the tactile system provides information about objects in the environment. Individuals with autism spectrum disorders often exhibit touch sensitivity. At its extreme, tactile hypersensitivity, or defensiveness, involves physical discomfort when coming into contact with someone or something that others might not register. Standing in line, shopping for clothing, bathing, eating, and using a glue stick all present potentially stressful situations for tactilely defensive individuals. In contrast, individuals who are hyposensitive fail to respond to the touch of others, yet often use touch to explore the environment for the tactile input they crave.

*See also* sensory integration; sensory integration disorder.

KELLY M. PRESTIA

## TACTILE DEFENSIVENESS

Tactile defensiveness is a behavior or coping mechanism exhibited by individuals who may be sensitive to certain tactile sensory stimuli. Observable behaviors of tactile defensiveness may include pulling away from the touch of others or wearing tagless undershirts.

KELLY M. PRESTIA

## TARGET BEHAVIOR

A desired or target behavior is a single, clearly defined, observable behavior. The behavior is defined to allow observations, data recording, and/or teaching of the specific behavior. A target behavior may be a negative or undesired behavior or a positive behavior being taught. For example, in **discrete trial training**, the specific skill or response being taught within a program is called the target behavior. It is of utmost importance that the desired or target behavior be clearly defined so that anyone reading its description would know exactly what is being addressed. This definition is referred to as an operational definition. Having a good operational definition provides clarity for staff and students alike and ensures accurate data and consistent instruction.

KATIE BASSITY

## TASK ANALYSIS

A task analysis is a breakdown of the individual steps involved in a complex behavior. For example, for hand washing, the task analysis would identify each step: turn on water, get hands wet, get soap, rub hands, rinse hands, turn off water, dry hands. The degree to which a behavior is broken down depends upon the individual and the task. Once a task analysis is performed, **chaining** is often used to teach the behavior.

*See also* applied behavior analysis.

KATIE BASSITY

## TESTIMONIAL

Testimonial is a written or verbal statement often given by an individual or group of individuals in support of a particular truth, fact, or claim. This anecdotal evidence is typically used to persuade others to support their belief.

*See also* anecdotal report.

THERESA L. EARLES-VOLLRATH

## TEST OF ADOLESCENT AND ADULT LANGUAGE– FOURTH EDITION (TOAL4)

The Test of Adolescent and Adult Language–Fourth Edition (TOAL4; Hammill, Brown, Larsen, & Wiederholt, 2007) measures expressive and receptive language skills from individuals ages 12 to 24. This **norm-referenced assessment** yields scores in the following areas: listening, speaking, reading, writing, spoken language, written language, vocabulary, grammar, **receptive language**, and **expressive language**.

**REFERENCE**

Hammill, D. D., Brown, V. L., Larsen, S. C., & Wiederholt, J. L. (2007). *Test of adolescent and adult language–fourth edition.* Austin, TX: Pro-Ed.

JEANNE HOLVERSTOTT

## TEST OF LANGUAGE COMPETENCE (TLC)

The Test of Language Competence (TLC; Wiig & Secord, 1989) determines student language strategies, assists in developing remediation plans, and aids in the development of **Individual Education Plan** goals and objectives. Subtests of this assessment include Ambiguous Sentences, Listening Comprehension: Making Inferences, Oral

Expression: Recreating Speech Acts, Figurative Language, and a supplemental memory subtest. Two levels of the TLC can be administered to children ages 5–9 and 10–18.

**REFERENCE**

Wiig, E. H., & Secord, W. (1989). *Test of language competence*. New York: Harcourt Publishing.

JEANNE HOLVERSTOTT

## TEST OF LANGUAGE DEVELOPMENT–INTERMEDIATE, THIRD EDITION (TOLD-I)

The Test of Language Development–Intermediate, Third Edition (TOLD-I; Hammill & Newcomer, 1997) consists of five subtests that measure components of spoken language. Students ages 8–0 through 12–11 are given tasks in combining sentences, understanding word relationships, constructing sentences with appropriate word order, knowing abstract relationships, recognizing grammatical sentences, and correcting ridiculous or absurd sentences.

**REFERENCE**

Hammill, D. D., & Newcomer, P. L. (1997). *Test of language development–intermediate, third edition*. Austin, TX: Pro-Ed.

JEANNE HOLVERSTOTT

## TEST OF LANGUAGE DEVELOPMENT–PRIMARY (TOLD-P)

The Test of Language Development–Primary (TOLD-P; Hammill & Newcomer, 1996) consists of nine subtests that measure components of spoken language. Picture Vocabulary, Relational Vocabulary, and Oral Vocabulary assess the understanding and meaningful use of spoken words. Grammatic Understanding, Sentence Imitation, and Grammatic Completion subtests assess differing aspects of grammar. Word Articulation, Phonemic Analysis, and Word Discrimination are supplemental subtests that measure the ability to say words correctly and to distinguish between words that sound similar.

**REFERENCE**

Hammill, D. D., & Newcomer, P. L. (1996). *Test of language development–primary*. Minneapolis, MN: Pearson Assessments.

JEANNE HOLVERSTOTT

## TEST OF PRAGMATIC LANGUAGE (TOPL)

The Test of Pragmatic Language (TOPL; Phelps-Teraski & Phelps-Gunn, 1992) is an individually administered test designed to assess an individual's ability to use pragmatic language. The test includes 44 items, each of which establishes a social context. After a verbal **stimulus** prompt from the examiner, who also displays a picture, the student responds to the dilemma. TOPL test items provide information within six core subcomponents of pragmatic language: physical setting, audience, topic, purpose (speech acts), visual-gestural cues, and abstraction.

**REFERENCE**

Phelps-Terasaki, D., & Phelps-Gunn, T. (1992). *Test of pragmatic language*. Austin, TX: Pro-Ed.

JEANNE HOLVERSTOTT

## TEST OF PROBLEM SOLVING–ADOLESCENT (TOPS-A)

The Test of Problem Solving–Adolescent (TOPS-A; Bowers, Huisingh, Barret, Orman, & LoGiudice 2007) assesses problem solving, critical thinking skills, and expressive language skills of adolescents ages 12–18. The 13 problem-solving items are composed of passages and open-ended questions designed to assess skills in clarifying, evaluating, fair-mindedness, analyzing, thinking independently, and affect.

### REFERENCE

Bowers, L., Huisingh, R., Barret, M., Orman, J., & LoGiudice, C. (2007). *Test of problem solving–adolescent.* East Moline, IL: LinguiSystems, Inc.

JEANNE HOLVERSTOTT

## TEST OF PROBLEM SOLVING–ELEMENTARY (TOPS-E)

The Test of Problem Solving–Elementary (TOPS-E; Bowers, Huisingh, & LoGiudice, 2005) assesses the ability of children ages 6 to 11 years to organize thoughts and express thoughts clearly. Performance is assessed in problem solving, determining solutions, drawing inferences, empathizing, predicting outcomes, using contextual cues, and vocabulary comprehension.

### REFERENCE

Bowers, L., Huisingh, R., & LoGiudice, C. (2005). *Test of problem solving 3–elementary.* East Moline, IL: LinguiSystems, Inc.

JEANNE HOLVERSTOTT

## THEORY OF MIND

Theory of mind refers to the ability to understand and impute to people mental states such as feelings, beliefs, or intentions that are different from our own (Baron-Cohen, Leslie, & Frith, 1985; Cumine, Leach, & Stevenson, 1998; and Klin, Volkmar, & Sparrow, 2000). There are two levels of theory of mind. First order comprises the ability to predict a mental state of someone else (e.g., I think that Katy thinks), the second order involves the ability to predict one person's mental state about another person's mental state (e.g., Katy thinks that Mark thinks). The theory of mind hypothesis related to autism proposes that persons with autism have difficulty or are unable to perceive the desires, intentions, or beliefs of others. The significance of this deficit is the inability of a person to develop and understand social relationships and answer appropriately to the social demands of his or her environment.

*See also* social skills training; social thinking.

### REFERENCES

Baron-Cohen, S., Leslie, A. M., & Frith, U. (1985). Does the autistic child have a theory of mind? *Cognition, 21,* 37–46.

Cumine, V., Leach, L., & Stevenson, G. (1998). *Asperger syndrome, a practical guide for teachers.* London: David Fulton Publishers.

Klin, A., Volkmar, F. R., & Sparrow, S. S. (2000). (Eds.). *Asperger syndrome.* New York: Guilford Press.

### FURTHER INFORMATION

Baron-Cohen, S. (1997). *Mindblindness: An essay on autism and theory of mind.* Cambridge, MA: The MIT Press.

Baron-Cohen, S. (2004). *Mind READING The interactive guide to emotions* [DVD edition]. London: Jessica Kingsley Publishers.

Charman, T., Baron-Cohen, S., Swettenham, J., Baird, G., Cox, A., & Drew, A. (2000). Testing joint attention, imitation, and play as infancy precursors to language and theory of mind. *Cognitive Development, 4*, 481–498.

Howlin, P., Baron-Cohen, S., & Hadwin, J. (1998). *Teaching children with autism to mind-read: A practical guide for teachers and parents.* New York: John Wiley.

McAfee, J. (2002). *Navigating the social world: A curriculum for individuals with Asperger's syndrome, high functioning autism, and related disorders.* Arlington, TX: Future Horizons.

SUSANA BERNAD-RIPOLL

## TIC DISORDERS

A tic is a brief, nonrhythmic, recurrent, and rapid movement caused by a problem in the brain with neurons that use dopamine. Tics can involve the skeletal muscles, which produce motor tics, or the smooth muscles, which produce vocal tics. Tics can be simple, involving only one muscle group, or complex, involving multiple groups. Common motor tics include simple ones such as eye blinking, head turning, or jaw movements, as well as complex ones such as hand gestures, jumping, or twirling. Vocal tics most commonly involve simple ones like clearing the throat or snorting. Complex vocal tics are rarer and can include saying words or phrases, including curse words. These words, like many tics, are unrelated to the situation and are potentially very embarrassing. Kurlan, McDermott, Deeley, Como, Brower, et al. (2001) found that around 20 percent of typical grade school children exhibited at least one tic. Most of these children and their families did not attach significance to their tics, and therefore they did not reach medical attention.

When tics interfere with a person's ability to function, a tic disorder may be diagnosed and treatment considered. The ***Diagnostic and Statistical Manual of Mental Disorders–Fourth Edition–Text Revision*** (DSM-IV-TR; APA, 2000) identifies four basic tic disorders: chronic motor or vocal tic disorder, transient tic disorder, tic disorder NOS, and Tourette's disorder. Individuals with a chronic motor tic disorder present only motor tics and no vocalizations. Chronic vocal tic disorder is similar except that the individual exhibits vocal tics with no motor involvement. Transient tic disorder patients have motor and/or vocal tics not for more than one year for at least four weeks. To be diagnosed with tic disorder NOS, the duration or frequency does not match the stipulations of the other conditions. Additionally, tic disorders must start before age 18 and cannot be secondary to substance abuse or another known medical condition. Tourette's disorder, sometimes referred to as Tourette's syndrome or TS, combines vocal and motor tics, though both do not have to be consistently present. The DSM-IV-TR (APA, 2000) states that in both chronic tic disorders and Tourette's, tics must be present for at least one year with no tic-free periods longer than 3 months. With Tourette's disorder, the intensity of tics fluctuates across time, with new ones starting and old ones subsiding, only to re-emerge later. Tics usually worsen with stress or excitement, such as during the school year.

The treatment of tics involves the use of dopamine antagonist medications such as pimozide or haloperidol. Newer medications such as risperidone and aripiprazole are also being used, but are not yet FDA-indicated treatments.

379

REFERENCES

American Psychiatric Association. (2000). *Diagnostic and statistical manual of mental disorders* (4th ed., text rev.). Washington, DC: Author.

Kurlan, R., McDermott, M. P., Deeley, C., Como, P. G., Brower, C., Eapen, S., et al. (2001). Prevalence of tics in schoolchildren and association with placement in special education. *Neurology, 57,* 1383–1388.

FURTHER INFORMATION

Adams, R. D., Victor, M., & Ropper, A. H. (1985). *Principles of neurology* (3rd ed.). New York: McGraw-Hill.

JAMES R. BATTERSON

## TIME-OUT

Time-out is a form of **punishment** intended to decrease the likelihood of a behavior reoccurring. Time-out simply removes the individual from reinforcement, whether that is attention, computers, playtime, or another situation or activity. There are two types of time-out: seclusionary and nonseclusionary. Seclusionary time-out removes the individual from the setting where the reinforcement is offered; nonseclusionary keeps the individual in the setting while still denying her access to reinforcement. It is important to remember that time-out is only effective and should only be used if it decreases the likelihood of the undesired behavior occurring again. In addition, time-out must remove the individual from all forms of reinforcement. For these reasons, time-out is not effective for all behaviors, all situations, or all children.

*See also* reinforcer.

KATIE BASSITY

## TOE WALKING/EQUINUS GAIT

*Toe walking,* also called *equinus gait* for its similarity to the way a horse walks, is normal for typically developing youngsters up to age 3. For those with autism spectrum disorders or other disabilities, toe walking may be seen well into childhood. Toe walking can be caused by a number of factors including habit, immature nervous system, visual problems, and various neuromuscular disorders.

FURTHER INFORMATION

Edelson, S. M. (2005). *Toe walking.* Retrieved June 5, 2006, from http://www.autism.org/toewalk.html.

Schwentker, E. P. (2004). *Toe walking.* Retrieved June 5, 2006, from http://www.emedicine.com/orthoped/topic451.htm.

PAUL G. LaCAVA

## TOKEN ECONOMY

Token economy is an individualized reinforcement system that uses a conditioned **stimulus,** or token, such as a coin, a poker chip, or even a mark on a paper, to represent progress towards the receipt of a predetermined **reinforcer** for a certain predetermined behavior. The tokens are earned for performing appropriate behavior and are then traded for reinforcement, which are tangible goods or privileges desired by the individual (Alberto & Troutman, 1999). Token economies can take many forms. The tokens can be traded one token for one reinforcer, or can be traded at a higher rate of multiple tokens for one reinforcer. Token economies are beneficial for several reasons. They assist in the delay of reinforcement over time and between different places or settings and decrease the satiation of reinforcement (Cooper, Heron, & Heward, 1987).

*See also* applied behavior analysis.

**REFERENCES**

Alberto, P. A., & Troutman, A. C. (1999). *Applied behavior analysis for teachers* (pp. 235–247). Upper Saddle River, NJ: Merrill.

Cooper, J. O., Heron, T. E., & Heward, W. L. (1987). *Applied behavior analysis*. Upper Saddle River, NJ: Prentice Hall.

JESSICA KATE PETERS AND TARA MIHOK

## TOTAL COMMUNICATION

Total communication is an educational philosophy for children who are deaf or hearing impaired. This philosophy promotes the use of all modes of communication that are most effective for the child in any given moment. This allows the child to use all available modes of communication such as speech, lip-reading, sign language, writing, visual supports, or a combination of these. This philosophy was meant to find a middle ground between advocates for oral language only and advocates for sign language only as methods of communication.

The term *total communication* was first coined by Roy Holcomb in 1967 in California and developed by David Denton at the Maryland School for the Deaf. By the mid 1970s, most of the schools for children who were deaf incorporated such philosophy in their instructional curriculums.

**FURTHER INFORMATION**

Baker, R., & Knight, P. A. (1998). Total communication: Current policy and practice. In S. Gregory, P. Knight, W. McCracken, S. Powers, & L. Watson (Eds.), *Issues in deaf education* (pp. 77–78). London: David Fulton, Publisher.

Evans, L. (1982). *Total communication: Structure and strategy*. Washington, DC: Gallaudet University Press

Gibbs, E., & Springer, A. (1994). *Early use of total communication: An introductory guide for parents*. Baltimore: Brookes Publishing Co.

SUSANA BERNAD-RIPOLL

## TOUCH PRESSURE

Touch pressure is also known as **proprioception**, which involves firm but gentle touch to strategic parts of the body as an intervention to calm and reorganize the body and nervous system.

KELLY M. PRESTIA

## TOUCH THERAPY

Touch therapy is an intervention that attempts to desensitize an individual who may be overly sensitive to touch by slowly increasing the amount and types of touch that the individual will tolerate.

KELLY M. PRESTIA

## TOWER OF HANOI (TOH)

The Tower of Hanoi (TOH; Lawrence Hall of Science, n.d.) is a mathematical puzzle invented by the French mathematician Edouard Lucas in 1883. TOH consists of a tower of eight disks, initially stacked in increasing size on one of three pegs. The objective is to transfer the entire tower to one of the other pegs, moving only one disk at a time and never a larger one onto a smaller.

### REFERENCE

Lawrence Hall of Science (n.d.). *Tower of Hanoi facts.* Retrieved December 10, 2006, from http://www.lawrencehallofscience.org/Java/Tower/index.html.

JEANNE HOLVERSTOTT

## TOXICOLOGY

Toxicology refers to the study of the **symptoms**, treatments, and detection of the adverse effects of chemicals on living organisms, typically referred to as poisoning. The chief criterion regarding the toxicity of a chemical is the dose or the amount of exposure to the substance.

JEANNE HOLVERSTOTT

## TRAIL-MAKING TEST

The Trail-Making Test (TMT; Reitan, 1958) requires participants to draw a single, continuous line (a trail) through randomly located items on a sheet of paper. In TMT's Form A, the trail is drawn through numbers to be connected in numerical order from 1 to 25. In Form B, the trail is through spatially intermingled numbers and letters, alternating between the two kinds of items, 1, A, 2, B, and so forth. The total time to complete each form is measured and performance is summarized by scoring each test separately, computing the difference between the two total times, or by their ratio. TMT is used to assess executive functioning; specifically, differential performance on the two forms has been linked to the ability to perform complex **executive functions**, such as planning of actions and switching between activities (Kuhlman, Little, and Sekuler, in press).

### REFERENCES

Kuhlman, A., Little, D., & Sekuler, R. (in press). An interactive test of serial behavior: Age and practice alter executive function. *Journal of Clinical and Experimental Neuropsychology.*

Reitan, R. M. (1958). *Trail making test: Manual for administration, scoring and interpretation.* Indianapolis, IN: Indiana University Medical Center.

JEANNE HOLVERSTOTT

## TRANSITION PLANNING

The **Individuals with Disabilities Education Act** (IDEA; 2004) provides for functional transition planning beginning no later than age 16 years and designed to support the movement of the individual learner from school-age services and supports (to the greatest extent possible) to the postschool world of adult independent living. IDEA defines transition planning as a coordinated set of activities that focus on improving the academic and functional achievement of the student and facilitate

**Figure 19  Initial Employment Experience Goal**

---

**Student: Mark Doe Age: 14 years**

*Transition to Employment Goal*: To obtain an employment experience in a field/location where:

There are clear completion criteria

He will be able to listen to his music on a Walkman

He will be able to consistently get to the location, and

He will work directly with one primary supervisor.

*Short-term (3 Month) Objectives & Person Responsible*:

Investigate employment opportunities meeting these criteria—*School Staff*

Assess specific instructional opportunities in terms of production (the work he will do), social (the interaction environment of the workplace), navigation (e.g., ability to independently access the Men's Room) and safety demands (potential hazards such a complex machinery)— *Transition Specialist*

Develop instructional programs to meet noted skill demands in new environment—*Transition Specialist*

Develop brief coworker training protocol focusing on the strengths of Mark Doe and what he may need to support effective communication—*Transition Specialist and Newly Identified Employer*

Obtain bus pass for ride to work—*Mark and His Parents*

Obtain state issued photo identification and age-appropriate wallet—*Mark and His Parents*

Purchase work specific clothes (if necessary)—*Mark and His Parents*

Schedule next meeting—*All Concerned*

---

movement from school to postschool activities. Additionally, IDEA requires that the transition services be based on the student's strengths, as well as their preferences and interests, and that the transition process is driven by a "results-oriented" philosophy of instruction and program development.

In practice, there is general agreement as to the overall importance of comprehensive transition planning. Comprehensive, in this case, can best be understood as including input from all relevant sources (e.g., the individual and family, school personnel, interested community members, representatives from postsecondary agencies/services, potential employers, etc.) with goals developed across all relevant domains (e.g., academics, behavior support, communication and social skills, community independence, safety, navigation, employability) and across all relevant environments (e.g., home, community, work, recreation). The central question to be addressed across all areas of comprehensive transition planning is, quite simply, "To what is the learner with ASD transitioning and what skills, competencies, services or supports will they need once they get there?" Failure to adequately answer this question results in a process best described by Lewis Carroll (1832–1898) when he wrote, "If you don't know where you are going, any road will take you there." In other words, in the absence of good planning quite a bit of time and effort will be exhausted with few, if any, discernable outcomes. A sample results-oriented goal for the development of a first employment experience may look something like this:

## The Role of the Family

There is little disagreement as to the critical role the family plays in effective transition planning. Beyond their personal knowledge of, and relationship with, their son or daughter, many parents with learners with autism spectrum disorders (ASD) are well versed in the current state of ASD research, services, and supports through their attendance at conferences, reading of journal articles, access of relevant texts, and extensive networking. Any reduction in parent involvement, either through the implementation of policies or procedures that restrict parental involvement or familial fear of "rocking the boat" denies the transition team access to both valuable information and, in many cases, an educated colleague.

Perhaps the most important role, among many, that parents and family members can play in the transition process is their continuing role as an advocate for their child. Despite a bevy of new stressors that may appear during the transition years (e.g., an unfamiliarity with the adult system of services and supports; the potential inability of this system to meet the needs of their, now, nearly adult child; the stress associated with life-cycle transitions in general and, uncertainty regarding the future), the need for parents to forcefully advocate on behalf of their son or daughter does not diminish with age. For all aspects of comprehensive transition planning to be effectively implemented, the critical role that parent advocacy plays cannot be overstated.

Transition planning, in summary, is a complex, complicated, dynamic, and highly individualized (or person-centered) process. Based on an almost backwards process, good transition planning begins not where the student is, but rather where the student wants to be as the initial, school-based process winds to a close. Individual goals and objectives are developed accordingly. It is important to note that good transition planning actually continues across a person's postschool life with new goals and objectives developed on a regular basis to provide the skills necessary to meet such challenges as moving into a new apartment, starting a new job, graduating from college, or meeting new people. Comprehensive transition planning, it seems, does not terminate as a function of one's high school graduation but instead, is only temporarily suspended at times as a function of one's attaining a preferred, active, and included quality of life.

*See also* Individualized Transition Plan; postsecondary education; vocational rehabilitation.

## Reference

*Individuals with Disabilities Education Improvement Act of 2004.* Public Law No. 109-446, § 20 U.S.C. (2004).

## Further Information

Bannerman, D. J., Sheldon, J. B., Sherman, J. A., & Harchik, A. E. (1990). Balancing the right to habilitation with the right to personal liberties: The rights of people with developmental disabilities to eat too many doughnuts and take a nap. *Journal of Applied Behavior Analysis, 23,* 79–89.

Ford, A., Schnorr, R., Meyer, L., Davern, L., Black, J., & Dempsey, P. (Eds.). (1989). *The Syracuse community-referenced curriculum guide for students with moderate to severe disabilities.* Baltimore: Brookes Publishing Co.

Gerhardt, P. F., & Holmes, D. L. (2005). Employment: Options and issues for adolescents and adults with autism. In F. Volkmar, R. Paul, A. Klin, & D. Cohen (Eds.), *Handbook of autism and pervasive developmental disorders* (3rd ed., pp. 1087–1101). New York: Wiley.

Gerhardt, P. F. (2003). Transition support for learners with Asperger syndrome: Toward successful adulthood, In T. Gullota & R. Ducharne (Eds.), *Aspergers syndrome* (pp. 159–174). New York: Klewer/Plenum.

Griffiths, D. M., Richards, D., Fedoroff, P., & Watson, S. L. (Eds.) (2002). *Ethical dilemmas: Sexuality and developmental disabilities.* Kingston, NY: NADD Press.

Howlin, P., Goode, S., Hutton, S., & Rutter, M. (2004). Adult outcome for children with autism. *Journal of Child Psychology and Psychiatry, 45,* 212–229.

Jefferson, G. L., & Putnam, G. L. (2002, May). Understanding transition services: A parent's guide to legal standards and effective practices. *Exceptional Parent Magazine,* 70–77.

Koller, R., (2000). Sexuality and adolescents with autism. *Sexuality and Disability, 18,* 125–135.

Steere, D. E., Rose, E., & Cavaiuolo, D. (2006). *Growing up: Transition to adult life for students with disabilities.* Boston: Allyn & Bacon.

Wehman, P. (2002). *Individual transition plans: The teacher's curriculum for helping youth with special needs* (2nd ed.). Austin, TX: Pro-Ed.

Wehman, P. (2006). *Life beyond the classroom: Transition strategies for young people with disabilities.* Baltimore: Brookes Publishing Co.

PETER GERHARDT

## TREATMENT EFFECTIVENESS

Treatment effectiveness refers to the ability of a particular treatment (e.g., pharmacological, psychosocial) to remediate the **symptoms** of a psychological disorder. Because **anecdotal reports** from providers and clients typically provide flawed data, treatment effectiveness is typically assessed through empirical research.

*See also* empirical evidence.

JEANNE HOLVERSTOTT

## TRIAL

A trial is the individual, distinct unit of behaviorally based instruction. It is comprised of four parts: the **discriminative stimulus** (SD), the response (R), the reinforcing stimulus (SR), and the intertrial interval. In addition, a prompt may be added, in which case it would immediately follow the SD and precede the response. The SD is the command or demand, and it may be verbal, such as "touch head," nonverbal, or a combination of the two. The R is the student's response to the given command, and the SR is the instructor's response to the student's response. While it is desired that the SR is a conscious reinforcement provided by the instructor, dependent on the student's response, some form of SR occurs regardless of the teacher's intent because it is virtually impossible to not react to the student's response. An intertrial interval follows each SD-R-SR sequence to separate it from the next SD-R-SR sequence; this is what makes the trial an individual unit of instruction. There are a wide variety of prompts which can be used within a trial, and instructors should be fully conscious of themselves while carrying out a trial to be sure prompts are only given when and how they are intended.

*See also* discrete trial training; prompting.

KATIE BASSITY

## TUBEROUS SCLEROSIS COMPLEX

Tuberous sclerosis complex is a genetic disorder in which multiple tumors appear in the skin, brain, heart, and kidneys of affected children. Infants born with this disease may have facial skin lesions (called angiofibromas), tumors of the central nervous system (called astrocytomas), and other lesions, producing mental retardation and seizures.

JEANNE HOLVERSTOTT

## TWENTY QUESTIONS TASK

The Twenty Questions Task (Denny & Denny, 1973) is a test of abstract thinking and problem solving involving two participants. One participant selects a topic, typically a person, place, object, or idea. The other participant can ask up to 20 yes-or-no questions in order to discover the other participant's topic. Success typically results from employing efficient strategies and effective communication.

### REFERENCE

Denny, D. R., & Denny, N. W. (1973). The use of classification for problem-solving: A comparison of middle and old age. *Developmental Psychology, 9,* 275–278.

JEANNE HOLVERSTOTT

## TWIN STUDIES

Autism research studies involving twins as subjects have been conducted since the 1970s. These twin studies have provided some of the most conclusive evidence for the genetic contribution to autism. Scientists calculate the chances of disabilities such as autism within twin pairs by studying identical twins (who share one embryo and have identical DNA) and fraternal twins (who have separate embryos and share only 50 percent of DNA). Twin studies have shown that autism and other autism spectrum disabilities, as well as other developmental problems, are much more likely in both identical twins as compared to a set of fraternal twins, non-twin siblings, or the typical population.

### FURTHER INFORMATION

Le Couteur, A., Bailey, A., Goode, S., Pickles, A., Robertson, S., Gottesman, I., et al. (1996). A broader phenotype of autism: The clinical spectrum in twins. *Journal of Child Psychology and Psychiatry, 37,* 785–801

Pericak-Vance, M. A. (2003). Discovering the genetics of autism. *USA Today, 131,* 56–57.

Rutter, M. (2005). Aetiology of autism: Findings and questions. *Journal of Intellectual Disability Research, 49,* 231–238.

The Tech Museum of Innovation. (March 31, 2006). *Ask a geneticist.* Retrieved July 25, 2006, from http://www.thetech.org/genetics/ask.php?id=168.

PAUL G. LaCAVA

# U

## UNIVERSAL NONVERBAL INTELLIGENCE TEST (UNIT)

The Universal Nonverbal Intelligence Test (UNIT; Bracken & McCullum, 1998) is designed to provide a thorough assessment of general intelligence for students from ages 5 through 17 years of age who may be at a disadvantage with traditional language-based intelligence tests. Students who may benefit from the UNIT are individuals previously identified with or thought to be diagnosed from many diverse areas such as different cultural backgrounds, intellectually gifted, limited English proficiency, deaf or hearing impaired, mental retardation, speech and language difficulties, autism, serious emotional disturbance or psychiatric disorders, and/or learning disabilities.

The UNIT is administered primarily through nonverbal gestures, and students respond via symbolic representations and gestures. The UNIT must be given by a psychologist trained and licensed in intelligence testing.

### REFERENCE
Bracken, B. A., & McCullum, R. S. (1998). *The universal nonverbal intelligence test*. Chicago: Riverside Publishing.

BROOKE YOUNG

# V

## VACCINATIONS (THIMEROSAL)

Vaccinations containing the preservative thimerosol are a controversial issue related to one of the possible causes of autism. Despite the fact that the Centers for Disease Control and Prevention and the American Academy of Pediatrics issued the statement, "the available scientific evidence has not shown thimerosol-containing vaccines to be harmful" (World Net Daily, 2004), the U.S. Food and Drug Administration in 1999 decided to no longer use thimerosol in vaccinations. Today several national organizations continue to raise funds to search for the causes of autism, with vaccinations containing thimerosol being one the leading causes.

### REFERENCES

World Net Daily (2004, April 3). *Feds won't warn people about vaccine*. Retrieved December 13, 2006, from http://wnd.com/news/article.asp?ARTICLE_ID=37874.

U.S. Food and Drug Administration. (n.d.). *Thimerosol in vaccines frequently asked questions*. Retrieved December 13, 2006, from www.fda.gov/cber/vaccine/thimfaq.htm.

### FURTHER INFORMATION

Autism Research Institute: www.autismwebsite.com.

Autism Speaks: www.autismspeaks.org.

Centers for Disease Control (n.d.). *National immunization program*. Retrieved December 13, 2006, from www.cdc.gov/nip/vacsafe/concerns/thimerosal/faqs-thimerosal.htm.

TERRI COOPER SWANSON

## VALIDITY

Validity refers to a study measuring information based on its design and the absence of logical errors in drawing conclusions from the data. Many different types of validity exist, all concerning the threats and biases that would undermine the meaningfulness of research.

*See also* concurrent validity.

JEANNE HOLVERSTOTT

## VAN DIJK APPROACH

The van Dijk approach is an integrated model of assessment and educational curriculum tailored for individuals who are deaf-blind and who may have intellectual disability and/or physical disability. The approach is based on the understanding that combined loss of vision and hearing affects communication, socialization, conceptualization, and movement (MacFarland, 1995).

### ASSESSMENT MODEL

In 1960, Dr. Jan van Dijk and his colleagues in the Netherlands developed a series of assessment strategies that focused on the process of how children who are deaf-blind learn rather than focusing on individual, discrete skills (Nelson, 2002). Such processes include: (a) preferred learning channels; (b) ability to maintain and modulate state; (c) ability to learn, remember, and anticipate routines; (d) ability to accommodate new experiences with existing schemes; (e) problem-solving approach; (f) ability to develop social attachments and interaction with others; and (g) communication modes.

The basis of this type of assessment is the establishment of a secure relationship between the child and the evaluator. To this end, the child is given time to explore and become comfortable in the new environment. Parents, or persons with whom the child feels secure, do not leave until a safe relationship is developed with the evaluator.

The evaluator is responsible for adjusting his emotional level and communication to the child and the child's interests and abilities. In fact, it is the child's interests and abilities that determine what materials are used and the direction of the assessment. The child initiates the conversation, and the assessor reproduces what the child is doing, adding new information as turn-taking routines are built. Communication signals are elicited by stopping the pleasurable routine and waiting for the child to sign that she wants to continue (Nelson, 2002). During these interactions, the child is able to demonstrate her ability to learn, and the evaluator is able to identify methods and educational objectives for teaching the child.

It is important to note that this process is tailored to each child; therefore, there are no standard materials or instructions. However, van Dijk and Nelson have developed an interactive CD with multiple videos of strategies for assessments (see references).

### CURRICULUM MODEL

The van Dijk curriculum uses a holistic approach implemented through the student's daily program. This curriculum model seeks to develop four child outcome characteristics: (a) initial attachment and security; (b) concepts of near senses (touch, smell, and taste) and distance senses (hearing and vision) in relation to the world; (c) ability to structure the world; and (d) natural communication systems.

The four outcomes are organized in 14 instructional strategies. These instructional strategies are teacher-applied methods (McFarland, 1995).

This curricular approach addresses several major principles such as sensory deprivation, integration of sensory information, concept formation, attachment and security, progressive distancing from concrete to more symbolic concepts, organizing and structuring the world, anticipatory learning, natural symbol development, pragmatic communication, and symbolic language (McFarland, 1995).

According to van Dijk's educational theory, there is an interrelationship between the neurological state of the student with dual sensory loss, vision and hearing, and the external influences of the student's environment. Depending on how this interrelation is presented and encouraged, the student will develop a rich and meaningful world of interaction or a limited and self-absorbed one (McFarland, 1995).

In this model, the teacher plays a fundamental role in guaranteeing that all components are correctly executed through the student's educational program and integrated simultaneously in his or her daily activities (McFarland, 1995).

### References
McFarland, S. (1995). Teaching strategies of the van Dijk curricular approach. *Journal of Visual Impairments and Blindness, 89*, 222–228.
Nelson, C. (2002). *The van Dijk approach to child guided assessment.* Retrieved April 10, 2006, from http://www.tsbvi.edu/Outreach/seehear/winter02/vnadijk.htm.

### Further Information
van Dijk, J., & Nelson C. (2002). Child-guided strategies for assessing children who are deaf blind or have multiple disabilities [CD Rom]. Available at http://www.tsbvi.edu/Outreach/seehear/winter02/vnadijk.htm and http://www.aapnootmuis.com/.

SUSANA BERNAD-RIPOLL

## VERBAL BEHAVIOR

**Applied behavior analysis** (ABA) and verbal behavior (also known as AVB-applied verbal behavior) are based on the works of B. F. Skinner. In his book, *Verbal Behavior* (1957), Skinner's theories regarding language classify speech and other forms of communication as behaviors. Skinner's study of the ecology of behaviors (1953) aided in the development of the field of **behavior modification** and the principles of ABA. For example, reinforcement, motivation, discrete trial instruction, and **shaping** are all components of ABA directly applied in AVB. With regard to verbal behavior, the verbal operant is the "behavior" serving as the object of study. The operants of verbal behavior include: **mand**, echoic, **tact**, receptive function feature class (RFFC), and **intraverbal**. Each verbal operant is taught separately and used for language assessment.

### The Mand

Typically used as the first type of language taught, a mand is simply a request for something (the **reinforcer**) that an individual is motivated to request. The level of motivation serves as the establishing operation (EO) demonstrating how effective a reinforcer is at a particular time or place. An effective EO increases the probability that a particular behavior will occur, thus creating more opportunities to reinforce the behavior.

According to Skinner (1957), observation of the child, an interview of the child, parents, and past teachers, and the administration of reinforcement inventories are necessary to discover what a child finds motivating. It is preferable to select items or activities that can be used more than once such as a toy that lights up and/or plays music. Skinner further suggests (1957) that the innately high level of motivation in the natural environment should be harnessed as much as possible. Moreover, a student should never be prompted to mand for items that are not preferred as this decreases motivation quickly. Another "motivation killer" is to offer some of the reinforcing items for "free" sometimes. The use of errorless teaching procedures, while limiting aversives and punishment, keeps the training enjoyable. Considerations should be made with regard to consistency across teachers and environments and with regard to mastery criteria and the accessibility of reinforcers. Skinner also suggests that generalization be a consideration from the initial stages of manding (1957) by varying the pace of instruction, materials, people, and environment whenever possible.

## THE ECHOIC

The echoic is verbal behavior that is controlled by another's verbal behavior, more commonly known as verbal imitation. Students with a limited verbal repertoire (e.g., babbling) and some indication of motor imitation can benefit from the use of pairing sign language with manding to develop vocalizations. In doing so, the focus should not be on the sign but on shaping the vocalizations (Sundberg & Partington, 1998), which is accomplished through differential reinforcing for closer and closer approximations of the vocalization (differential reinforcement). In this way, signing can be used as a "bridge" to arrive at the correct vocalization (Sundberg & Partington, 1998). At this stage, imitation (e.g., teacher says, "Do this," and claps and the student claps), receptive language (e.g., student is able to follow a verbal direction) and matching to sample (e.g., can match items that vary only by color or size in a field of eight) should be taught as soon as possible with the echoic.

## THE TACT

The tact is verbal behavior as a result of a nonverbal stimulus, commonly referred to as labeling (e.g., the teacher holds up a cup and the child states, "cup"). Before teaching the tact, a student should have some words/signs that he can imitate, and he should have some independent mands (Sundberg & Partington, 1998). Trials of other acquired skills should be interspersed with tact trials (e.g., echoic, receptive, matching, imitation). At this stage it is important that the student be able to respond to these "mixed" trials effectively and that the mand, tact, and receptive operants are strong and generalized before moving on to the next stage. When this basic repertoire has been achieved, it is time to consider the receptive function, feature, class, and intraverbal operants.

## THE RECEPTIVE FUNCTION FEATURE CLASS (RFFC)

Receptive means the ability to respond to the instructions or requests of others. The response depends upon the verbal behavior of someone else; for example, if the teacher says "clap," the student claps. The receptive feature, function, class process teaches students to distinguish items by how they look (e.g., "give me the one that is orange"), how they are used (e.g., "give me the one that you drive"), or by the class of items a particular object belongs to ("give me the one that is a food").

## THE INTRAVERBAL

An intraverbal is a verbal response to a verbal behavior without the presence of nonverbal stimuli (Skinner, 1957). For example, one might answer "dog" when asked,

"What is your favorite pet?" A more basic example requires a child to fill in the words to familiar songs. The response is not an echoic, rather an "answer." The goal is to teach a student to respond in a conversational manner. It can be difficult for a student to distinguish how to respond to the many different word combinations that people use to say the same thing (e.g., "Where do you live?" vs. "What's your address?").

Intraverbals are introduced at the same time as RFFC and when a student has at least 50 mands and tacts (Sundberg & Partington, 1998). Instruction typically begins with simple fill-in-the-blank responses using songs and nursery rhymes and moves to teaching a student to give his name, address, phone number, and the names of animals. Intraverbals pose the most difficult verbal behavior to teach, and many direct teaching trials are needed to master the intraverbal operant.

Skinner's analysis of verbal behavior provides a framework for assessment and language training (Sundberg & Partington, 1998). Therefore, each of the verbal operants should be considered as part of language assessment in addition to the physical properties of a student's response form (e.g., syntax, pitch, intonation). Verbal behavior breaks down language into these separate verbal operants in the same way that we break down any new skill or behavior we want to teach into the individual steps of that skill. In doing so, we are provided with a more informative language assessment and a more clearly defined "roadmap" of how to teach language to our students with developmental delays.

*See also* discrete trial training; echoic/verbal behavior.

**REFERENCES**

Skinner, B. F. (1953). *Science and human behavior*. New York: Free Press.

Skinner, B. F. (1957). *Verbal behavior*. New York: Appleton-Century-Crofts.

Sundberg, M. L., & Partington, J. W. (1998). *Teaching language to children with autism or other developmental disabilities*. Pleasant Hill, CA: Behavior Analyst, Inc.

**FURTHER INFORMATION**

Lovaas, O. I. (1981). *Teaching developmentally disabled children: The me book*. Baltimore: University Park Press.

Lovaas, O. I. (2003). *Teaching individuals with developmental delays: Basic intervention techniques*. Austin, TX: Pro-Ed.

Maurice, C., Green, G., & Luce, S. C. (1996). *Behavioral intervention for young children with autism: A manual for parents and professionals*. Austin, TX: Pro-Ed.

MICHELE MULLENDORE

# VESTIBULAR

Responsible for balance and movement, the *vestibular* system resides in the inner ear and is stimulated by movements and changes in head position. Individuals with vestibular hypersensitivity have low tolerance for activities involving movement and exhibit difficulties with changing speeds and directions. They may experience nausea and/or headaches from spinning and have difficulty sitting still. Hyposensitivity is observed in the individual who seeks out vestibular input by rocking or swinging; this individual might also be clumsy and have difficulty "switching gears."

*See also* hyperresponsiveness; hyporesponsiveness; proprioception; sensory.

KELLY M. PRESTIA

## VIDEO MODELING

Video modeling is a technique that involves demonstration of desired behaviors, outcomes, and attitudes through active, visual representation. When using a video-modeling intervention, an individual typically watches a video demonstration and then imitates the behavior of the model. Video modeling can be used with peers, adults, or self as a model.

The concept of modeling as an intervention technique was first introduced by Albert Bandura in the early 1960s. Bandura demonstrated that children were more aggressive towards a toy after an age-matched model demonstrated aggressive behavior towards the same toy (Bandura & Huston, 1961). Bandura later demonstrated that watching an individual receive reinforcement for a particular behavior (i.e., vicarious reinforcement) would later increase the rates of the behavior in the individual observing the model.

Over the past two decades, modeling has been further explored and implemented using video technology. Thus, video modeling has been used across multiple disciplines and populations to teach a wide variety of skills, including motor behaviors, increased athletic performance, and even to decrease anxiety (Dowrick, 1999). Further, it has been effectively used to teach children with autism spectrum disorders (ASD), social skills (Nikopoulos & Keenan, 2004), conversation skills (Charlop & Milestein, 1989), **self-help skills** (Pierce & Schreibman, 1994), and purchasing skills (Alcantara, 1994).

As theorized by Bandura, attention is a necessary component of modeling. That is, a person cannot imitate the behavior of a model if he does not attend to the model's behavior. Individuals with ASD tend to exhibit overselective attention or attend to irrelevant details of the environment. The use of video modeling allows interventionists to remove irrelevant elements of the modeled skill or behavior through video editing. The removal of irrelevant stimuli, in turn, allows the individual with ASD to better focus on essential aspects of the targeted skill or behavior. In addition, individuals with ASD often exhibit anxiety and distress related to social interactions, which may significantly impact their ability to attend to a learning task. Video modeling can be implemented with minimal human interaction, thereby reducing much of the distress and anxiety related to social interactions. Charlop-Christy and Daneshvar (2003) noted that the children with ASD in their study demonstrated increased motivation to watch the model in the video-modeling procedure compared to the live-modeling procedure. Finally, the effectiveness of video modeling might be a result of preference for visual learning. This notion is supported by Sherer, Pierce, Paredes, Kisacky, Ingersoll et al. (2001), who noted that video modeling was most effective for the children in their study who demonstrated prior preference for visual learning, such as video viewing and the use of visual support strategies.

Many skills learned via video modeling have been found to generalize across settings and conditions (Dowrick, 1999), and the positive gains made during the video-modeling intervention are maintained for months following the conclusion of the intervention. Classroom teachers, professionals, and parents may find video modeling a promising technique when working with children with autism.

*See also* social skills training.

REFERENCES

Alcantara, P. R. (1994). Effects of videotape instructional package on purchasing skills of children with autism. *Exceptional Children, 61*(1), 40–55.

Bandura, A., & Huston, A. (1961). Transmission of aggression through imitation of aggressive models. *Journal of Abnormal and Social Psychology, 63,* 575–582.

Charlop, M. H., & Milestein, J. P. (1989). Teaching autistic children conversational speech using video modeling. *Journal of Applied Behavior Analysis, 22,* 275–285.

Charlop-Christy, M. H., & Daneshvar, S. (2003). Using video modeling to teach perspective taking to children with autism. *Journal of Positive Behavior Interventions, 5*(1), 12–21.

Dowrick, P. W. (1999). A review of self-modeling and related interventions. *Applied & Preventative Psychology, 8,* 23–39.

Nikopoulos, C. K., & Keenan, M. (2004). Effects of video modeling on social initiations by children with autism. *Journal of Applied Behavior Analysis, 37,* 93–96.

Pierce, K., & Shreibman, L. (1994). Teaching daily living skills to children with autism in unsupervised settings through pictorial self-management. *Journal of Applied Behavior Analysis, 27,* 471–481.

Schrer, M., Pierce, K. L., Paredes, S., Kisacky, K. L., Ingersoll, B., & Schreibman, L. (2001). Enhancing conversation skills in children with autism via video technology. *Behavior Modification, 25,* 140–159.

SCOTT BELLINI AND JENNIFER M. AKULLIAN

## VIDEO SELF-MODELING

Video self-modeling (VSM) is a modeling strategy that allows individuals to learn targeted behaviors by watching videos of themselves successfully performing the behaviors.

For children with autism spectrum disorders (ASD), VSM integrates a powerful learning medium (visually cued instruction) with an effective evidence-based intervention modality (modeling). VSM capitalizes on the well-documented success of visually cued instruction in this population by presenting a visual representation of the target skill or behavior (e.g., showing a video of the child initiating or responding during social interactions).

The use of VSM has been effective in treating children with a variety of disorders, including **selective mutism, autism, attention deficit hyperactivity disorder** (ADHD), social anxiety, aggressive/disruptive behavior, and motor problems (Buggey, 1999; Dowrick, 1999). Further, an emerging body of research has demonstrated great promise for the use of VSM as a therapeutic intervention for individuals with ASD (Buggey, Toombs, Gardener, & Cervetti, 1999; Schrer, Pierce, Paredes, Kisacky, Ingersoll, et al. 2001; Wert & Neisworth, 2003).

According to Dowrick (1999), VSM interventions typically fall within two categories, positive self-review (PSR) and video feed-forward.

PSR refers to individuals viewing themselves successfully engaging in a behavior or activity that is currently in their behavioral repertoire. PSR is best used with low-frequency behaviors or behaviors that were once mastered, but are no longer. In this case, the individual is videotaped while engaging in the low-frequency behavior and then shown a video of the behavior.

PSR is a relatively simple strategy to use from a technological standpoint. However, for very low-frequency behaviors, it requires extensive amounts of raw video footage to capture even a small amount of the target behavior.

Video feed-forward, another category of VSM interventions, may be used when an individual already possesses a component of the target skill in her behavioral repertoire, or is performing the skill at a low level of mastery or autonomy. While feedforward requires additional editing capabilities, as compared to PSR, it typically requires a smaller quantity of raw video footage. "Hidden supports" are an important component of video feed-forward interventions. For instance, the child could be videotaped interacting with peers while an adult provides assistance through cueing and prompting. The adult prompt could then be edited out (hidden) so that when the child views the video segment, she sees herself as independent and successful.

Motivation to watch oneself on a video may be enhanced by the portrayal of predominantly positive behaviors. According to Buggey (1999), showing predominantly positive behaviors to children is beneficial because of the confidence they develop from observing their own success. Watching primarily positive and/or successful behaviors of oneself, as opposed to negative and/or unsuccessful behaviors, is also thought to increase attention and motivation to attend to the modeled behaviors. In addition, Buggey states that VSM is preferable to peer and adult modeling because peers or adults do not possess the exact characteristics of the target child. That is, the target individual is more likely to relate to the model because she is the model. Finally, anecdotal evidence and clinical experience suggest that watching videos is a highly desired activity for many children with and without ASD, leading to increased motivation and attention to task.

REFERENCES

Buggey, T. (1999). Videotaped self-modeling: Allowing children to be their own models. *Teaching Exceptional Children, 4*, 27–31.

Buggey, T., Toombs, K., Gardener, P., & Cervetti, M. (1999). Training responding behaviors in students with autism: Using videotaped self-modeling. *Journal of Positive Behavior and Intervention, 1*(4), 205–214.

Dowrick, P.W. (1999). A review of self modeling and related interventions. *Applied & Preventative Psychology, 8*, 23–39.

Schrer, M., Pierce, K. L., Paredes, S., Kisacky, K. L., Ingersoll, B., & Schreibman, L. (2001). Enhancing conversation skills in children with autism via video technology. *Behavior Modification, 25*, 140–159.

Wert, B. Y., & Neisworth, J. T. (2003). Effects of video self-modeling on spontaneous requesting in children with autism. *Journal of Positive Behavior Interventions, 5*(1), 30–34.

SCOTT BELLINI AND JENNIFER M. AKULLIAN

## VINELAND ADAPTIVE BEHAVIOR SCALES–SECOND EDITION (VABS-II)

The Vineland Adaptive Behavior Scales–Second Edition (VABS-II; Sparrow, Cicchetti, and Balla, 2005) is used to assess children with autism spectrum disorders in the areas of communication, socialization, motor skills, daily living skills, and maladaptive behavior skills. The VABS-II is available in three forms: interview edition, survey, and expanded forms. The assessment requires between 20 and 60 minutes for parents, caretakers, and teachers to fill out and provide information to the psychologist or social worker. The layout of the assessment allows for comprehensive data collection across settings and individuals. VABS-II has been proven to be an effective tool in diagnosing Asperger syndrome, **autism**, **developmental delays**, **mental retardation**, and speech and language impairments.

**REFERENCE**

Sparrow, S. S., Cicchetti, D. V., & Balla, D. A. (2005). *Vineland Adaptive Behavior Scales, Second Edition*. Circle Pines, MN: America Guidance Service.

TYI-SANNA JONES

## VIRTUAL ENVIRONMENT

The virtual environment is one form of computer-based learning that has advantages for people with autism in that computer-based programs are logical, predictable, impersonal, and limit distractions and anxiety while permitting the user to repeat a lesson as many times as necessary to learn the material or skill taught. Virtual environments are three-dimensional simulations of an environment created by a computer program. The environment may be imaginary or designed to represent a specific location. Research to date has shown that users with autism spectrum disorders (ASD) generally enjoy working with virtual environments and learn to use programs as or more quickly than peers without **autism**.

Virtual environments can take the form of virtual reality or immersion environments in which the user wears headgear and other equipment that displays the visual component directly in front of the user's eyes and translates the user's movements into movements on the visual display. Another form of virtual environment is represented on a computer monitor, much like a typical computer game. The equipment used to immerse a user in a virtual reality is expensive, heavy, and cumbersome, and some users report nausea, headaches, and dizziness. The virtual environments displayed on a desktop computer monitor have no such side effects and are far less expensive, utilizing existing computers and accessory equipment, such as a mouse, keyboard, and joystick. The ability to use standard computer equipment also increases the possibility that the user with autism can use a program at home as well as at school or a training site.

Within the virtual environment, the user "occupies" an avatar, a figure representing the user, and generally "sees" the environment through the viewpoint of the avatar, although the user may also be provided with a view of the activity from above. Interaction with the environment takes place through the avatar being controlled by the accessory equipment.

Users with autism have reported that their experiences with virtual environments are interesting and fun, and they tend to learn to use the equipment and interact with the environment fairly quickly. There are two types of virtual environments. Those designed for one user at a time are called single-user virtual environments (SVEs) and allow the user to interact with the environment and to have limited, preprogrammed interactions with another. Programs designed for multiple users are called collaborative virtual environments (CVEs).

SVEs have been designed to allow users to practice daily activities around home, work, transportation, and café settings, and other settings can be developed to allow for a highly varied and flexible training program. Programs introducing new skills can be highly structured with limited choices to allow rehearsal of the new skill in realistic but safe settings. As only the user is involved with the lesson, the user can practice each skill and scenario at a comfortable speed and as frequently as necessary to master the skill. As the person progresses in mastery of the skill, the programs can introduce more choices and some randomness in placement of objects and simulated people and variations in prompts to encourage flexibility. Once a skill is learned in one setting (for instance, asking if a seat is available in a café), it can be practiced in other settings, such as a theater, bus, or social event. Since only one person uses the SVE at a time, the user can learn the skills and visit the same scenario many times without the difficulty and unpredictability of interacting with other people, and without anxiety or fear about any consequences for making an error. The session can be recorded and reviewed by the user and a teacher in order to discuss the user's performance and any problems that the user may have. To increase social interaction and generalization, a teacher, coach, or peer may sit beside the user during some sessions, particularly after the user has become somewhat familiar with the skill being taught.

A CVE involves more than one user in a shared environment where users can interact, work together, and communicate through their avatars. Interaction through avatars, rather than face to face, provides a sense of anonymity and reduces the stress and sense of risk that can occur during direct interaction with another person, but still provides the flexibility and reality of interacting with people rather than strictly with a preprogrammed computer. By reducing the level of threat in communication, and by bringing people who may be widely dispersed together, CVEs function as an assistive technology to improve communication and reduce isolation and the sense of social exclusion for people with autism. Virtual meetings and networks of people with autism can facilitate communication between people with and without autism, since communication through CVEs is slower than face-to-face conversation and can provide people with autism extra time to respond to the avatar of a communication partner. Since avatars can be programmed to show facial expressions, users may have an opportunity to consider and convey their own emotions as well as be aware of the expressions of other avatars.

CVEs can also be used for group lessons for dispersed students with autism and can provide a setting for more advanced and flexible social skills instruction than is possible in a SVE where the user can "interact" with characters only in the ways that are built into the program. Users of a CVE can also work together in role-playing scenarios to practice social skills, and can discuss problems that arise with each other or with a teacher, as CVEs can also be recorded to allow a user to review the session and consider alternative ways of handling problems that arise.

Although the use of SVEs and CVEs for the teaching of skills is promising, they are not appropriate for all users, nor do they offer a complete training program by themselves. Studies to date have involved only persons with autism spectrum disorders who do not have mental retardation. A minority of users in studies have shown difficulty staying on task in virtual environments, and another minority have had difficulty understanding that virtual environments are representational of real-life settings and activities. Thus when an individual with autism is first introduced to the use of virtual environments, a teacher should observe to make sure that the student is able to follow instructions and stay on task, and should talk with the user and make sure that the user is able to understand that the virtual environment represents reality and that other avatars represent people.

Another problem with using virtual environments to teach skills is that no study to date has provided evidence that users of virtual environments and computer-based learning are able to generalize the learned skills to different environments at significant levels. However, existing studies have been of very short duration and have had few participants. Even in those studies, however, individuals who have used the programs more have shown a greater ability to generalize than participants who used the programs for shorter periods of time. Thus it is possible that studies that involve longer periods of use may provide empirical evidence of generalization by users. Finally, it should be noted that the use of virtual environments is only one part of any learning package, especially for social skills. Although SVEs and CVEs can help the user develop appropriate skills and a sense of self-confidence that may make real-life experiences less stressful and more productive, the use of SVEs and CVEs should be combined with group work, discussion, and experience in real-world settings to improve mastery and generalization.

*See also* assistive technology; social skills training.

### FURTHER INFORMATION

Cobb, S., Beardon, L., Eastgate, R., Glover, T., Kerr, S., Neale, H., et al. (2002). Applied virtual environments to support learning of social interaction skills in users with Asperger's syndrome. *Digital Creativity, 13*(1), 11–22.

Golan, O., & Baron-Cohen, S. (2006). Systemizing empathy: Teaching adults with Asperger syndrome and high functioning autism to recognize complex emotions using interactive multimedia. *Developmental and Psychopathology, 18,* 591–617.

Moore, D., Cheng, Y., McGrath, P., & Powell, N. J. (2005). Collaborative virtual environment technology for people with autism. *Focus on Autism and Other Developmental Disabilities, 20,* 231–243.

Moore, D., McGrath, P., & Thorpe, J. (2000). Computer-aided learning for people with autism—a framework for research and development. *Innovations in Education and Training International, 37*(3), 218–228.

Parsons, S., & Mitchell, R. (2002). The potential of virtual reality in social skills training for people with autistic spectrum disorders. *Journal of Intellectual Disability Research, 46,* 430–443.

Parsons, S., Mitchell, P., & Leonard, A. (2004). The use and understanding of virtual environments by adolescents with autistic spectrum disorders. *Journal of Autism and Developmental Disorders, 34*(4), 449–466.

Parsons, S., Mitchell, P., & Leonard, A. (2005). Do adolescents with autistic spectrum disorders adhere to social conventions in virtual environments? *The National Autistic Society, 9*(1), 95–117.

Rajendran, G., & Mitchell, P. (2000). Computer mediated interaction in Asperger's syndrome: The bubble dialogue program. *Computers and Education, 35,* 189–207.

Silver, M., & Oakes, P. (2001). Evaluation of a new computer intervention to teach people with autism or Asperger syndrome to recognize and predict emotions in others. *The National Autistic Society, 5*(3), 299–316.

HYUN-JEONG CHO

## VIRUSES

A virus is a submicroscopic infectious organism that reproduces itself in biological entities (such as human cells) and may cause damage or disease. It has been claimed that, like other diseases, autism can be caused by slow-moving viruses that affect brain development. The cytomegalovirus is one virus that has been connected to autism spectrum disorders. Maternal rubella is another virus that has been studied for connections to autism. Rubella was once a very common disease, but since inoculation efforts has been almost unheard of in the United States. Although rubella has been much less of a concern due to mass vaccinations, in light of the controversy over the possible connections between autism and vaccinations, and with the possibility of some people forgoing inoculations of childhood, the rubella virus cannot be forgotten as a possible culprit.

### FURTHER INFORMATION

Merriam-Webster. (2005). *Virus*. Retrieved June 30, 2006, from http://www2.merriam-webster. com/cgi-bin/mwmednlm?book=Medical&va=virus.

Rutter, M. (2005). Aetiology of autism: Findings and questions. *Journal of Intellectual Disability Research, 49*, 231–238.

PAUL G. LaCAVA

## VISUAL-MOTOR

Visual-motor describes any activity that requires the use and coordination of vision and movement simultaneously. Examples of visual-motor skills include drawing, completing a puzzle, or painting.

KELLY M. PRESTIA

## VISUAL STRATEGIES

Visual strategies refer to ways of using visual stimuli such as photos, drawings, and so on, to enhance the communication process. A primary purpose for using visual strategies is to support understanding. Visual strategies provide information in a form that many students can understand more easily than auditory information. Other terms used include visual supports, visual tools, visual cues, or visually mediated communication.

Most students with autism spectrum disorders (ASD) and many others with communication or behavior challenges demonstrate strength in visual learning compared to their auditory abilities. That means they understand what they see better than what they hear. Yet we tend to communicate with them primarily by talking (Hodgdon, 1995). Temple Grandin, a well-known speaker and author with autism, describes her unique visual learning style in her book *Thinking in Pictures* (1995).

Using visual strategies to support communication capitalizes on a person's ability to gain information from the sense of sight. Photographs, line drawings, computer clip art, pictures from catalogs or magazines, food labels, signs, logos, objects, and written language can be used as visual tools to support communication. Video is another visual medium that is proving effective.

Visual supports can include the following:

### Body Language
Facial expressions, body movement, pointing, eye contact.

### Cues in the Natural Environment
Furniture arrangement, signs in the environment (in/out, men/women), menus, directions on a vending machine.

**Commonly Used Tools for Organizing and Gaining Information**
Calendar, day planner, TV guide, shopping list, cooking instructions.

**Specially Designed Tools for Giving Information**
To develop schedules, provide choices, give information, give directions, establish rules, teach skills, develop self-regulation, and more.

One goal when using visual strategies is to teach students to identify, understand, and respond appropriately to the visual cues and information that already exist in the environment. Another goal is to identify their specific communication needs and challenges as a basis for creating visual tools that give the specific information they need to understand.

Visual tools are easy to use. We can become more effective communicators if we use simple language and support our communication by showing the student something visual to help him understand what we are saying. Sometimes visual tools are hung on the wall or refrigerator or placed in communication books so the student can easily access them when he needs them.

REASONS TO USE VISUAL STRATEGIES

Visual strategies assist students in processing language, organizing their thinking, remembering information, and many other skills necessary to participate and communicate effectively. The following are some of the possibilities.

Visual tools can *provide structure* to help create an environment that is more predictable and understandable as well as present information. They can be used at home or school or transported to other environments. For example:

- *Schedules* are the most common visual tools. They help students know what is happening during the day and anticipate transitions from one activity to another.
- *Visual timers* create a visual way for students to understand the passage of time and to assist with transition.
- *Task organizers or step-by-step directions* guide students through a series of steps to accomplish a task.
- *Choice boards* display the options available to choose from.
- *Classroom or home rules* help students remember what to do or state options to unacceptable behavior.

A powerful purpose for visual strategies is to *give students information*. It is common to give students information verbally and to assume they understand. Anxiety or behavior problems can emerge when students really don't understand, or they don't remember what to do or how to handle a situation. For example:

- *People locators* help students understand where significant people are, when they will leave, or when they will return.
- *Transition and travel helpers* can prepare students for predictable activities and routines or for excursions that are not part of the normal routine.
- *Behavior helpers* guide students to prepare for activities and anticipate what will happen and what will be expected of them.

Video as a teaching medium is a comparatively new visual tool. It is becoming useful for teaching appropriate social and communication behavior. The value of video is that it captures the movement of the social world. It has been used successfully for teaching a variety of skills including imaginative play, correct behavior, and perspective taking (Hodgdon, in press).

## WHY STUDENTS BENEFIT FROM VISUAL STRATEGIES

Communication is one of the core deficits in ASD. Communication is complex and there are many reasons why students may have difficulty. For example, research suggests these students experience difficulty shifting and reestablishing attention (Courschene, 1991). Children with autism tend to have particular difficulty attending to auditory input and may prefer visual input (Anzalone & Williamson, 2000). Greenspan and Wieder (1998) found that 97 percent of their sample of children with autism showed significant receptive language deficits.

Many of the difficulties these students encounter as they attempt to follow life routines, handle change and transition, demonstrate appropriate behavior, or participate in social opportunities are directly related to their communication challenges. Speech is transient. Consider that an auditory message may disappear before a student has focused his attention enough to receive it. These children do not easily understand what is happening around them, what is changing, or what the rules are. The result can be frustration, anxiety, tantrums, and more.

In contrast, most of these students demonstrate a preference for visual information. Visual supports are helpful because the visual message stays long enough for the student to establish attention and receive information.

Using visual strategies to support understanding can significantly affect a student's ability to communicate more successfully, develop appropriate social skills, regulate behavior in various environments, and participate more independently. The challenge is to determine how using visual supports will meet each student's individual needs.

## COMMON QUESTIONS

Traditionally, communication boards and other augmentative communication supports have been used to help nonverbal students or those with limited verbal ability express themselves better. The current use of visual strategies for supporting understanding has shifted that focus. It is appropriate to use visual tools to aid understanding for both nonverbal and verbal students.

Visual strategies are not just for young children. They are appropriate for students of all ages. Most of us use a calendar or a day planner and other visual supports to help organize our own lives. Students with ASD can benefit from the same tools; however, they generally need more visual supports. Visual strategies are tools for life that can be modified and adapted to meet students' changing needs as they grow into adulthood. Visual strategies provide the support students need to participate more appropriately and independently in their life activities.

## CASE STUDY
### Problem

Stacy's Mom was taking her to the doctor for a check-up. Stacy began to cry and bite her wrist. She kept yelling, "No shot!" Her behavior escalated, making it difficult for Mom to try to get her into the car.

## Cause

Even though Mom told Stacy she was not going to get a shot this time, Stacy was nervous because she remembered her last trip to the doctor. She remembered getting a shot that hurt. Stacy needs a lot of information because she has a memory of fear and pain. She doesn't have the communication skills to discuss the situation adequately, so she is expressing her fear with her behavior.

## Solution

Giving Stacy information in a form that she understands will help her anticipate the event and demonstrate more appropriate behavior. One or more of the following options should help the situation: (a) tell her verbally and *visually* where she is going; (b) give her visual information about the sequence of events; (c) give her information in a visual form about what will happen and what will not happen; and (d) create a visual tool that will prompt something to say or do when she goes to the doctor's office.

## Result

Mom developed some visual tools to communicate the information Stacy needed. When Stacy had more information, she had a successful doctor visit (Hodgdon, 1999).

## REFERENCES

Anzalone, M. E., & Williamson, G. G. (2000). Sensory processing and motor performance in autism spectrum disorders. In A. Wetherby & B. Prizant (Eds.), *Autism spectrum disorders: A transactional developmental perspective* (pp. 145–146). Baltimore: Brookes Publishing Co.

Courschene, E. (1991). A new model of brain and behavior development in infantile autism. *Autism Society of America Conference Proceedings*. Indianapolis, IN.

Grandin, T. (1995). *Thinking in pictures: And other reports from my life with autism*. New York: Doubleday.

Greenspan, S., & Wieder, S. (1998). *The child with special needs: Encouraging intellectual and emotional growth*. Reading, MA: Addison-Wesley.

Hodgdon, L. (1995). *Visual strategies for improving communication*. Troy, MI: QuirkRoberts Publishing.

Hodgdon, L. (1999). *Solving behavior problems in autism*. Troy, MI: QuirkRoberts Publishing.

Hodgdon, L. (in press). *How to teach social skills with visual strategies*. Troy, MI: QuirkRoberts Publishing.

## FURTHER INFORMATION

Hodgdon, L. (1995). Solving social-behavioral problems through the use of visually supported communication. In K. A. Quill (Ed.), *Teaching children with autism: Strategies to enhance communication and socialization* (pp. 265–286). New York: Delmar Publishers Inc.

Hodgdon, L. (2005). *25 reasons to use visual strategies. Another view with Linda Hodgdon: Effective solutions for autism, Asperger's syndrome and more*, 1(4). Retrieved April 23, 2005, from http://www.lindahodgdon.com/newsletters.html.

Quill, K. A. (1995). Visually cued instruction for children with autism and pervasive developmental disorders. *Focus on Autistic Behavior*, 10(3), 10–20.

LINDA HODGDON

**VISUAL SUPPORTS.** *See* Visual Strategies

## VOCATIONAL REHABILITATION

The Division of Vocational Rehabilitation Services (VR) is a federally funded agency that provides job training for adult individuals with disabilities. A vocational rehabilitation counselor is assigned when the individual applies for services. Therefore, the individual with the disability needs to seek out the services from VR; VR will not seek out the individual. The counselor will assess the needs of the individual to determine whether the individual is eligible for services. Eligibility is determined based on the level of disability the individual has and the amount of work the individual is capable of doing.

Service funding availability changes depending on the amount of money the federal government provides. When funding is low, VR goes on "Order of Selection," which only allows monies for individuals with moderate to severe disabilities who were assessed as able to work in the community with some support. An example of a person with a moderate to severe disability that VR would still consider employable in the community is an individual with bipolar disorder who is taking medication but still needs assistance with social interactions, anger management, and controlling negative thoughts and actions. This individual would be eligible for job placement services and job coach support on the job to maintain employment and develop appropriate job social skills.

Students who are 18 months prior to graduation from high school can apply with VR services to begin the assessment process and paperwork. Upon graduation, if the individual qualifies, the VR counselor will assist the individual in finding and maintaining competitive, paid employment in the community. Short-term job coaching assistance is provided depending on the need of the individual and the demands of the job. Job coaching ceases after a determined amount of time (usually 90 days), at which time the individual will need to maintain performance on the job with natural supports from employees within the job. If the individual wants to change employment, is promoted within his or her current job, or has job tasks change within the job, the VR counselor can reopen the case and provide job training services again for the benefit of promotion and job retention.

*See also* Individualized Transition Plan; transition planning.

BETH CLAVENNA-DEANE

## VOCATIONAL REHABILITATION PROGRAMMING

Each state has a vocational rehabilitation (VR) agency that is designed to help people with disabilities enter the workforce, learn a new skill or trade, or return to the workforce after an extended absence. High school students with disabilities can receive transition services that are designed to make the move from the school environment into the community as a young adult more successful. Students are taught work readiness skills such as teamwork, communication, how to dress, the importance of timeliness and basic office skills such as copying, collating, and filing. These services can be provided in a variety of settings to maximize the student's developmental potential. For those who are able, VR services can include enrollment in a local college or trade school and community job placements where skills can be learned or advanced. Job coaches or VR counselors often follow the individual into the community for a period of time to provide appropriate levels of supervision or support to both the individual and the employer. To increase access to other federal programs, VR agencies are also able to help people apply for Supplemental Security Income (SSI), subsidized housing, and health care programs, among many things. As with SSI and most other federal programs, the actual services available at VR agencies do vary from state to state, so it is best to contact your state agency directly to get information about what is in your area. The Social Security Administration maintains the following Web site with direct links to each state agency to facilitate access to services: http://www.ssa.gov/work/ServiceProviders/rehabproviders.html.

*See also* Individualized Transition Plan; postsecondary education; transition planning.

SHERRY MOYER

## VOTING

One context in which disability is defined is in federal and state laws, which address the electoral participation of individuals with disabilities. Federal laws pertaining to individuals with disabilities and their voting rights include the National Voter Registration Act of 1993 (NVRA), and; the **Americans with Disabilities Act** (ADA, 1990), which provides that no qualified individual with a disability may be excluded from participation in, or denied the benefits of the services, programs, or activities, or subjected to discrimination by public entities, such as state and local government. Specially, the NVRA requires that all state-funded agencies offer voter registration. State-funded facilities may include public schools, facilities providing disability services, and voter registration agencies. The ADA ensures that polling sites provide reasonable accommodations, technical assistance materials, and assistance with registering to vote and casting a ballot. In contrast to these federal laws, state laws specifying the qualifications of the electorate typically disenfranchise some individuals with disabilities. A majority of states disenfranchise on the basis of "mental incompetence," or "mental incapacity," to characterize who will not be allowed to vote.

Federal law acknowledges the physical and communication barriers that affect electoral participation, but fails to appreciate implications of state policies that exclude people based on perceived incompetence of cognitive and emotional impairments. The issue of physical accessibility has required states to ensure voters with cognitive and emotional disabilities have access to the electoral process and not be subject to accessibility barriers (ADA, 1990). In 1982, before the ADA was passed, the American Bar Association proposed that competency testing be objective, and suggested a competent voter be defined as any person able to provide the information, orally, in writing, through an interpreter, or interpretive device that is reasonably required of all persons seeking to register to vote, to be considered a qualified voter, and shall be registered to vote and allowed to cast a ballot in any election held (Schriner, Ochs, & Shields, 2000).

In October 2002 President George W. Bush signed into law the Help America Vote Act (HAVA), Public Law 107-252. HAVA was designed to modernize election equipment, facilitate easy use of equipment, maintain confidentiality and independence, and increase accessibility for persons with disabilities. HAVA was further intended to provide "talking" voting machines, large print or braille, interpretation for the hearing-impaired, a more simplified process to make it understandable for the intellectually impaired, and to protect the privacy rights of such voters.

Many resources lend to simplification of the electoral process. Because many individuals use written communication rather than face-to-face interactions, a large number of resources are available online. The use of computers and the Internet has made it possible for many individuals to present their perspective when they lack adequate communication and socialization skills.

For individuals who want to participate in the democratic process, they must be registered to vote prior to an election and have appropriate identification. For further information, contact the local election office or go to www.declareyourself.org/index.php.

## REFERENCES

Americans with Disabilities Act, 42 U.S.C. §§ 12101-12213 (1990).

Help America Vote Act. (2002). Public Law 107-252. U.S. Code. 42, 2002. [section] 15301 et seq.

National Voter Registration Act (1993). Public Law 103-131. U.S. Code 42, 1993. Sec. 2 et seq.

Schriner, K., Ochs, L., & Shields, T. (2000). Democratic dilemmas: Notes on the ADA and voting rights of people with disabilities. *Berkeley Journal of Employment and Labor Law*, *21*(1), 437–472.

## FURTHER INFORMATION

*Declare yourself*. (n.d.). Retrieved November 9, 2006 from www.declareyourself.org/index.php.

U.S. Department of Justice (2005). *A guide to disability rights laws*. Retrieved November 9, 2006, from www.usdoj.gov/crt/ada/cguide.htm.

STACEY L. BROOKENS

# W

## WAIT TRAINING

Wait training is teaching a child to wait using structured, incremental training sessions. Waiting is taught through short trials or sessions in which something desirable to the child is placed in front of her with the command to wait. **Prompting** as needed, the student is given the item after waiting a set period of time. Normally a **baseline** is recorded, and this type of program begins at or slightly above the baseline. To begin, the wait interval could be as short as 1–2 seconds. Wait training is most often done in the early stages of intervention.

KATIE BASSITY

## WEAK CENTRAL COHERENCE. *See* Central Coherence

## WECHSLER INDIVIDUALIZED ACHIEVEMENT TEST– SECOND EDITION (WIAT-2)

The Wechsler Individualized Achievement Test–Second Edition (WIAT-2; Wechsler, 2001) is a very common assessment tool used in schools to measure the academic achievement of students. The WIAT-2 consists of nine subtests: word reading, pseudoword decoding, reading comprehension, spelling, written expression, numerical operations, math reasoning, listening comprehension, and oral expression. The WIAT-2 is a measurement tool for individuals ranging in age from 4 to 85 years and can be used to assess both low- and high-functioning individuals. It is useful for assessing achievement skills, determining educational placement, as well as developing curriculum. Administration time ranges from 30 to 75 minutes.

### REFERENCE

Wechsler, D. (2001). *Wechsler individualized achievement test* (2nd ed.). San Antonio, TX: Psychological Corporation.

AMY BIXLER COFFIN

## WECHSLER INTELLIGENCE SCALES FOR CHILDREN–FOURTH EDITION (WISC-IV)

The Wechsler Intelligence Scales for Children–Fourth Edition (WISC-IV; Wechsler, 2003) is a cognitive assessment generally given by a psychologist to determine cognitive ability of school-aged children. This test provides a full-scale IQ score obtained from subtests in two subscales: verbal and performance scales. The two scales allow the examiner to assess a child in tasks that require verbal and nonverbal activities to evaluate performance and knowledge in: (a) memory; (b) factual information; (c) language; (d) attention; (e) concentration; (f) abstract, spatial, and visual problem solving; (g) fine motor and visual coordination; and (h) processing speed. This assessment tool is widely used and known to be helpful in diagnostic, placement, and planning for children with an array of exceptionalities.

REFERENCE

Wechsler, D. (2003). *Wechsler intelligence scales for children–fourth edition.* San Antonio, TX: Harcourt Assessment, Inc.

TYI-SANNA JONES

## WELCH METHOD THERAPY

### THE TREATABLE BASIS OF AUTISM

Clinical observations in the 30-year psychiatric practice of Martha G. Welch, MD, form the framework for her innovative treatment and research efforts. It is widely agreed that autism spectrum disorders (ASD) stem from genetic/environmental insults that are not yet identified. Whatever the cause, we are now focused on intervening in the subsequent events that stem from the insults. Further, we theorize that such insults share a common physiological effect: interruption and/or arrest of key developmental programs. Over time, if uncompensated, the cascade leads to adverse conditioning of stress adaptation networks, in which case the infant will present with various interrelated psychological, neurological, and immunological pathology, including autism. Our clinical experience has shown that it is possible, regardless of etiology, for the family to successfully treat autism and related developmental disorders by reinstating components of intense parent-child interaction. Our experimental research and laboratory findings support the idea that it will be possible at some point in the future to treat autism and related developmental disorders by intervening in stress mechanisms of the child with administration of exogenous brain/gut peptide combinations.

In Dr. Welch's practice, two seemingly disparate groups of patients, autistic children and maternally deprived orphans, shared two symptom complexes: (a) behavioral symptoms, such as lack of direct eye contact, indiscriminate approaches toward strangers, inability to respond to normal maternal nurturing; and (b) gastrointestinal (GI) symptoms, such as gut motility abnormalities, discomfort, diarrhea, and odd and restricted food preferences. Dr. Welch developed an intervention that engages intense parent-child interactions as a means of positively conditioning stress adaptation responses. This intervention has led to concurrent amelioration of both behavioral and gut symptoms. In many cases following intensive intervention, direct eye contact between mother and child ensued, the child was able to benefit from normal nurturing, adverse behaviors were dramatically reduced, and GI symptoms abated. Because mothers often described feeling as though they had just given birth after the therapy, Welch theorized that the bonding peptide oxytocin had been released. She attributed the striking post-treatment changes observed in the child's behavioral and gut health to the simultaneous release of natural endogenous peptides, including brain/gut peptides secretin as well as oxytocin. These collective clinical observations led to a theory that brain and gut disorders in autism and behavioral disorders of low-nurture orphans share a common dysregulation of underlying stress mechanisms.

RESEARCH BACKGROUND

The Welch Laboratory of Childhood Regulatory Disorders and the Ruggiero Laboratory of Behavioral Neuroanatomy at Columbia University are engaged in efforts to translate this clinical experience into an experimental design of new treatments for autism. The work supports a new paradigm for the treatment of mental illness, based on a theory that emotions and emotional behavior stem from dysregulations of a unified stress-adaptation brain-gut network. Peptide mechanisms critical in the conditioning of the infant adaptive behavioral patterns are abnormal in developmental disorders such as autism. Neuropeptides such as secretin and oxytocin are being tested in animal models to determine their role in compensating for the effects of stress on the brain and gut. This idea originated from Welch's clinical experience treating genetic/congenital ASD, late-onset ASD, and children with other developmental disorders, all of whom shared GI symptoms (see Figure 20).

Medical examination of children with autism reveals inflammation in the brain (Vargas, Nascimbene, Krishnan, Zimmerman, & Pardo, 2005) and gut, as well as abnormalities of **neurotransmitters**, brain/gut peptides, and cytokines (Ashwood, Anthony, Torrente, & Wakefield, 2004). The high incidence of **seizure disorders** and familial autoimmunity suggests that autism is a visceral disorder. Pathological visceral

**Figure 20 Differentiating the Welch Method**

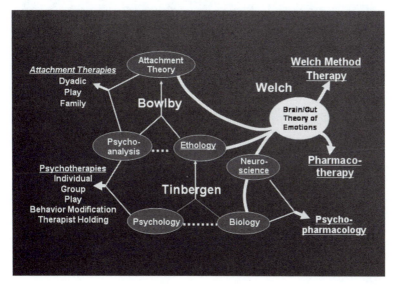

activity patterns transmit via the vagus nerves and neurohumorally to visceral/emotional brain regions abnormal in autistic children. We theorize that the viscera may be a site of pathology causing secondary developmental delays of brain regions abnormal in autism spectrum disorders. Deserving of clinical study is the functional integrity of the GI tract in family members of children with autism.

During critical periods of development, visceral diseases generating pathological stress-related activity lead to impairments of perceptual, emotional, and social development, all of which are observed in children with autism. The research literature provides ample evidence that these children exhibit classic stress-induced inflammatory symptoms in gut and brain areas that are acted upon by neuropeptides. Peptides are important in determining stress-response patterns. Their actions are the molecular basis of optimal mother-infant interactions, and they are naturally secreted on physiological demand in response to stress. As such, they are critical in regulating stress and maintaining homeostasis. It follows that therapies intervening in the peptide mechanisms activated by mother-infant interaction will be most effective in treating developmental disorders such as autism.

The role of secretin and oxytocin in the treatment of autism is emerging (see Figure 21).

Patients with autism demonstrate symptoms and sites of pathology that respond in experimental animal models to secretin and oxytocin administration. For example, a recent clinical study concluded that **secretin** ameliorated symptoms of autism in a subgroup of children with GI abnormalities (Kern, Espinoza, & Trivedi, 2004). Another clinical study showed that behavioral symptoms in autism have responded to oxytocin peptide treatment (Hollander et al., 2003). In addition, a growing body of research is providing important information about the role of secretin and oxytocin in both the gut and the brain. In an example of environmental insult, our preliminary studies of induced colitis in a rat model demonstrated that systemic combined treatment with

**Figure 21  The Role of Secretin and Oxytocin**

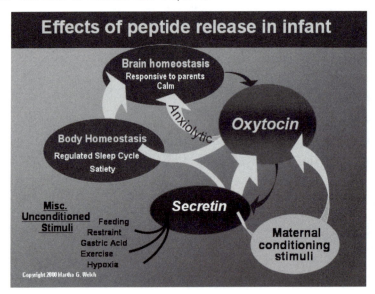

secretin and oxytocin reduced peripheral inflam-mation and its neurological manifestations in the brain (Welch et al., 2003b).

In studies designed to determine behavioral regulatory actions, secretin and oxytocin were found to activate the visceral thalamic and hypothalamic stress axes (Welch et al., 2003a). Secretin and oxytocin were synthesized by hypothalamic and gut and vascular cells in response to homeostatic challenges, such as vis-ceral stress or metabolic stressor (Welch et al., 2003a). Visceral inflammation activated vis-ceral/emotional brain regions known to be abnormal in autism, thus, providing important evidence of a connection between visceral inflammation and brain disturbance (Welch et al., 2005). In another experiment that further demonstrated a connection between brain/gut disturbance and peptides, we showed that secre-tin, like oxytocin, activated many of the same visceral/emotional brain regions that are dysre-gulated in chronic disorders such as autism. In a third experiment we clarified the structural basis for the mechanisms of individual action of

**Figure 22  Secretin and Oxytocin Research**

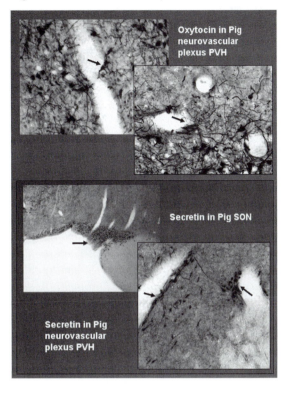

secretin and oxytocin (see Figure 22). That is, we found that secretin as well as oxyto-cin are synthesized in the hypothalamus and may act on structures involved in the pathophysiology of autism (Welch & Ruggiero, in press).

In the future, the long-term benefit of **peptide** therapy may be demonstrated by the reversal of the actions of stress transmitters and stress peptides as well as the alteration of receptor numbers or combinations abnormal in chronic mental and visceral meta-bolic disorders. Clinical trials will be necessary to assess the efficacy of systemic administration of combined secretin/oxytocin or other combinations of peptides in resolving visceral inflammation, autism, and autism with GI symptoms. We also seek a marker expressed by brain and gut that can identify a precursor stage of autism, pro-viding a means of early diagnosis and early intervention, which would in turn halt the progression of the brain changes that are stress induced.

## ABNORMAL STRESS ADAPTATION IN AUTISM

The development of the infant's stress adaptation response patterns is largely de-pendent on caregiver-infant interactions. This interaction up-regulates neuropeptides and activates key genetic developmental programs. Key developmental genetic pro-grams are altered or silenced when the mother-infant interaction is rendered ineffec-tive (Caldji, Diorio, Anisman, & Meaney, 2004). The infant is thus unable to respond to the parental care on which his physiological state depends. Unable to receive stress modulation, the infant reacts with adverse behavioral symptoms: inabil-ity to nurse, inability to maintain direct eye contact, abnormal face recognition with

Figure 23 Positive Stress-Response Conditioning Cycle

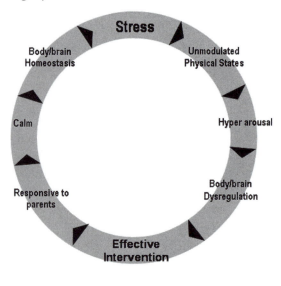

failure to respond to normal cues, inability to learn or attend to important environmental stimuli, inability to habituate to background stimuli, stereotypes, and bizarre fixations on objects or actions. If left untreated—if normal responsiveness is not restored—some of the child's critical developmental programs may remain inactivated or silenced. In this event, the stress effects on the brain and viscera continue on a downward course that gets progressively worse and eventually ends in a range of psychological, neurological, behavioral, and immunological pathology, including autism spectrum disorders.

Professionals and parents may never know what caused the child's abnormal response patterns, or in the case of late-onset autism, what precisely caused the regression in behavior. Causes may include any number of **environmental stressors**, possibly **vaccinations**, with or without periods of physical illness in a child genetically predisposed to autoimmunity. In our experience, the cause of the abnormality is less important than the fact that the abnormal stress responses can be reversed (see Figure 23).

If reversal of stress cascades is accomplished early enough in the child's development—in the case of autism before age 4 or 5, or in the case of other autism spectrum disorders before age 10 or 11—the negative cascade of stress responses may be reduced greatly or completely reversed.

TREATMENT PROGRAM

The earlier the family starts to address the brain and behavioral problems by reinstating important components of parent-child interaction, the sooner typical development will resume (see Figure 24).

We believe that very early reversal of adverse stress response patterns can reverse the on-going cascade of brain damage. If the family is performing the therapy effectively after training, they should achieve results in the child's ability to handle stress almost immediately, such as at the end of a successful 2-day treatment program. Even the most resistant child responds to the therapy. Such relatively rapid results may be supported by recent research at McGill University in Canada, where it has been discovered that genetic programs are activated in an animal model by intense mother-infant interaction (Weaver et al., 2004). It takes just 96 hours for this

Figure 24 Effects of Family Therapy

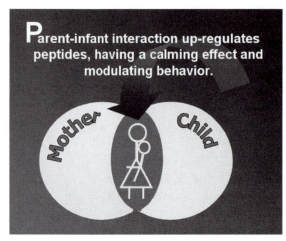

activation of genetic stress management programs to occur. It is important to note that these genes are conserved throughout mammalian development, and humans and animals express similar genetic stress adaptation programs. We theorize that intense parent-child therapy releases peptides and helps the family to activate those silenced genetic programs.

In summary, the etiology and pathophysiology of autism are little understood. However, inasmuch as autism involves adverse stress response patterns, interventions that target mechanisms of stress adaptation offer a promising approach. Systemic administration of antistress peptides may be an effective preventive measure. Our research efforts continue to seek support for therapeutic administration of neuropeptide combinations. Outcomes of such experiments could accelerate the development of novel naturalistic pharmacological treatments that do not have the side effects of current drugs. Until then, Welch Method therapy allows the parents to intervene naturally in the stress adaptation conditioning of autistic spectrum disorder children, thereby activating, as we theorize, important antistress gene programs and halting the harmful cascade that results from unmitigated stress.

*See also* environment; genetics.

## REFERENCES

Ashwood, P., Anthony, A., Torrente, F., & Wakefield, A. J. (2004). Spontaneous mucosal lymphocyte cytokine profiles in children with autism and gastrointestinal symptoms: Mucosal immune activation and reduced counter regulatory interleukin-10. *Journal of Clinical Immunology, 24,* 664–673.

Caldji, C., Diorio, J., Anisman, H., & Meaney, M. J. (2004). Maternal behavior regulates benzodiazepine/GABAA receptor subunit expression in brain regions associated with fear in BALB/c and C57BL/6 mice. *Neuropsychopharmacology, 29,* 1344–1352.

Hollander, E., Novotny, S., Hanratty, M., Yaffe, R., DeCaria, C. M., Aronowitz, B. R., et al. (2003). Oxytocin infusion reduces repetitive behaviors in adults with autistic and Asperger's disorders. *Neuropsychopharmacology, 28,* 193–198.

Kern, J. K., Espinoza, E., & Trivedi, M. H. (2004). The effectiveness of secretin in the management of autism. *Expert Opinions on Pharmacotherapy, 5,* 379–387.

Uvnas-Moberg, K. (1989). The gastrointestinal tract in growth and reproduction. *Science America, 261,* 78–83.

Vargas, D. L., Nascimbene, C., Krishnan, C., Zimmerman, A. W., & Pardo, C. A. (2005). Neuroglial activation and neuroinflammation in the brain of patients with autism. *Annual Neurology, 57,* 67–81.

Weaver, I. C., Cervoni, N., Champagne, F. A., D'Alessio, A. C., Sharma, S., Seckl, J. R., et al. (2004). Epigenetic programming by maternal behavior, *National Neuroscience, 7,* 847–854.

Welch, M. G., & Ruggiero, D. A. (in press). GABA in autism and related disorders: Predicted therapeutic role of secretin and oxytocin in autism: Implications for treatment of mental illness. *International review of neurobiology.* Burlington, MA: Elsevier.

Welch, M. G., Keune, J. D., Welch-Horan, T. B., Anwar, M., Anwar, N., & Ruggiero, D. A. (2003a). Secretin activates visceral brain regions in rats including areas abnormal in autism. *Cellular and Molecular Neurobiology, 23,* 817–837.

Welch, M. G., Welch-Horan, T. B., Keune, J. D., Anwar, N., Anwar, M., Ludwig, R. J., et al. (2003b). Neurohormonal resolution of genetic and acquired IBD and secondary brain activation in areas abnormal in autism. *(Prog. # 318.5 2003 Abstracts).* Washington, DC: Society for Neuroscience Abstracts.

Welch, M. G., Welch-Horan, T. B., Anwar, M., Keune, J. D., Anwar, N., Ludwig, R. J., et al. (2004). Secretin: hypothalamic distribution and hypothesized neuroregulatory role in autism. *Cellular Molecular Neurobiology, 24,* 219–241.

Welch, M. G., Welch-Horan, T. B., Anwar, M., Anwar, N., Ludwig, R. J., & Ruggiero, D. A. (2005). Brain effects of chronic IBD in areas abnormal in autism and treatment by single neuropeptides secretin and oxytocin. *Journal of Molecular Neuroscience, 25,* 259–274.

MARTHA G. WELCH AND DAVID A. RUGGIERO

## WILBARGER PROTOCOL

Designed by Patricia Wilbarger, the Wilbarger Protocol is a specific brushing technique to reduce tactile defensiveness by providing deep pressure to the skin on the arms, back, and legs using a surgical brush.

KELLY M. PRESTIA

## WISCONSIN CARD SORTING TEST (WCST)

The Wisconsin Card Sorting Test (WCST; Grant & Berg, 2003) is a neuropsychological test of "set-shifting." The WCST is used to assess perseveration, abstract reasoning, and the capacity to modify problem-solving strategies when needed. It has been considered a measure of executive function because of its reported sensitivity to frontal lobe dysfunction. The assessment includes 128 response cards and 4 stimulus cards. The subject taking the test is asked to sort the response cards onto the stimulus cards based upon sorting rules. The WCST has been widely used with individuals ages 6.5–89 years. Administration time ranges from 20 to 30 minutes.

REFERENCE
Grant, D. A., & Berg, E. A. (2003). *Computerized Wisconsin card sorting test version 4.* Lutz, FL: Psychological Assessment Resources, Inc.

AMY BIXLER COFFIN

## WOODCOCK-JOHNSON PSYCHOEDUCATIONAL BATTERY–REVISED: TESTS OF COGNITIVE ABILITY

The Woodcock-Johnson Psychoeducational Battery–Revised: Tests of Cognitive Ability (WJPB-R; Mather & Jaffe, 2003) is both an individual cognitive and achievement test. There are two batteries of tests, the Standard Battery and the Extended Battery. Both versions include 11 subtests incorporating reading, math, and writing/spelling concepts. The WJPB-R is a useful measure for the assessment of school performance across a variety of academic areas and ages. The tool assesses cognitive achievement as well as scholastic interests. The WJPB-R can be administered on individuals ranging in ages 3 through 80.

REFERENCE
Mather, N., & Jaffe, L. (2003). *Woodcock Johnson III–reports.* Indianapolis, IN: Wiley.

AMY BIXLER COFFIN

## WORK ADJUSTMENT PERIOD

The work adjustment period is offered through most **vocational rehabilitation** agencies to allow for opportunities to train people who have either never entered the workforce or have few work readiness skills. Training provided during a work adjustment may include interviewing skills, resume writing, staying on-task, hygiene, time management, assessing vocational interests or skills, and potential job matches. For the person with an autism spectrum disorder, the very notion of how to plan a future can be quite overwhelming simply because of a lack of exposure to community or employment experiences. Many of the skills we take for granted, like organizing our priorities and successfully planning to carry them out, are a great challenge, requiring direct instruction and support to be completed successfully. The work adjustment period is a safe test period for people to test out their skills, gain self-confidence, and discover what social expectations are associated with the work environment.

### FURTHER INFORMATION

Nuehring, M., & Sitlington, P. (2003). Transition as a vehicle: Moving from high school to an adult vocational service provider. *Journal of Disability Policy Studies, 14*(1), 23–36.

SHERRY MOYER

# Y

## YEAST-FREE

Yeast–free refers to a **diet** that controls yeast intake and strives to starve the yeast organism of sugars and simple carbohydrates. Complex carbohydrates (whole grains) and foods with low sugar content typically replace these foods. It is argued that the chemical compounds produced by yeast are toxic to the nervous system. In relation to their ability to remediate the **symptoms** of **autism**, yeast-free diets are not substantiated by empirical data.

*See also* empirical evidence.

JEANNE HOLVERSTOTT

# Z

## ZERO REJECT

Zero Reject refers to one of the founding principles of the **Individuals with Disabilities Education Act** of 1975 (PL 94-142; formerly Education of All Handicapped Children Act), which states that all children with a disability should be provided full educational opportunities and are eligible for free and appropriate education. Zero Reject ensures that no child with a disability as qualified under the Individuals with Disabilities Education Act should be fully, physically, or functionally excluded from educational opportunities because of disability or a need for special education and related services. In practice, the application of Zero Reject has included the creation of appropriate education programs as well as the transport of students to schools providing appropriate education programs.

REFERENCE

Education of All Handicapped Children Act of 1975, 20 U.S.C. Sec. 1400(d).

JEANNE HOLVERSTOTT

## ZIGGURAT MODEL

The Ziggurat Model (Aspy & Grossman, 2006) is a system for designing comprehensive interventions for individuals of all ages with autism spectrum disorders (ASD). The model is based on the premise that there are critical factors that must be addressed in all intervention plans for individuals on the spectrum—the five levels of the Ziggurat. An additional premise is that most social, emotional, and other behavioral difficulties experienced by individuals with ASDs stem from the autism itself. In other words, these difficulties are symptoms of the underlying disorder; therefore, in order to be effective, interventions must target underlying factors rather than simply alleviate surface symptoms. The Ziggurat Model incorporates assessment tools used to identify those aspects of autism that manifest as social, emotional, and other behavioral concerns. Underlying elements then become targets for intervention. A third premise of the model is that comprehensive intervention plans include preventative strategies, strategies for teaching new skills, and effective reinforcement—the three elements of a functional behavioral assessment (antecedent, behavior, and consequence).

INTERVENTION ZIGGURAT

The Intervention Ziggurat is the centerpiece of the Ziggurat Model (see Figure 25). It contains five levels in a hierarchal structure. Each level is based on fundamental needs of individuals with ASDs. The levels are interdependent, each contributing to the effectiveness of other levels.

The base or foundation of the Ziggurat represents what is, in one sense, the basis of all behavior—biology. Consideration of biological factors is especially important in the case of **autism**—a disorder with strong genetic and neurological underpinnings. Unmet sensory and biological needs will result in changes in behavior—highlighting the importance of including strategies to address these needs.

The second level of the Ziggurat represents another fundamental need—Reinforcement. Reinforcement is defined as "a situation or event that follows a particular behavior, resulting in an increased likelihood that a behavior will recur in the future" (Bregman & Gerdtz, 1997, p. 611). The ultimate goal of comprehensive interventions is to help individuals develop skills that will increase their success. This cannot occur without reinforcement.

Individuals on the spectrum require instruction and reinforcement for skills that are generally assumed to have been mastered by same-age peers. This mistaken assumption often results in punishment for failure to display a skill that has actually never been acquired. In order to counter this tendency, the Ziggurat Model includes the reinforcement level to facilitate skill acquisition and maintenance.

**Figure 25  The Five Levels of the Intervention Ziggurat**

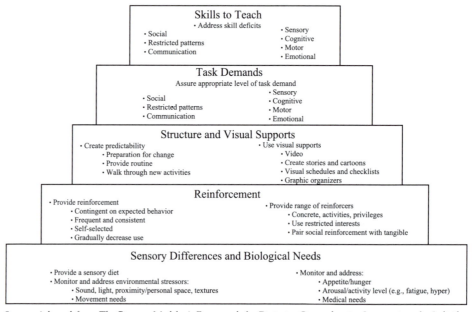

Source: Adapted from *The Ziggurat Model: A Framework for Designing Comprehensive Interventions for Individuals with High-Functioning Autism and Asperger's Syndrome*, by R. Aspy & B. G. Grossman. Copyright 2006. Shawnee Mission, KS: Autism Asperger Publishing Company. Reprinted with permission.

The third level of the Ziggurat, Structure and Visual Supports, is a response to the communication deficits and strong need for routine and order often displayed by individuals with ASDs. Structure is the systematic organization of the environment that increases predictability. The term *visual supports* refers to a range of techniques that incorporates visual media. Visual supports draw upon a strength of individuals with autism spectrum disorders—the processing of visual information. Structure and visual supports are interrelated concepts. Visual supports are a frequent means of providing increased structure. Further, both increase the ability of individuals on the spectrum to predict and understand the world. Visual reminders (e.g., visual schedules and checklists) or visual instruction techniques (e.g., cartooning and video modeling), called visual supports, are often provided to address these concerns. Visual supports and structure often result in the prevention of problem behaviors, making these strategies critical to an effective intervention plan.

Individuals with ASDs are asked to function in a world designed for neurotypicals. Even seemingly simple situations present multilayered demands (e.g., social, communication, cognitive, sensory, social, motor, etc) that can be overwhelming and result in behavioral concerns for those with ASDs. Task difficulty is the focus of the fourth level of the Ziggurat. The goal is to make certain that the balance of supports offered and independence expected are appropriate for the task presented.

In general, Task Demand interventions involve identifying prerequisite and component skill deficits and reducing the demands of a task. If skills are lacking or supports are not provided, the demand will be too difficult and expectations cannot be met. The Ziggurat Model incorporates Vygotsky's concept of the zone of proximal development (ZPD), describing the ideal conditions for skill development, as a guide for determining the level of task demand (1978, as cited in Miller, 1993). Expectations must be reasonable; that is, an individual must be capable of succeeding either independently or with assistance.

The first four levels of the Ziggurat set the stage for acquisition of skills. Skills to Teach is the final level of the model. The focus of this level is the teaching of skills across a range of areas—motor, sensory, emotional, social, communication, cognitive, etc. Those with ASDs often require direct instruction in skills and concepts that typically developing individuals acquire effortlessly—this is referred to as the seemingly obvious or "hidden" curriculum (Myles, Trautman, & Schelvan, 2004). As skills increase, less intensive interventions will be required on the lower levels of the Ziggurat because it is the learning of new skills that makes a permanent difference for the person on the spectrum. Table 10 lists examples of strategies on each level of the Intervention Ziggurat.

## UNDERLYING CHARACTERISTICS

The social and behavioral challenges presented by individuals with ASDs most often are manifestations of autism itself. Addressing behaviors without ascertaining and attending to what underlies them is a common intervention mistake. This surface or "band-aid" approach often fails to establish long-term gains because it ignores the true need—underlying hidden deficits.

Underlying needs and characteristics related to autism must be addressed (the third premise of the Ziggurat Model). To that end, the Ziggurat Model includes two

## Table 10. Examples of Interventions on Each Level of the Intervention Ziggurat

| Level | Examples of Interventions |
|---|---|
| Sensory Differences and Biological Needs | • Sensory diets<br>• Pharmacotherapy<br>• Breaks<br>• Headphones<br>• Physical activities<br>• Allowing for personal space<br>• Relaxation strategies |
| Reinforcement | • Reinforcer menu<br>• Token systems<br>• First-then charts<br>• Self-selection of activity |
| Structure and Visual Supports | • Cartooning<br>• Social Stories (Gray, 1998)<br>• Power Cards<br>• Social Autopsies<br>• Calendars (paper or electronic)<br>• Lists<br>• T-chart<br>• Video<br>• Visual map<br>• Scheduled work systems<br>• Preparation in advance of changes<br>• Visual timers<br>• Checklists<br>• Individualized work stations<br>• Picture schedules<br>• Portable transition pictures |
| Task Demands | • Copies of lecture notes<br>• Laptop computer for note taking<br>• Extra time for written work<br>• Personal Digital Assistant (PDA)<br>• Organizational skills support<br>• Coping cards<br>• Circle of Friends<br>• Narration<br>• High interest activities to encourage social interaction<br>• Peer buddies<br>• Highlighted text<br>• Monitoring teacher<br>• Safe place<br>• Breaks<br>• Preparation in advance of changes<br>• Minimizing transitions<br>• Scheduled work system<br>• PECS<br>• Modeling social/communication skills<br>• Tactile teaching aides |

|  | |
|---|---|
|  | • Individualized work station<br>• Verbal prompts<br>• Repeated exposure to activities<br>• Adult-directed play routines |
| Skills to Teach | • Social Stories (Gray, 1998)<br>• Adult-directed play routines<br>• Modeling social/communication skills<br>• Scheduled work system to teach skills for independence<br>• Video modeling |

assessment tools—the Underlying Characteristics Checklist (UCC) and the ABC-Iceberg (ABC-I)—designed to identify these underlying factors. The UCC is a descriptive assessment instrument that can be completed by multiple respondents and provides a "snapshot" of how autism is expressed for an individual in the following areas: social, restricted patterns of behavior, interests, and activities, communication, sensory differences, cognitive differences, motor, and emotional vulnerability. The ABC-I incorporates a traditional functional behavioral assessment and helps to illustrate patterns of behavior (i.e., ABCs–antecedent, behavior, and consequence). By including underlying factors, the ABC-I goes beyond the **functional behavioral assessment**. The user identifies items endorsed on the UCC that are related to the behaviors analyzed in the functional behavior assessment portion of the ABC-I. The process of completing the ABC-I (functional assessment and identification of related underlying factors) highlights the link between the behavior and the underlying autism. The identified antecedent, behavior, and consequences provide three points of intervention. The purpose of behavior interventions is to teach new skills. Antecedent interventions alter the events that "trigger" behavior difficulties and thus are preventative, while consequence interventions alter the events that follow behavior. The Ziggurat Model emphasizes positive consequences in order to reinforce appropriate behaviors and skill development.

### INTERVENTION DESIGN PROCESS

The Ziggurat Model is not a collection of intervention strategies. It is a *framework* for intervention *design*. The Ziggurat Worksheet is a tool to assist in this process. Use of the worksheet assures that the three required elements for comprehensive intervention are included. These are: (1) five levels of the Intervention Ziggurat; (2) underlying characteristics, and; (3) three points of intervention A-B-C. The authors of the model emphasize the importance of incorporating evidenced-based strategies. Further, the model provides for ongoing monitoring of progress.

The Ziggurat Model presents two paths for intervention: general and specific. General interventions address more global needs based on the UCC, while specific interventions address identified behaviors of concern based on the ABC-I and UCC. Following the assessment process, actual intervention strategies are selected with the aid of the Ziggurat Worksheet in order to create a comprehensive plan.

While the Ziggurat Model can be used by an individual, its components lend themselves to collaboration among multiple caregivers. The assessment tools are designed to incorporate the perspectives of multiple team members while assuring that they work from the same reference point—the individual's underlying characteristics of autism. The Ziggurat Worksheet also promotes collaboration by helping parents and professionals to understand their part in the larger intervention picture. Because of this capacity to promote collaboration, the Ziggurat Model is an ideal consultation tool for those serving individuals with ASDs. Through the use of the Ziggurat Model, the whole truly is greater than the sum of its parts.

*See also* genetic factors/heredity.

REFERENCES

Aspy, R., & Grossman, B. G. (2006). *The Ziggurat Model: A framework for designing comprehensive interventions for individuals with high-functioning autism and Asperger syndrome.* Shawnee Mission, KS: Autism Asperger Publishing Company.

Bregman, J. D., & Gerdtz, J. (1997). *Behavioral interventions.* In D. J. Cohen & F. R. Volkmar (Eds.), *Handbook of autism and pervasive developmental disorders* (2nd ed., pp. 606–630). New York: John Wiley and Sons.

Gray, C. A. (1998). Social stories and comic strip conversations with students with Asperger syndrome and high functioning autism. In E. Schopler, G. B. Mesibov, & L. J. Kunce (Eds.), *Asperger syndrome or high functioning autism* (pp. 167–198). New York: Plenum Press.

Miller, P. (1993). *Theories of developmental psychology* (3rd ed.). New York: W. H. Freeman and Company.

Myles, B. S., Trautman, M. L., & Schelvan, R. L. (2004). *The hidden curriculum: Practical solutions for understanding unstated rules in social situations.* Shawnee Mission, KS: Autism Asperger Publishing Company.

RUTH ASPY AND BARRY G. GROSSMAN

## ZONE OF PROXIMAL DEVELOPMENT (ZPD)

A student's zone of proximal development, or ZPD, is the student's range of ability with and without assistance from a teacher or capable peer. On one end of the range is the student's ability level without assistance. On the other end of the range is the student's ability level with assistance. The ZPD bridges that gap between what is known and what can be known. This theory requires the teacher and student to collaborate so that the student can create his own meaning from the information presented.

JAN L. KLEIN

# APPENDIX A: Newsletters

# Compiled by Lynn Dudek

## AANE NEWSLETTER (ASPERGER'S ASSOCIATION OF NEW ENGLAND)
AANE members receive a semiannual newsletter that contains valuable articles for those with Asperger syndrome, as well as important news and events.

182 Main Street
Watertown, MA 02472
Phone: 617.393.3824
Fax: 617.393.3827
E-mail: info@aane.org
Web site: www.aane.org

## AHA E-LIST (ASPERGER SYNDROME AND HIGH FUNCTIONING ASSOCIATION E-LIST)
Asperger Syndrome and High Functioning Association subscribers receive articles of interest, relevant research abstracts and updates about our group.

Web site: www.ahaNY.org

## THE ANDI NEWS (AUTISM NETWORK FOR DIETARY INTERVENTION)
*The ANDI News* is a quarterly publication that covers the dietary aspects of autism. The ANDI Web site offers links to resources and frequently asked questions. E-mailed inquiries may take up to several weeks to receive a response.

Web site: www.AutismNDI.com

## ASCEND NEWS
ASCEND Group Inc., the Asperger Syndrome Alliance for Greater Philadelphia, is a nonprofit organization founded in 2001. It was launched by parents of children with Asperger syndrome (AS) as a means to create a community of people who are concerned about the many ways that AS and other autism spectrum disorders affect children and adults and their families in the home, at school, and in every area of their lives. The *ASCEND News* is a twice-yearly newsletter from ASCEND Group, Inc.

ASCEND Group, Inc.
P.O. Box 531
Ardmore, PA 19003-0531

Phone: 610.449.6776
Fax: 610.853.6137
E-mail: membership@ascendgroup.org
Web site: www.ascendgroup.org

## THE ASPEN NEWSLETTER

ASPEN (Asperger Syndrome Education Network, Inc.) is a source of education, support, and advocacy for families and individuals whose lives are affected by autism spectrum disorders. *The ASPEN Newsletter* is included as a benefit of membership in ASPEN.

The ASPEN Newsletter
Asperger Syndrome Education Network, Inc.
Aspen Newsletter
9 Aspen Circle
Edison, NJ 08820
Phone: 732.321.0880
Web site: www.aspennj.org

## ATC NEWSLETTER

Periodically published by the Autism Training Center of Marshall University, *ATC Newsletter* is a pdf format newsletter concerning the activities in and around the Autism Training Center at Marshall.

Virginia Autism Training Center at Marshall University
College of Education
One John Marshall Drive
Huntington, WV 25755-2430
Phone: 800.344.5115
Web site: www.marshall.edu/coe/atc/newsletter.html

## AUTISM ADVOCATE MAGAZINE

The *Autism Advocate* Magazine, distributed by the Autism Society of America, is a collection of the latest autism news, chapter highlights, first-person accounts of families living with and growing with autism, and tips from parents and professionals. It is distributed to Autism Society of America members five times a year.

Autism Society of America
7910 Woodmont Avenue, Suite 300
Bethesda, MD 20814-3067
Phone: 800.3AUTISM
Web site: www.autism-society.org

## AUTISM ASPERGER PUBLISHING COMPANY (AAPC) NEWSLETTER

The *AAPC Newsletter* is a free online publication that covers a variety of topics including emotions, diet, school, and relationships. The AAPC Newsletter provides a community of support for parents, professionals, and people on the spectrum.

Autism Asperger Publishing Company
P.O. Box 23173
Shawnee Mission, KS 66283
Phone: 877.277.8254
Fax: 913.681.9473
Web site: www.asperger.net

## AUTISM-ASPERGER'S DIGEST

This bimonthly magazine features original articles and materials related to autism spectrum disorders. The magazine is written specifically for parents, teachers, and related service providers.

Web site: www.autismdigest.com

## AUTISM RESEARCH REVIEW INTERNATIONAL NEWSLETTER

*Autism Research Review International Newsletter* is published quarterly through the Autism Research Institute (ARI). The ARI Web site and newsletter are clearinghouses for biomedical and educational research on autism.

Autism Research Institute
4182 Adams Avenue
San Diego, CA 92119
Fax: 612.563.6840
Web site: www.autism.com/ari

## AUTISM SPECTRUM QUARTERLY

*Autism Spectrum Quarterly* (ASQ) provides information for individuals on the autism spectrum as well as their families. Articles are written by individuals on the autism spectrum as well as leading professionals in the field.

*Autism Spectrum Quarterly*
c/o Starfish Specialty Press LLC
P.O. Box 799
Higganum, CT 06441-0799
Phone: 877.STARFISH, ext. 3
Fax: 860.345.4471
Web site: www.ASQuarterly.com

## DAN! PROTOCOL (DEFEAT AUTISM NOW!)

The DAN! Protocol outlines guidelines for biological treatments of autism. It is published through the Autism Research Institute.

Web site: www.autism.com/ari/dan/dan.htm

## FASTIMES (FLORIDA ASPERGER SYNDROME TIMES)

*FASTimes* is published by the University of Miami Center for Autism & Related Disabilities. The newsletter contains tips, articles, resources, and practical intervention strategies for parents and educators of children with Asperger syndrome.

*FASTimes*
5665 Ponce de Leon Boulevard
Coral Gables, FL 33124
Phone: 305.284.6556
Web site: www.umcard.org

## F.E.A.T. DAILY AUTISM NEWSLETTER
## (FAMILIES FOR EARLY AUTISM TREATMENT)

This newsletter is sent daily via e-mail. It includes updates on research, interventions, publicity, and other news in the autism world.

Web site: www.feat.org

## THE MAAP

The MAAP is the quarterly publication for the families of MAAP Services (More Able Autistic Persons). Each issue includes: a letter from the editor, letters from parents and individuals with ASD, and an FYI section.

MAAP Services, Inc.
P.O. Box 524
Crown Point, IN 46307
Phone: 219.662.1311
Fax: 219.662.0638
Web site: www.maapservices.org

## THE NEW ENGLAND CENTER FOR CHILDREN RESEARCH NEWSLETTER

The New England Center for Children (NECC) publishes the *Research Newsletter*, through which we hope to let families, practitioners, researchers, and others in the NECC community know about some of the research being conducted here.

The New England Center for Children
33 Turnpike Road
Southborough, MA 01772-2108
Phone: 508.481.1015
Fax: 508.485.3421
Web site: www.necc.org

## THE OARACLE

*The OARacle* is a monthly e-newsletter from The Organization for Autism Research (OAR). Topics include articles on strategies and interventions, empirical research, personal perspectives, and updates on OAR's yearly conference.

Organization for Autism Research
2000 North 14th Street, Suite 480
Arlington, VA 22201
Phone: 703.243.9710
Web site: www.researchautism.org

## THE OPEN DOOR NEWSLETTER

*The Open Door* is the official newsletter of The New England Center for Children. Published twice a year, *The Open Door* provides profiles of students, parents, staff, donors, and board members, along with news and announcements from all around NECC.

The New England Center for Children
33 Turnpike Road
Southborough, MA 01772-2108
Phone: 508.481.1015
Fax: 508.485.3421
Web site: www.necc.org

## USAA NEWSLETTER (U.S. AUTISM AND ASPERGER ASSOCIATION, INC. NEWSLETTER)

The *USAA Newsletter* is an e-newsletter that addresses a range of topics on autism and Asperger syndrome.

Web site: www.usautism.org

# APPENDIX B: Journals

## Compiled by Lynn Dudek and Terri Cooper Swanson

### AMERICAN JOURNAL OF HUMAN GENETICS

The *American Journal of Human Genetics* explores topics such as behavioral genetics, biochemical genetics, clinical genetics, cytogenetics, dysmorphology, gene therapy, genetic counseling, genetic epidemiology, genomics, immunogenetics, molecular genetics, neurogenetics, and population genetics.

*American Journal of Human Genetics*
1427 East 60th Street
Chicago, IL 60637
Phone: 877.705.1878
Fax: 877.705.1879
E-mail: subscriptions@press.uchicago.edu
Web site: www.journals.uchicago.edu/AJHG

### AMERICAN JOURNAL OF OCCUPATIONAL THERAPY

The *American Journal of Occupational Therapy* is a peer-reviewed journal related to research and professional development in occupational therapy.

AOTA Subscriptions—AJOT
P.O. Box 31220
Bethesda, MD 20824-1220
Phone: 301.652.2682, ext. 2769
Web site: www.aota.org

### AMERICAN JOURNAL OF SPEECH LANGUAGE PATHOLOGY

The *American Journal of Speech Language Pathology* pertains to all aspects of clinical practice in speech-language pathology. Articles address screening, assessment, and treatment techniques, and professional issues.

ASHA
10801 Rockville Pike
Rockville, MD 20852
Phone: 888.498.6699
Fax: 301.897.7355
E-mail: subscribe@asha.org
Web site: www.asha.org

## ARCHIVES OF GENERAL PSYCHIATRY

The *Archives of General Psychiatry* publishes original, state-of-the-art studies and commentaries of general interest to clinicians, scholars, and research scientists in psychiatry, mental health, behavioral science, and allied fields.

Subscriber Services Center
American Medical Association
P.O. Box 10946
Chicago, IL 60610-0946
Phone: 800.262.2350
E-mail: ama-subs@ama-assn.org
Web site: http://archpsych.ama.assn.org

## ASSESSMENT FOR EFFECTIVE INTERVENTION (FORMERLY DIAGNOSTIQUE)

*Assessment for Effective Intervention* is the official diagnostic journal for the Council for Exceptional Children. This peer-reviewed journal publishes empirical research that is applicable to diagnosticians, special educators, psychologists, and others related to psychoeducational assessment.

The Council for Exceptional Children
1110 North Glebe Road, Suite 300
Department K03082
Arlington, VA 22201-5704
Phone: 888.232.7733
Fax: 703.264.9494
Web site: www.ideapractices.org/bk/catalog2/divjourn.html

## AUTISM: THE INTERNATIONAL JOURNAL OF RESEARCH AND PRACTICE

*Autism* is an international journal for research of direct practical relevance to improving the quality of life for individuals with autism or autism-related disorders.

The National Autistic Society
393 City Road,
London, EC1V 1NG, United Kingdom
Phone: +44.0.20.7833.2299
Fax: +44.0.20.7833.9666
E-mail: nas@nas.org.uk
Web site: www.sagepub.co.uk

## BRAIN (THE JOURNAL OF NEUROLOGY)

*Brain* provides researchers and clinicians with original contributions in the field of neurology. Leading studies in neurological science are balanced with practical clinical articles.

*Brain*
Journals Subscription Department
Great Clarendon Street
Oxford OX2 6DP, United Kingdom
Phone: +44.0.1865.353907
Fax: +44.0.1865.353485
E-mail: jnls.cust.serv@oupjournals.org
Web site: http://brain.oxfordjournals.org

## BRITISH JOURNAL OF DEVELOPMENTAL PSYCHOLOGY

*British Journal of Developmental Psychology* publishes full-length empirical, conceptual, review, and discussion papers, as well as brief reports on all aspects of developmental psychology, including: motor, perceptual, cognitive, social, and emotional development in infancy; social, emotional, personality, cognitive, and sociocognitive development in childhood, adolescence, and adulthood; atypical development, including developmental disorders and learning difficulties/disabilities; factors that impact upon psychological development; theories of psychological development.

The British Psychological Society
St Andrews House
48 Princess Road East
Leicester, LE1 7DR, United Kingdom
Phone: +44.0.116.254.9568
Fax: +44.0.116.247.0787
E-mail: enquiry@pbs.org.uk
Web site: www.bps.org.uk

## CAREER DEVELOPMENT OF EXCEPTIONAL INDIVIDUALS

*Career Development of Exceptional Individuals* is the official journal for the Council for Exceptional Children Division on Career Development and Transition. This peer-reviewed journal is published twice a year on issues related to transition and career development.

The Council for Exceptional Children
1110 North Glebe Road, Suite 300
Department K03082
Arlington, VA 22201-5704
Phone: 888.232.7733
Fax: 703.264.9494
Web site: www.dcdt.org and www.ideapractices.org/bk/catalog2/divjourn.html

## EDUCATION AND TRAINING IN DEVELOPMENTAL DISABILITIES

*Education and Training in Developmental Disabilities* is a peer-reviewed journal published by the Council of Exceptional Children Division on Developmental Disabilities. The journal is published quarterly.

The Council for Exceptional Children
1110 North Glebe Road, Suite 300
Department K03082
Arlington, VA 22201-5704
Phone: 888.232.7733
Fax: 703.264.9494
Web site: www.ideapractices.org/bk/catalog2/divjourn.html

## FOCUS ON AUTISM AND OTHER DEVELOPMENTAL DISABILITIES

*Focus on Autism and Other Developmental Disabilities* is published by Council for Exceptional Children Division on Developmental Disabilities. *Focus* covers a variety of issues related to autism and developmental disabilities in education, psychology, therapies, and other related areas.

Phone: 800.897.3203
Fax: 800.397.7633
Web site: www.proedinc.com

## INTERVENTION IN SCHOOL AND CLINIC

*Intervention in School and Clinic* provides user-friendly information for teachers and related practitioners. Topics include information related to children with learning disabilities and behavior disorders.

Phone: 800.897.3203
Fax: 800.397.7633
Web site: www.proedinc.com

## JOURNAL OF APPLIED BEHAVIORAL ANALYSIS

*Journal of Applied Behavioral Analysis* is a peer-reviewed journal that publishes empirical research related to the field of applied behavioral analysis.

Kathy Hill, Business Manager
Department of Applied Behavioral Sciences
1000 Sunnyside Avenue
Lawrence, KS 66045-2133
Phone: 785.841.4425
Fax: 785.841.0846
E-mail: behavior@ku.edu
Web site: http://seab.envmed.rochester.edu/jaba

## JOURNAL OF AUTISM AND DEVELOPMENTAL DISORDERS

*Journal of Autism and Developmental Disorders* is a peer-reviewed journal that specializes in severe childhood psychopathologies, including autism and childhood schizophrenia. The journal features experimental research on biochemical, neurological, and genetic aspects of particular disorders, case studies, and advances in the diagnosis and classification of disorders.

Springer
233 Spring Street
New York, NY 10013
Phone: 800.SPRINGER
E-mail: springerlink-ny@springer.com
Web site: www.springer.com

## JOURNAL OF CHILD PSYCHOLOGY AND PSYCHIATRY AND ALLIED DISCIPLINES

*The Journal of Child Psychology and Psychiatry* is an international journal covering both child and adolescent psychology and psychiatry. Articles published include experimental and developmental studies.

Blackwell Publishing Inc.
Commerce Place
350 Main Street
Malden, MA 02148
Phone: 781.388.8200
Fax: 781.388.8210
Web site: www.blackwellprofessional.com

## JOURNAL OF NEUROPSYCHIATRY & CLINICAL NEUROSCIENCES

The *Journal of Neuropsychiatry and Clinical Neurosciences* presents original research and clinical reports related to the assessment and treatment of neuropsychiatric disorders.

*Journal of Neuropsychiatry and Clinical Neurosciences*
1000 Wilson Boulevard, Suite 1825
Arlington, VA 22209-3901
Phone: 800.368.5777
E-mail: appi@psych.org
Web site: http://neuro.psychiatryonline.org

## JOURNAL OF POSITIVE BEHAVIOR INTERVENTIONS

*Journal of Positive Behavior Interventions* is a peer-reviewed journal that publishes information on empirical research and programs and is a forum on controversial issues and published materials.

Phone: 800.897.3203
Fax: 800.397.7633
Web site: www.proedinc.com

## JOURNAL OF SPEECH HEARING LANGUAGE RESEARCH

The *Journal of Speech, Language, and Hearing Research* pertains broadly to studies of the processes and disorders of hearing, language, and speech and to the diagnosis and treatment of such disorders.

ASHA
10801 Rockville Pike
Rockville, MD 20852
Phone: 888.498.6699
Fax: 301. 897.7355
E-mail: subscribe@asha.org
Web site: www.asha.org

## JOURNAL OF THE AMERICAN MEDICAL ASSOCIATION

The *Journal of the American Medical Association* is an international peer-reviewed general medical journal published 48 times per year. JAMA is the most widely circulated medical journal in the world.

Subscriber Services Center
American Medical Association
P.O. Box 10946
Chicago, IL 60610-0946
Phone: 800.262.2350
E-mail: ama-subs@ama-assn.org
Web site: http://jama.ama-assn.org

## JOURNAL OF THE INTERNATIONAL NEUROPSYCHOLOGICAL SOCIETY

*Journal of the International Neuropsychological Society* publishes peer-reviewed articles covering all areas of neuropsychology with either an experimental or clinical focus.

Cambridge University Press
100 Brook Hill Drive
West Nyack, NY 10994-2133
Phone: 800.872.7423
Fax: 845.353.4141
E-mail: subscriptions_newyork@cambridge.org
Web site: www.cambridge.org/journals

## NEUROLOGY

*Neurology* is directed to physicians concerned with diseases and conditions of the nervous system. The journal's purpose is to advance the field by presenting new basic and clinical research with emphasis on knowledge that will influence the way neurology is practiced.

Lippincott Williams & Wilkins
Customer Service Department
16522 Hunters Green Parkway
Hagerstown, MD 21740
Phone: 866.489.0443
Fax: 301.223.2398
E-mail: customerservice@lww.com
Web site: www.neurology.org

## NEUROSCIENCE & BIOBEHAVIORAL REVIEWS

This journal publishes original and significant review articles dealing with all aspects of neuroscience, where the relationship to the study of psychological processes and behavior is clearly established.

Customer Service Department
6277 Sea Harbor Drive
Orlando, FL 32887-4800
Phone: 877.839.7126
Fax: 407.363.1354
E-mail: usjcs@elsevier.com
Web site: www.elsevier.com

## NEW ENGLAND JOURNAL OF MEDICINE

The *New England Journal of Medicine* is a weekly general medical journal that publishes new medical research findings, review articles, and editorial opinions on a wide variety of topics of importance to biomedical science and clinical practice.

Customer Services
860 Winter Street
Waltham, MA 02451-1413
Phone: 800.843.6356
Fax: 781.893.0413
E-mail: nejmcust@mms.org
Web site: www.nejm.org

## PEDIATRICS

*Pediatrics* is a peer-reviewed journal of the American Academy of Pediatrics. The journal's vision since 1948 continues to be "intended to encompass the needs of the whole child in his physiologic, mental, emotional, and social structure."

American Academy of Pediatrics
141 Northwest Point Boulevard
Elk Grove Village, IL 60007-1098
Phone: 866.843.2271
Fax: 847.228.1281
E-mail: journals@aap.org
Web site: http://pediatrics.aappublications.org

## PSYCHOLOGICAL MEDICINE

*Psychological Medicine* is an international journal in the fields of psychiatry, related aspects of psychology, and basic sciences. Each issue features original articles reporting key research being undertaken worldwide.

Cambridge University Press
100 Brook Hill Drive
West Nyack, NY 10994-2133
Phone: 800.872.7423
Fax: 845.353.4141
E-mail: subscriptions_newyork@cambridge.org
Web site: www.cambridge.org/journals

# APPENDIX C: Organizations

**AMERICAN ACADEMY OF CHILD AND ADOLESCENT PSYCHIATRY**

The American Academy of Child and Adolescent Psychiatry is a national professional medical association dedicated to treating and improving the quality of life for children, adolescents, and families affected by mental, behavioral, or developmental disorders. The AACAP is composed of over 7,400 child and adolescent psychiatrists and other physicians. These physicians actively research, evaluate, diagnose, and treat individuals with such psychiatric disorders.

The American Academy of Child and Adolescent Psychiatry

3615 Wisconsin Avenue, NW

Washington, DC 20016-3007

Phone: 202.966.7300

Fax: 202.966.2891

Web site: www.aacp.org

AMY BIXLER COFFIN

**AMERICAN HYPERLEXIA ASSOCIATION**

American Hyperlexia Association (AHA) is a nonprofit organization represented by children with hyperlexia, parents, educators, and professionals devoted to identifying and promoting effective interventions for hyperlexia. Members of AHA receive quarterly newsletters, notice of conferences, and a directory of membership to encourage networking.

195 W. Spangler Road, Suite B

Elmhurst, IL 60126

Phone: 630.415.2212

Fax: 630.530.5909

Web site: www.hyperlexia.org

KATHERINE E. COOK

**AMERICAN MEDICAL ASSOCIATION**

The American Medical Association (AMA) is the professional association that organizes and serves the needs of medical doctors, defines a code of ethics, and determines the standards of practice. This organization creates policy on the management and treatment of health care issues, ethics, and internal governance. Detailed information is available on the AMA's Web site.

515 N. State Street

Chicago, IL 60610

Phone: 800.621.8335
Web site: www.ama-assn.org

LYNN DUDEK

## AMERICAN MUSIC THERAPY ASSOCIATION

The American Music Therapy Association (AMTA) is the professional association that organizes and serves the needs of Certified Music Therapists. The organization was founded in 1998, and it sets the educational and clinical standards necessary to be certified as a music therapist.

American Music Therapy Association, Inc.
8455 Colesville Road, Suite 1000
Silver Spring, MD 20910
Phone: 301.589.3300
Fax: 301.589.5175
Web site: www.musictherapy.org

LYNN DUDEK

## AMERICAN OCCUPATIONAL THERAPY ASSOCIATION

The American Occupational Therapy Association (AOTA) is the professional association that organizes and attends to the needs of occupational therapists, occupational therapy assistants, and students studying to become occupational therapists.

The AOTA, through the Accreditation Council for Occupational Therapy Education (ACOTE), has developed standards for the profession of occupational therapy. Included in the standards of AOTA are accountability, respect, and service excellence.

4720 Montgomery Lane
P.O. Box 31220
Bethesda, MD 20824-1220
Phone: 301.652.2682
Fax: 301.652.7711
Web site: www.aota.org

LYNN DUDEK

## AMERICAN PHYSICAL THERAPY ASSOCIATION

The American Physical Therapy Association (APTA) is the professional association that organizes and serves the needs of physical therapists, physical therapy assistants, and students studying to become physical therapists. APTA defines and administers the rules and terms of membership for its members, as well as serves as a resource for continuing education, information, and research.

American Physical Therapy Association
1111 N. Fairfax Street
Alexandria, VA 22314-1488
Phone: 703.684.APTA (2782)
Fax: 703.684.7343
Web site: www.apta.org

LYNN DUDEK

## AMERICAN PSYCHIATRIC ASSOCIATION

The American Psychiatric Association includes over 35,000 U.S. and international member physicians working together to make certain that all persons with mental disorders, including mental retardation and substance-related disorders, are provided with benevolent care and accessible quality psychiatric diagnosis and effective treatment. The basic eligibility requirement of being a member is to have completed a residency program in psychiatry. Applicants for membership must hold a valid medical license, with the exception of those in residency or medical school, and must provide a reference from an already existing APA member (American Psychiatric Association, 2006).

American Psychiatric Association
1000 Wilson Boulevard, Suite 1825
Arlington, VA 22209-3901
Phone: 703.907.7300
Web site: www.psych.org

AMY BIXLER COFFIN

## AMERICAN PSYCHOLOGICAL ASSOCIATION

The American Psychological Association (APA) is the largest association of psychologists. The APA seeks to advance the profession of psychology through education, establishment, and maintenance of high standards, research, and encouragement of psychology across all its branches.

American Psychological Association
750 First Street, NE
Washington, DC 20002-4242
Phone: 800.374.2721
Web site: www.apa.org

MEGAN MOORE DUNCAN

## AMERICAN SPEECH-LANGUAGE-HEARING ASSOCIATION

The American Speech-Language Hearing Association (ASHA) is the professional association that organizes and serves the needs of speech language pathologists and audiologists, as well as those students studying to become speech pathologists and audiologists. ASHA defines and administers the rules and requirements for certification for its members, as well as serves as a resource for continuing education, clinical information, and research.

10801 Rockville Pike
Rockville, MD 20852
Phone: 800.638.8255
Fax: 240.333.4705
Web site: www.asha.org

LYNN DUDEK

## THE ARC OF THE UNITED STATES

The Arc of the United States is a national organization represented by people with mental retardation and their families. The Arc advocates at the local, state, and federal levels and is dedicated to advancing supports and services, and providing resources, educational assistance, and technical support.

The Arc of the United States
1010 Wayne Avenue, Suite 650
Silver Spring, MD 20910
Phone: 301.565.3842
Fax: 301.565.5342
E-mail: info@thearc.org
Web site: www.thearc.org

KATHERINE E. COOK

## ASSOCIATION FOR BEHAVIOR ANALYSIS

The Association for Behavior Analysis is a nonprofit professional membership organization with the goal of developing, improving, and supporting the growth and vivacity of behavior analysis through research, education, and practice. The organization is dedicated to promoting the experimental, theoretical, and applied analysis of behavior. Memberships include both individual and organization memberships.

1219 South Park Street
Kalamazoo MI 49001
Phone: 269.492.9310
Fax: 269.492.9316
Web site: www.abainternational.org

AMY BIXLER COFFIN

## ASSOCIATION FOR BEHAVIORAL AND COGNITIVE THERAPIES

The Association for Behavioral and Cognitive Therapies (formerly known as Association for Advancement of Behavior Therapy) is a nonprofit professional, interdisciplinary organization consisting of over 4,500 mental health professionals and students who use and/or are interested in empirically based behavior therapy or cognitive behavior therapy. Members of the organization yearn to understand human behavior, develop interventions to improve the human condition, and promote the appropriate utilization of these interventions.

Association for Behavioral and Cognitive Therapies
305 7th Avenue, 16th Fl.
New York, NY 10001
Phone: 212.647.1890
Fax: 212.647.1865
Web site: www.aabt.org

AMY BIXLER COFFIN

## ASSOCIATION FOR SCIENCE IN AUTISM TREATMENT

The Association for Science in Autism Treatment (ASAT) strives to distribute accurate and scientifically based information about autism. ASAT distributes a free newsletter, *Science in Autism Treatment*, and hosts Science in Autism Treatment conferences geared towards improving access to effective, science-based interventions for all individuals with autism.

Association for Science in Autism Treatment
389 Main Street, Suite 202
Malden, MA 02148
Phone: 781.397.8943
Fax: 781.397.8887
Web site: www.asatonline.org

KATHERINE E. COOK

## ASSOCIATION OF UNIVERSITY CENTERS ON DISABILITY

Association of University Centers on Disability (AUCD; formerly American Association of University Affiliated Programs) is a nonprofit organization striving to advance the lives of individuals with developmental disabilities and their families by promoting and supporting the national network of university centers on disabilities, as they conduct research, advance policy, and develop educational interventions.

Association of University Centers on Disabilities
1010 Wayne Avenue, Suite 920

Silver Spring, MD 20910
Phone: 301.588.8252
Fax: 301.588.2842
Web site: www.aucd.org

KATHERINE E. COOK

## AUTISM INTERNATIONAL NETWORK

Autism Network International (ANI) is an organization run by individuals with autism that provides a medium for autistic persons to share information and problem-solve. ANI provides an advocacy voice for individuals with autism seeking equal opportunities and rights. Additionally, ANI provides social opportunities for individuals with autism through Autreat, a 3-day retreat and conference specifically designed for individuals with autism.

Autism Network International
P.O. Box 35448
Syracuse, NY 13235-5448
Web site: www.ani.autistics.org

KATHERINE E. COOK

## AUTISM RESEARCH INSTITUTE

Autism Research Institute (ARI) is a nonprofit organization, committed to conducting research and providing parents and professionals with identified results related to the cause, prevention, diagnosis, and treatment of autism spectrum disorders. ARI publishes a quarterly newsletter, *The Autism Research Review International*, which provides up-to-date information and is available by subscription.

4182 Adams Avenue
San Diego, CA 92116
Fax: 619.563.6840
Web site: www.AutismResearchInstitute.com

KATHERINE E. COOK

## AUTISM SOCIETY OF AMERICA

The Autism Society of America (ASA) advocates and supports lifelong accessibility opportunities for individuals with autism spectrum disorders. ASA is one of the leading advocacy groups for individuals with autism spectrum disorders at the local, state, and federal level. ASA provides valuable resources to parents, educators, and professionals, including an on-line resource directory, free e-newsletter, current news and media events, and an annual conference. Most states within the United States have local ASA chapters. In addition, ASA founded the ASA foundation to support quality research in the area of autism spectrum disorders.

Autism Society of America
7910 Woodmont Avenue, Suite 300
Bethesda, MD 20814-3067
Phone: 800.328.8476
Web site: www.autism-society.org

KATHERINE E. COOK

## AUTISM SPEAKS

Autism Speaks is dedicated to conducting research on the causes, prevention, treatments, and the cure for autism. Bob and Suzanne Wright, whose grandson is diagnosed with autism, founded Autism Speaks in 2005 in an effort to find a cure. Their mission is to raise awareness and the funds to quicken the pace of research. Most recently Autism Speaks joined forces with the National Alliance for Autism Research.

2 Park Avenue
11th Floor
New York, NY 10016
Phone: 212.252.8584
Fax: 212.252.8676
Web site: www.autismspeaks.org

TERRI COOPER SWANSON

## CENTER FOR THE STUDY OF AUTISM

Center for the Study of Autism (CSA) provides up-to-date information regarding autism spectrum disorders to parents, educators, and professionals. Additionally, CSA in collaboration with the Autism Research Institute conducts on-going research looking at the efficacy of various therapeutic interventions utilized with individuals with autism spectrum disorders.

Center for the Study of Autism
P.O. Box 4538
Salem, OR 97302
Web site: www.autism.org

KATHERINE E. COOK

## CENTERS FOR DISEASE CONTROL AND PREVENTION

Founded in 1946, the Centers for Disease Control and Prevention (CDC) is one of the 13 major operating components of the Department of Health and Human Services, which is the principal agency in the United States government for protecting the health and safety of all Americans and for providing essential human services, especially for those people who are least able to help themselves.

1600 Clifton Road
Atlanta, GA 30333
Phone: 800.311.3435
Web site: www.cdc.gov

PATRICIA R. SCHISSEL

## CHILDREN'S DEFENSE FUND

Children's Defense Fund (CDF) is a private, nonprofit organization that advocates, lobbies, and educates in the need for preventative care for America's poor, minority, and disabled children. Programs include Head Start and Healthy Start. CDF provides a calendar of upcoming events impacting America's children.

25 E Street, NW
Washington, D.C. 20001
Phone: 202.628.8787
Web site: www.childrensdefense.org

KATHERINE E. COOK

## CLOSING THE GAP

Founded in 1983 by Budd and Dolores Hagen, parents of a child who is deaf, Closing the Gap, Inc. is an organization that focuses on computer technology for individuals with special needs. The organization produces a bimonthly newspaper highlighting hardware and software products appropriate for people with special needs. Closing the Gap, Inc. also hosts an annual international conference, which is held each fall in Minneapolis, Minnesota. The conference allows participants to explore the many ways that technology can be used to improve the lives of persons with disabilities.

526 Main Street
P.O. Box 68
Henderson, MN 56044
Phone: 507.248.3294
Fax: 507.248.3810
Web site: www.closingthegap.com

AMY BIXLER COFFIN

## COLLABORATIVE PROGRAMS FOR EXCELLENCE IN AUTISM

In 1997, the National Institute for Child Health and Development (NICHD), in collaboration with the National Institute on Deafness and Other Communication Disorders (NIDCD), started a 5-year, $45 million international Network on the Neurobiology and Genetics of Autism. The Network included 10 Collaborative Programs of Excellence in Autism (CPEAs) designed to conduct research about the possible causes of autism, targeting genetic, immunological, and environmental factors. In 2002, the NICHD and NIDCD renewed funding for the CPEA Network, agreeing to provide $60 million over a period of 5 years. The CPEAs link 129 scientists from 23 universities in the United States, Canada, Britain, and five other countries, and more than 2,000 families of people with autism. As a result of the CPEAs, researchers now have data on the genetics and outward characteristics of the largest group of well-diagnosed persons with autism in the world.

6100 Executive Boulevard, Room 4B09F, MSC 7510
Bethesda, MD 20892-7101
Phone: 800.370.2943
Fax: 301.496.3791
Web site: www.nichd.nih.gov/autism/research/cpea.cfm

KATHERINE E. COOK AND PATRICIA R. SCHISSEL

## COUNCIL FOR EXCEPTIONAL CHILDREN

The Council for Exceptional Children (CEC) is a professional organization that focuses on improving the education of children who are gifted or have disabilities. The CEC advocates for these children, provides professional development, and publishes journals and newsletters.

1110 North Glebe Road
Suite 300
Arlington, VA 22201
Phone: 888.915.5000
Fax: 703.264.9494
Web site: www.cec.sped.org

LYNN DUDEK

## CURE AUTISM NOW

Cure Autism Now (CAN) is an organization of parents, medical professionals and researchers devoted to lobbying and raising money for autism research, education, and support. The principle research goals of CAN are to fund programs seeking to identify the cause(s) of autism so that prevention and treatment options may be implemented.

5455 Wilshire Boulevard, Suite 715
Los Angeles, CA 90036-4234
Phone: 888.8.AUTISM
Fax: 323.549.0500
Web site: www.cureautismnow.org

KATHERINE E. COOK

## FAMILY FOR EARLY TREATMENT OF AUTISM

Family for Early Autism Treatment (FEAT) is a nonprofit organization composed of parents and professionals who are devoted to providing education, advocacy, and support regarding autism spectrum disorders, pervasive developmental disorder, and Asperger syndrome to families, educators, and professionals. FEAT organizations are located throughout the United States.

Families for Early Autism Treatment
P.O. Box 255722
Sacramento, CA 95865-5722
Web site: www.feat.org

KATHERINE E. COOK

## INSTITUTE OF EDUCATION SERVICES

The Institute of Education Services (IES) is part of the U.S. Department of Education. IES is responsible for finding evidence to support the foundations of education policy and practice.

U.S. Department of Education
400 Maryland Avenue, SW
Washington, DC 20202
Phone: 200.872.5327
Fax: 202.401.0689
Web site: www.ed.gov/ies

TERRI COOPER SWANSON

## INTERAGENCY AUTISM COORDINATING COMMITTEE

The Interagency Autism Coordinating Committee (IACC) was mandated by The Children's Health Act of 2000 to facilitate the exchange of information on autism research and activities. The IACC meets biannually at the National Institute for Health (NIH). The committee is chaired by the director of the National Institute of Mental Health (NIMH) and is composed of directors or lead administrators from all the agencies of the National Institute of Health (NIH) plus public members from agencies and universities (i.e., Autism Society of America, Cure Autism Now, a university professor whose child has autism).

National Institute of Mental Health
Public Information and Communications Branch
6001 Executive Boulevard, Room 8184, MSC 9663
Bethesda, MD 20892-9663
Phone: 866.615.6464
Fax: 301.443.4279
Web site: www.nimh.nih.gov/autismiacc/index.cfm

PATRICIA R. SCHISSEL

## INTERNATIONAL RETT SYNDROME ASSOCIATION

The International Rett Syndrome Association (IRSA) provides individuals with accurate information and resources on Rett syndrome including books, materials, conferences, a web page, and a quarterly newsletter. IRSA has funded over $2.33 million dollars for the sole purpose of research related to Rett syndrome. In addition, IRSA provides a toll-free help line, RettNet, which provides personal answers to individual questions.

9121 Piscataway Road
Clinton, MD 20735
Phone: 800.818.RETT
Fax: 301.856.3336
Web site: www.rettsyndrome.org

KATHERINE E. COOK

## LEARNING DISABILITY ASSOCIATION OF AMERICA

The Learning Disability Association of America (LDA) provides support to individuals with learning disabilities while providing timely, accurate, and objective information, solutions, and resources for specific learning disabilities, including a calendar of events and an online bookstore. In addition, LDA specifically provides information regarding learning disabilities under the categories of parents, teachers, and professionals and for adults.

4156 Library Road
Pittsburgh, PA 15234-1349
Phone: 412.341.1515
Fax: 412.344.0224
Web site: www.ldaamerica.org

KATHERINE E. COOK

## LOVAAS INSTITUTE FOR EARLY INTERVENTION

The Lovaas Institute for Early Intervention (LIFE) is a nationwide research-based educational program that provides an individualized comprehensive curriculum aimed at enhancing language, communication, social, preacademic, and independent living skills of young children with autism spectrum disorders. This program is designed to work with all students regardless of their functioning level.

11500 West Olympic Boulevard, Suite 460
Los Angeles, CA 90064
Phone: 310.914.5433
Fax: 310.914.5463
Web site: www.lovaas.com

KATHERINE E. COOK

## MAAP SERVICES FOR AUTISM AND ASPERGER SYNDROME

MAAP (More Abled Autistic Persons) Services for Autism and Asperger Syndrome is a nonprofit organization that provides information and advice to families of individuals with autism spectrum disorders via printed materials, phone calls, e-mails, and conferences. Additionally, MAAP distributes a quarterly newsletter that provides parents and professionals opportunities for timely and accurate information as well as a means for networking.

P.O. Box 524
Crown Point, IN 46307

Phone: 219.662.1311
Fax: 219.662.0638
Web site: www.maapservices.org

KATHERINE E. COOK

## NATIONAL ALLIANCE FOR AUTISM RESEARCH

National Alliance for Autism Research (NAAR) is a nonprofit organization dedicated to finding the causes, prevention, and effective treatments for autism spectrum disorders. NAAR promotes and funds research and science-based approaches through grants, pilot studies, fellowships, and collaborative research efforts with the objective being finding a cure for autism spectrum disorders.

99 Wall Street, Research Park
Princeton, NJ 08540
Phone: 888.777.NAAR
Fax: 609.430.9163
Web site: www.naar.org

KATHERINE E. COOK

## NATIONAL HUMAN GENOME RESEARCH INSTITUTE

In 1989, Congress established an organization called The National Human Genome Research Institute (NCHGR), which was the United States' contribution to the International Human Genome Project (HGP). In 1990 the HGP began to map the human genome. The Human Genome Project was the international, collaborative research program whose goal was the complete mapping and understanding of all the genes of human beings; this map is called the "genome."

In 1993, NCHGR expanded its role on the National Institute of Health (NIH) campus by establishing the Division of Intramural Research (DIR) to apply genome technologies to the study of specific diseases. In 1996, the Center for Inherited Disease Research (CIDR) was also established (cofunded by eight NIH institutes and centers) to study the genetic components of complex disorders.

In 1997, the United States Department of Health and Human Services (DHHS) renamed this organization, NCHGR, as the National Human Genome Research Institute (NHGRI), officially elevating it to the status of a research institute—1 of 27 institutes and centers that make up the NIH.

Now, with the human genome sequence complete since April 2003, scientists around the world have access to a database that greatly facilitates and accelerates the pace of biomedical research.

Communication and Public Liaison Branch
National Human Genome Research Institute
National Institutes of Health
Building 31, Room 4B09
31 Center Drive, MSC 2152
9000 Rockville Pike
Bethesda, MD 20892-2152
Phone: 301.402.0911
Fax: 301.402.2218
Web site: www.genome.gov

PATRICIA R. SCHISSEL

## NATIONAL INFORMATION CENTER FOR CHILDREN AND YOUTH WITH DISABILITIES

The National Dissemination Center for Children with Disabilities (NICHCY) is a national information center that provides individuals with information, resources, and issues related to specific disabilities. Specific information provided by NICHCY includes disabilities in infants, toddlers, children, and youth, IDEA, No Child Left Behind, resources for every state, disability and professional organizations, and parent materials.

P.O. Box 1492
Washington, DC 20013
Phone: 800.695.0285
Fax: 202.884.8441
Web site: www.nichcy.org

KATHERINE E. COOK

## NATIONAL INSTITUTE OF CHILD HEALTH AND HUMAN DEVELOPMENT

NICHD research on fertility, pregnancy, growth, development, and medical rehabilitation strives to ensure that every child is born healthy and wanted and grows up free from disease and disability. Established in 1962, the NICHD, part of the National Institutes of Health (NIH) within the U.S. Department of Health and Human Services, is one of several institutes doing research into various aspects of autism, including its causes, prevalence, and treatments.

P.O. Box 3006
Rockville, MD 20847
Phone: 800.370.2943
Fax: 301.984.1473
Web site: www.nichd.nih.gov/autism

PATRICIA R. SCHISSEL

## NATIONAL ORGANIZATION FOR RARE DISORDERS

The National Organization for Rare Disorders (NORD) is a consortium of health organizations (not a government agency) responsible for education, promotion of research, and information regarding rare diseases. NORD is dedicated to the identification, treatment, and cure of those rare disorders.

The definition of a rare disorder is one that affects fewer than 200,000 individuals in the Unites States (e.g., Huntington's disease, neurofibromatosis, and cri du chat syndrome).

55 Kenosia Avenue
P.O. Box 1968
Danbury, CT 06813-1968
Phone: 203.744.0100
Fax: 203.798.2291
Web site: www.rarediseases.org

LYNN DUDEK

## OFFICE OF SPECIAL EDUCATION AND REHABILITATION SERVICES

The Office of Special Education and Rehabilitation Services (OSERS) is the agency of the U.S. federal government responsible for the administration of the No Child Left Behind Act (NCLB) and supports local districts in the outcomes for children with disabilities. OSERS

447

provides support in three main areas: special education, vocational rehabilitation, and research. The OSERS Web site contains links to resources, research, and other government programs.

U.S. Department of Education
400 Maryland Avenue, SW
Washington, DC 20202
Phone: 800.872.5327
Fax: 202.401.0689
Web site: www.ed.gov/about/offices/list/osers/index.html

TERRI COOPER SWANSON

## OFFICE OF SPECIAL EDUCATION PROGRAMS

The Office of Special Education Programs (OSEP) is the agency of the U.S. federal government responsible for the administration of the Individuals with Disabilities Act (IDEA) and supports local districts in the improvement of results for children with disabilities. The OSEP Web site contains links to state organizations as well.

U.S. Department of Education
400 Maryland Avenue, SW
Washington, DC 20202
Phone: 800.USA.LEARN
Fax: 202.401.0689
Web site: www.ed.gov/about/offices/list/osers/osep/index.html?src=mr

MEGAN MOORE DUNCAN

## ORGANIZATION FOR AUTISM RESEARCH

Organization for Autism Research (OAR) is a parent-led organization that focuses on applied research. OAR's mission is to apply research to the challenges of autism spectrum disorders by funding applied pilot studies, commissioning directed studies, and communicating autism research in a family and community friendly manner.

2111 Wilson Boulevard, Suite 600
Arlington, VA 22201
Phone: 703.351.5031
Web site: www.researchautism.org

KATHERINE E. COOK

## PACER CENTER, INC.

PACER Center, Inc. provides support and resources for individuals with disabilities and their families. PACER is based on the model of parents helping parents and is able to provide one-on-one help, a newsletter, a catalog of publications, and PACER programs that address specific needs and resources disabilities.

8161 Normandale Boulevard
Minneapolis, MN 55437
Phone: 952.838.9000
Fax: 952.838.0199
Web site: www.pacer.org

KATHERINE E. COOK

## STUDIES TO ADVANCE AUTISM RESEARCH AND TREATMENT NETWORK

Congress passed the Children's Health Act of 2000, legislation that mandated many activities, among them the establishment of a new autism research network. In response, the five Institutes of the National Institute of Health Autism Coordinating Committee (NIMH, NICHD, NINDS, NIDCD, & NIEHS) have implemented the Studies to Advance Autism Research and Treatment (STAART) network program.

The STAART Network includes eight centers located at Boston University, Kennedy Krieger Institute (Baltimore), Mt. Sinai Medical School (New York City), University of California at Los Angeles, University of North Carolina at Chapel Hill, University of Rochester, University of Washington, and Yale University. Research currently being conducted at the eight sites includes early characteristics of autism, diet, and behavior in young children with autism, citalopram for children with autism and repetitive behavior, and relationship training for children with autism and their peers.

National Institute of Mental Health (NIMH)
Office of Communications
6001 Executive Boulevard, Room 8184, MSC 9663
Bethesda, MD 20892-9663
Phone: 866.615.6464
Web site: www.autismresearchnetwork.org/AN

KATHERINE E. COOK AND PATRICIA R. SCHISSEL

## TASH

TASH (formerly The Association for Persons with Severe Handicaps) is an international association of people with disabilities, family members, advocates, and professionals who believe in the inclusion of individuals with disabilities. TASH provides numerous printed and online materials and resources that are timely and accurate, including a monthly newsletter and an annual conference.

29 W. Susquehanna Avenue, Suite 210
Baltimore, MD 21204
Phone: 410.828.8274
Fax: 410.828.6706
Web site: www.tash.org

KATHERINE E. COOK

## UNITED STATES DEPARTMENT OF EDUCATION

The U.S. Department of Education was created in 1980 with a mission of creating access to education for all individuals and to promote excellence in education. The U.S. Department of Education Web site provides links to related government and state agencies.

U.S. Department of Education
400 Maryland Avenue, SW
Washington, DC 20202
Phone: 800.872.5327
Fax: 800.437.0833
Web site: www.ed.gov

TERRI COOPER SWANSON

## UNITED STATES DEPARTMENT OF HEALTH AND HUMAN SERVICES, NATIONAL INSTITUTE OF HEALTH

Founded in 1887, the National Institutes of Health is one of the world's foremost medical research centers, and the federal focal point for medical research in the United States. The NIH, comprising 27 separate institutes and centers, is one of eight health agencies of the Public Health Service, which, in turn, is part of the U.S. Department of Health and Human Services.

9000 Rockville Pike
Bethesda, MD 20892
Phone: 866.615.6464
Web site: www.nih.gov

PATRICIA R. SCHISSEL

## UNITED STATES DEPARTMENT OF HEALTH AND HUMAN SERVICES, NATIONAL INSTITUTE OF MENTAL HEALTH

The NIMH was founded in 1949 and is dedicated to understanding, treating, and preventing mental illnesses through basic research on the brain and behavior, and through clinical, epidemiological, and services research.

6001 Executive Boulevard, Room 8184, MSC 9663
Bethesda, MD 20892-9663
Phone: 866.615.6464
Web site: www.nimh.nih.gov

PATRICIA R. SCHISSEL

## UNITED STATES FOOD AND DRUG ADMINISTRATION

This agency is under the auspices of the Department of Health and Human Services and information on a myriad of products, consumer's rights, and policies can be accessed on their site.

5600 Fishers Lane
Rockville, MD 20857-0001
Phone: 888.463.6332
Web site: www.fda.gov

PATRICIA R. SCHISSEL

## WRIGHTSLAW

Wrightslaw is an excellent online resource for finding information related to special education law, education law, and advocacy for children with disabilities. This Web site is designed for parents, educators, advocates, and attorneys and provides access to articles, cases, and other free resources on topics related to the Individuals with Disabilities Education Act, special education, law, advocacy, and training and seminars.

Web site: www.wrightslaw.com

TERRI COOPER SWANSON

# APPENDIX D: Personal Perspectives

## THE CEMENT MIXER (FATHER)

As a dad, when your child is diagnosed with autism, you go through many different thoughts and emotions. Most are heavy and deep, much like cement in a mixer. One by one they come to the surface as your mind evaluates what is ahead for you, your child, and your family. Slowly the cement hardens into resolve as you chart your course of action.

In our family, it was no different. My wife and I have four kids, with our oldest dealing with Asperger syndrome and our youngest son diagnosed with autism almost 7 years ago at the age of 18 months. We have a boy and a girl in-between who are not on the spectrum.

By the time our youngest was several months old, we could see that he was not hitting the same developmental milestones that our others had. My wife started quickly in getting therapists (physical, occupational, and speech) in to evaluate and help out. The therapists were very careful NOT to diagnose, but they were AMAZING at helping Jordan develop where he had not been able to before.

By the time Jordan was 18 months old, I was looking forward to getting a complete diagnosis as a means to get him the help he needed and to "put a name" on what was "holding him back." I kept asking my wife, "Why can't we just put a name to this?" I thought it was going to be easy and that the neurologist was going to smile and say, "Folks, your son has autism (or PDD or Asperger syndrome)." And that would be that. The cement mixer was already churning and I just wanted solid answers.

Enter the neurologist. After examining Jordan and talking with us, he told us that he thought Jordan had autism. He looked at me and said, "That's what you wanted, right, a diagnosis?" He then proceeded to let us know what the probabilities were for everything that could go wrong (or right) for Jordan over the course of his life. "He has such and such percent chance of not talking … or being mentally retarded … or not being able to live independently … or …" It all kind of droned together and I ceased listening and became numb. The cement mixer churned a little faster that day as I found myself coming to grips with the new reality of things.

Knowing that your son is not meeting some developmental milestones and hearing that he might not talk or ever be independent were far apart in my mind and they came crashing together with surprising force that day. As the cement mixer inside of me churned, there were several repeating thoughts that floated to the top.

I was concerned for the life plans that my wife and I had made. We married and started a family quickly with the thought that we would have a few more "golden years" where we could enjoy grandkids and do missionary work in Korea (where we met). This was immediately followed by guilt for being so selfish as to think about "us," but I couldn't help it. This was altering our life plan and the trepidation that I felt about it was real.

The feelings churned some more . . .

Both Jen and I grew up with a strong sense of faith in our lives. Part of that was accepting that God had a plan for each of us and that we were all given obstacles as part of our life's journey. My mind was at peace when I thought of my own experience. My brother and I were born 10 weeks premature and the doctors had told my parents similar things to what I had heard. I turned out just fine after overcoming a few obstacles, so why not Jordan?

Our faith as a couple led us to look less for a cure and more towards being in the "obstacle removal business." We discussed it on the way home from the neurologist. We decided that we were going to help Jordan fulfill what God had in store for him and we were going to subordinate our desires for what we wanted him to be. This was a very "freeing" experience for me.

"Maybe God has enough basketball players on the earth and maybe he needs another scientist . . ." I told myself little affirmations like this to keep things on track and keep my confidence level up.

More churning . . .

How do I help? My thoughts turned to all of those "Super-Dads" out there. The ones who leap tall buildings in a single bound, cure their kids of whatever ails them, raise awareness, start a foundation, and name the wing of the local hospital after their son. I certainly did not fit that mold although I am certainly glad that some people do. Being an activist wasn't the right way for me personally. Some days I wished I was one of them, but I just wasn't.

My wife was naturally suited to be a great advocate for Jordan. She has a degree in teaching and was known and well liked in our school district. She had a knack for finding the right people, knowing when it was a good fit with our son and establishing rapport with them to get the needed help. I am not the type to patiently work with people in an Individualized Education Plan meeting or take the time to go to the myriad of conferences and support groups available.

If my role was not the activist or the advocate, then was it OK to be "just" a supportive dad? Would I be helping enough with that? Maybe I could be the source of "normal" in our family. Maybe the right role for me to play was just to be dad . . .

All kids like to have fun, to play games, and to be inside their comfort zone at times. Autism doesn't change that. It just makes them have different (and sometimes smaller) comfort zones. We needed money to pay therapists to work with Jordan. My middle kids needed to feel that they were not being overlooked. I decided that my role was to supply that comfort zone to each of our kids on their level, to help facilitate therapists and to provide general support where needed.

More churning . . .

What is it going to be like for Jordan? Since I didn't view Jordan's autism as something that needed to be cured, but rather an obstacle that he needed help with, what did he need? How could I give him enough confidence?

Jen and I took a lot of time to research on the Internet many possible therapies and strategies for dealing with autism. That seemed to be the only way for me to calm my fears. And yes, they were fears.

How am I going to deal with this with extended family? Everyone seemed to have their own opinion about autism and what we should do. Having a diagnosis only seemed to fuel the firestorm of opinions being thrown our way and the opinions were very seldom based on facts. Almost always, they came from hearsay or projected fear. More often than not, everyone REALLY wanted to help, but was unsure HOW.

Why does he have autism? Genetically whose "fault" is it? The questions and opinions were unending.

From my point of view as a dad, I wanted to scream at ALL of them. I just wanted to fix things ... That's what guys are supposed to do, right?

What came out of all the churning was a feeling of resolve. It was a unity between my wife and me as to how to proceed. We decided that we were going to enlist the help of the best people we could find to help Jordan and that we were going to pray for guidance as to who these people were.

I was not going to be an activist for Jordan, but rather I'd be a father and husband who was supportive of Jordan and helpful to Jen in being his advocate. I was going to be the "Director of Normalcy" for our home and try to keep it a safe comfort zone for everyone. I am above all else, a dad.

ERIC BLACKWELL

## FINDING FRIENDSHIP AND SUPPORT (MOTHER)

It seems strange to say my first reaction was relief, but quite honestly it was. The doctor's question was, "Have you ever heard of Asperger syndrome?" At that moment all of our worrying, wondering, and questions were, temporarily at least, answered. Our son had a disorder with a name, and if there was a name, then there must be answers too as to what to do to help him. More questions came later, and eventually the grief hit too, followed by many more struggles. But for a single moment, we had peace. It wasn't our fault; there was something "wrong" with our child.

Looking back with knowledgeable eyes, we can see so clearly the answers to the questions we'd asked for years. Why does our baby scream and pull at the feet of his footed pajamas desperate to take them off? Why does our preschooler insist on lining up all of his toys in rows, but never play with them? Why doesn't he respond when we speak to him? Why won't he eat anything but three or four foods? Why does he have meltdowns and tantrums seemingly out of the blue? The answer was in all accounts, Asperger syndrome.

And so our journey began. There were other revelations, some very painful. I visited the Web site the doctor suggested only to be shocked to learn Asperger syndrome also meant, gasp, autism.

The first day I was in shock, especially after reading the word, autism. I called my close friend, Sue, who said, "That's what Amy's son has just been diagnosed with." I knew Amy, she attended our church, and we often gave each other sympathetic looks as we passed each other in the hall. She was usually chasing her busy running child, while I was soothing my crying one. I called Amy hesitantly. I said, "My son has Asperger syndrome." Her son was diagnosed four months previously, and she was light years ahead of me. She began reeling off information, resources, and people to call. I knew so little (nothing at all in fact) that I couldn't respond to her, much less even have the least bit of an idea what to ask. Later she recounted, "I still remember how shocked you were." For 10 days I did nothing. I had taken the assessment test online for my son; I knew he had Asperger syndrome, and that's all I needed to do as far as I was concerned. Amy called to check on me. Dragging myself out of the thick volume of Chinese history I'd buried myself in, the fifth I'd read that week, I picked up the phone annoyed to be interrupted. I can't remember what Amy said, but I didn't want to talk with her. She wanted me to take some kind of action, I just wanted to read. Not think. Not cry. Not take action. Read about Chinese history. In other words, bask in denial.

At last the day came for our follow-up visit with the doctor. He said, "Did you take the test? Do you think it's a match?" I tried to show it to him, he waved it off, not necessary for him to see it. Suddenly I felt panic. Hopefully, plaintively I inquired, "What do we do now?" I still remember his face. He hesitated. He had no idea. I walked out, with sudden resolve. I would find out what to do. I would call Amy.

It was a torturous wait until a decent hour of the morning to call her. I'd been up most of the night checking the clock impatiently. I'd written out the various interventions listed online: diet, therapies, books to read, Web sites to go to. I was ready. The moment the clock hit 8:00 a.m. I picked up the phone. Amy had a list of her own, doctors' and therapists' names, therapy centers, and a list of phone numbers. While my previous coping mechanism had been withdrawal, hers had been not to leave her bedroom in the weeks following her son's diagnosis, and she had ferreted out quite a list of resources and interventions. Excitedly, I began dialing. Five hours of calling later, I laid my head down on the dining room table and cried for the first time. I sobbed inconsolably. Our insurance didn't cover any of these places, there were none in our area that they covered, no one could refer me elsewhere, and no one had any other solutions. I felt so completely helpless and hopeless. I did not know what to do. So I called Amy, and she walked me through it.

Amy had a pile of ideas, but what she had most was a clear understanding of how I felt, and she offered me support. That was the beginning of one of the closest relationships I have ever had (along with Sue, who made up the triad of "girls"). It was only the beginning. Amy and I had something in common besides the fact that our boys both had Asperger syndrome. Once we'd decided our course of action, we were both powerhouses. We each had our strengths to bring to the table. Although she read quite a number of books, I was the quick reader. The first time I realized I could go to a Web site, click on a book, give my credit card number and a package would show up at my doorstep two days later, I had found my niche. While I devoured every single Asperger syndrome book in print at the time (not exaggerating), Amy utilized her own gift. She was the conference-goer. She was the networking queen, soaking up information like a sponge and then carrying it back like an ant with breadcrumbs for me who waited salivating. She knew every presenter, every significant person in the autism community, testified for the state legislator, started a support group, and trained to be an advocate. I stayed home and read. Our boys became friends, too. I'll never forget the day we "introduced them." They'd been in Sunday school together for nearly 7 years, but as Amy said to Dylan, "This is Tom," they beamed, put out their hands and said, "Nice to meet you!" I'm sure the joy on Amy's face at that moment only matched mine.

We spoke daily; the only break in the routine was when she went to a conference, in which case she'd call me on the way there and on the way home. We had good days and bad days. I remember one day I heard my call waiting, I clicked over and it was Amy sounding as though she'd been crying, "I'll call you right back!" I hurriedly told her, I was on hold with the insurance company. I called her back in awhile crying, too. Our children's evaluations had both simultaneously been rejected for payment by the insurance company. We both wailed, "It's not fair!" Together we problem solved and devised strategies. Sometimes the strategies involved multiple phone calls, letters, and even complaints to the state insurance commissioner. Other times the strategies failed miserably and then we'd get on the phone to lament. We'd occasionally get impatient with each other, "Well, just submit it AGAIN!" That is true friendship, when you can say, "Shut up and just do it. I know you don't feel like doing it AGAIN, but you have to!"

Amy's second son was diagnosed, then my second. "We've got to stop hanging out" she said giggling, "it must be contagious!" We laughed hard and often, and quite inappropriately. We vented, we commiserated, we cried. Our friendship evolved to the point where we knew each other so well that we knew exactly what each other was going to say at almost any given moment, but our friendship was so close that we still let the other continue anyway.

Daily calling has waxed and waned as our lives changed, as my third child was diagnosed, she made the difficult decision as to whether she should have another baby and then welcomed a beautiful girl into their family. Our roles have shifted in the last couple of years. The home-body and the social butterfly have exchanged roles for various reasons. Amy stays home, while I trek around to conferences, both of us content with where we are. We laugh about this too. "Been there, done that!" We say to each other. If something significant happens, good or bad, it is still Amy I want to call. Recently she told me one of her favorite memories was of me calling her from the ladies room at the ASA conference a couple of years ago whispering furiously, "Aim! Brenda Myles just asked me to write a book!" She laughed, she had loaned me my first book by Dr. Myles, not to mention the fact that she'd been nagging me herself for years to write. "See! I told you so!" she said smugly. Time has passed, but never the love we have for each other; the years of friendship we have built are enduring. Whenever I start to get senti-mental and coo sappily how thankful I am for our friendship, and say, "What would I have ever done without you?!" Aim will retort, "Oh shut up! You would have figured it out!" Maybe, maybe not, but I'm glad I'll never know.

KRISTI SAKAI

## INDIVIDUAL EDUCATION PLAN IDEAS (MOTHER)

Many parents nervously face the ever dreaded eligibility and IEP meetings. If this is you, then you know why emotions run high. Nothing like just being a lowly parent surrounded by "experts" and teachers (which cause you to have elementary school flashbacks of being sent to the principal's office) followed by being told everything that is "wrong" with your child as you cringe painfully. While staff may have the best of intentions, they are often perplexed by the intensity of emotions we carry into these meetings. But no wonder! This is YOUR child they are talking about. This is his future, his life, your family. A seemingly small comment about your child eating lunch alone doesn't just mean, "My son is lonely." Our minds immediately jump to, "My son might never have friends, never date or get married, he is going to be alone forever. What is going to happen to him after I'm gone?" This is not an irrational thought. Living as lonely adults is the reality for many people who have autism spectrum disorder (ASD), and as parents we're well aware of this fact. We have a long-term, vested interest in our child, and we are poised and ready to fight to our last breath on his behalf. And, boy howdy, staff better know it, too! No wonder we so easily garner a reputation as a "difficult parent." While I generally like to think I'm a reasonable person, I've done what my friend referred to as having "left a trail of bodies" behind me when it's merited. Do I enjoy conflict? No. Is it sometimes necessary? Yes. But is it ALWAYS necessary? Absolutely not. So what do we do? If you are pre-pared, confident in your knowledge and abilities, and feel supported, you are better able to handle conflict or avoid it altogether.

*Know* your child and the characteristics of ASD and how they apply to him. Is he extremely reactive to noise? Crowds? Smells? Create a list and take it with you, include the strategies you have found effective. These can be adapted for school use. For example, if you allow your son to wear headphones in crowded places, perhaps he can do the same on the noisy bus. Providing staff with concrete solutions shows them you know your child and they are more likely to respectfully consider your input.

*Provide* documentation. Had a private evaluation done that backs up what you're saying about your child's strengths and areas that need attention? Take it with you. Don't assume, as I have mistakenly done at times, that something is SO OBVIOUS about your child that there is no question he is eligible for services. The written work with the signature of a qualified professional speaks more effectively than we ever can. In the case of eligibility this is especially crucial. Concrete evidence snuffs out many a conflict before it even sparks.

*Prepare* goals. Have a list of long-term goals you have for your child and the short-term steps necessary to achieve them. For example, if your child is currently unable to be in the general ed classroom, but your long-term goal is that he will be able to, a short-term goal might be that he be able to participate in occasional classroom activities. The meeting is a wonderful way to elicit ideas and brainstorm with staff about their own ideas to meet those goals. Be open to their suggestions, you might be surprised at how once they understand the plan how willing they are to try new accommodations.

*Trust* that you *do* know your child. Staff may be seeing a different child, that is, he may be exhibiting different behaviors you don't see at home. Knowing your child as you do, the fact that he is having difficulties at school is an important indicator. If he is displaying what you would consider unusual behavior for him, then obviously he is stressed and needs supports in place.

*Believe* the staff when they relate an incident, have empathy for those involved and resist the urge to immediately jump on them about how poorly they may have handled the situation. Instead, use this information to look for the hidden triggers that set him off, and a logical jumping-off point for creating supports. "My son has NEVER hit anyone at home. I'm shocked. Let's talk about what happened BEFORE that, and see if we can figure out what set him off." Remember that not everyone understands the characteristics of ASD and how they impact behavior. If staff feel you are listening to them they are more likely to consider what you have to say and implement change.

*Support* yourself in meetings by bringing an advocate. Having support means we won't feel ganged up on and are less likely to be defensive. Plus, everyone has different skill sets; perhaps yours isn't to remain cool under pressure (And who can when it comes to our kids? Certainly not me!). An advocate can balance you out with complementary skills, reframe a question, and bring up points you may not have considered. He or she can also be the quiet type who takes notes, or simply kicks you under the table if you start to get side-tracked. Great choice: someone who knows your child and how to help him. These can include such folks as his private occupational or speech therapist or counselor. Better choice: someone who knows both your child and your family well. Try bringing someone who is in a related field who also happens to be a close friend, and barring that, a friend of the family who can lend moral support. Always refer to this person as "my advocate." Also good: a professional who doesn't know your child but who understands the needs of kids on the spectrum. Last choice is a professional who doesn't know much, but who has a string of important letters after his name who is there to back you. But make sure you're on the same page ahead of time, you don't want to be blindsided by your own advocate.

*Emotional?* Yes, I'd rather not burst into tears during a meeting, but it's painful to be reminded in black-and-white documents what difficulties my child struggles with and on occasion it can be all too much. Sometimes there are tears, and embarrassing as I find that to be, I give myself that allowance because I'M THE MOM. This is my child and I'm doing my very best, but it's not enough. I need the school's support to help him grow into a productive adult. At times anger is what comes out instead of tears, but it all stems from the same place: our fears for our child, our frustrations that we aren't getting the help that we so desperately need. But instead of simply expressing our emotion without explanation or resorting to personal attacks (a big no-no), be clear and go back to the original issues at hand: focusing on the child's specific needs and how to meet them. And remember, if emotions are running high, it's all right to excuse yourself to calm down, or even to reschedule. If there is ONE staff member who is consistently disruptive, remember that the other team members may not be happy about the conflict either. Depending on who it is, you may be able to have that person removed from the invite list for the next meeting.

Pick you battles. It's a rare pigs flying kind of meeting for you to get everything you are asking for, but if it happens, thank your lucky stars. In most cases, however, you're going to have to decide what you're not willing to compromise on. Your child is best served by saving your fights for the significant issues; for example, I'd fight tooth and nail for appropriate placement. But bide your time on smaller issues that can be resolved over time if you build a close working relationship with the staff.

You are The Parent and simply human. But it's important to remember that although the staff is made up of professionals, underneath their credentials they are simply human beings, too, with their own fears, concerns, shortcomings, and desires. It takes a great deal of work and patience to build an effective IEP team, to get along, to balance give and take, but all relationships take effort, and most are well worth it. And when it comes to your child, no amount of effort is wasted.

KRISTI SAKAI

## INTERVIEW WITH CAMERON BLACKWELL (ADOLESCENT)

*Background.* Cameron is a freshman in high school, working towards an honors diploma. He was diagnosed with Asperger syndrome while in second grade. He has been very involved in his school and church, as well as attending autism-related conferences. His special passion is band. He marched with the high school band as an eighth grader and hopes someday to be a band director himself.

Q: What does it feel like to have Asperger syndrome?

Cameron: That's an interesting question. You know you're different from other people. You have different needs and other people are different from you. You realize that we're all individuals, that we're all different. Not everyone knows that I have Asperger's.

Q: Why don't they know?

Cameron: Several reasons: I'm very independent. I do a lot of things for myself. Some people I have told just because they're really close to me. It's just a sad fact about myself, something I need help with.

Q: Do you feel like other people see the world differently than you do?

Cameron: Yeah, I do. What I view about Asperger's and autism, I view it as a different perspective, a different way of thinking. I view it as a different perspective. People with Asperger's and autism, they *are* smart, we are just different from other people.

Q: Describe your sensory world: what in the environment bothers you, for example, particular lights, sounds, touch, tastes, movements?

Cameron: Yeah, I have gotten better. When I was eight, I was diagnosed with Asperger's syndrome and I had a lot of sound sensitivities, but not light sensitivities, not other senses. Mainly sound. Now I am in band. I used to have sound therapy where I listened to classical music. Listening therapy was used about a year or two. Sound is better. In middle school I joined in the band, and learned to play a brass instrument. I'm a French horn player right now. I've become less sensitive to loud sensitivity. I'm trying to become more tolerant of the flute, but that's not sound sensitivity. (Q: Any movement or balance problems?) I used to. I went to a gym and worked on balance beams. I learned a lot. I'm also in marching band. It takes a lot of stamina and balance to do that. I'm really progressing and I'm doing well and my balance is better because of that.

Q: What in the environment do you especially like?

Cameron: I like—I honestly don't know. I'm usually not aware of stuff like that.

Q: Do you have behavioral difficulties sometimes?

Cameron: No, I never do anything like that. I've never been in any disciplinary problems. I've always tried to follow the rules.

Q: How do you deal with your feelings or emotions?

Cameron: The way I deal with them is every day I try to jog for about an hour or so, so I'm away from everyone. I use that time to jog and think. That's the way I deal with my emotions.

Q: What do you want your teachers to know about you?

Cameron: I want them to know that I'm hard working, that I do my best no matter what, that I do have trouble with organization and handwriting. I have some difficulties, but that is just a part of me. I will work hard and do my best to have a good year.

Q: What do you want your peers to know about you?

Cameron: I want them to know that I'm good person, that I try hard, I like them a lot, I want to be around them, that I do have difficulties in my life, that I've overcome a lot. I have situations that I have to deal with, that I'm claustrophobic, but they are understanding of that.

Q: Describe your school experience. What do you do well?

Cameron: Academically, I do really well. I'm an A/B student. I take all honors courses and I do band for extracurricular activity, and I have a lot of friends from band and in my classes.

Q: What do you need help with?

Cameron: Organization and handwriting. I need people to be understanding. I get a little sensitive to sound. That happens very rarely. (Q: Do you have someone to help with organization?) I have an OT who I see every two or three weeks. My teachers understand when I am disorganized—they call a meeting if they see I'm carrying around a mess.

Q: What do you need to do to advocate for yourself?

Cameron: I'm learning to do more of it. I do not like it but I'm learning to like it. I have to go to more meetings now. I went to my IEP meeting last year. (Q: What was IEP meeting like?) It was OK. My mom always brings treats so I just ate. It was OK. We talked about what I needed to do last year. I was transitioning to high school so there was lot of talk about that.

Q: What type of recreational or community activities do you participate in?

Cameron: I used to be in Boy Scouts, not anymore. I go to a couple of meetings cause they're at church. I do participate in church activities, service activities, academic activities, band. My life is pretty busy with that. Not a whole lot else I can do.

Q: What do you want to do after you graduate from high school?

Cameron: First of all I may join a professional drum corps after high school. I may join one of those for a year. In my church I am expected to serve a mission for two years somewhere else in the world, so I'll do that then I'll go to college, hopefully on a band and some academic scholarships. I want to major in music and music education and be a band director after college.

Q: Any thoughts on dating?

Cameron: (laughs) Yeah. I'm gonna—I have to wait 'til I'm sixteen to date. I'll probably date people within my religion most of the time. I'll probably marry a girl after my mission.

Q: Any other thoughts?

Cameron: People with Asperger's and autism have potential but that can only be reached if the people around them realize it, then they will act on it to realize their potential. A lot of people don't realize the potential. We do have obstacles in our life; we just need help getting over them.

ANN PILEWSKIE

## INTERVIEW WITH CRAIG AND JAIME BLACKWELL (SIBLINGS)

*Background.* Craig is 12 years old and in his first year of middle school. He loves cooking, fishing, golf, and anything to do with dragons. He is in beginning band and enjoys attending his brother's marching band competitions. Craig has his own cooking Web site for kids. Jamie, 10 years old, is the lone sister among all the brothers. She is in her last year of elementary school and enjoying being "top dog" for the year. She loves to sing and not only has she sung with groups at church, she has performed songs in sign language for both school and church. She loves to spend time with her friends and family. Craig and Jamie are siblings to Jordan and Cameron. Both of whom have autism spectrum disorders.

Q: What do you most like about Cameron?

Craig: I really look up to him. It kind of started not that long ago. He's been in there [band] much longer than I have so I do a lot of learning from him. He helps me learn my instrument a little better.

Jamie: That I get to see him in band. It's fun just watching him out there.

Q: Is there anything you dislike about him?

Craig: One or two times he'll try to get mad or upset. He likes his personal space. He likes to be alone a lot.

Jamie: Since he's older, since he has Asperger's, when you're around him he gets mad if you whistle too much or something like that.

Q: What about Jordan?

Craig: It's nice to be around Jordan because he's very good at memorizing things. It's cool to have someone who can play video games at your level. He sometime doesn't listen very well. Sometimes he doesn't pay a lot of attention.

Jamie: That he stands up for what he wants and stuff. When he speaks his mind freely most of the time he doesn't know what he's saying.

Q: Do you ever feel left out, or that your parents spend too much time dealing with your brother's problems?

Craig: No not really. It's not as bad as other families have it. Sometimes yeah, I do, not very often, but sometimes.

Jamie: Yeah, sometimes when my mom has to deal with Jordan. She's talking to him and she doesn't know other things that he's doing, and I notice him and she doesn't really want to deal with them [the other things] right then.

ANN PILEWSKIE

## INTERVIEW WITH JEN BLACKWELL (MOTHER)

*Background.* Jen grew up in the Northeast until her family settled in southern Indiana where she attended high school and college. She earned her degree in secondary education from Indiana University Southeast and later taught boys with severe emotional disabilities in a group home. Jen met her husband, Eric, while serving as a missionary in Seoul, Korea and they were married in 1989. Currently, Jen works in an inclusive preschool run by the local school district. Favorite pastimes include photography, sports, coaching her kids' teams, and hanging out with her family.

Q: What was it about Cameron that made you seek professional assistance and diagnosis?

Jen: Way back when he was little we knew there was something. We had no idea what it was. We knew he had to have ideas given to him a certain way. If he didn't have things a certain way he didn't get it. He had language delays at age 3. He started with a speech pathologist in the school district who was awesome! She quickly figured out he had more than articulation problems. He had pragmatic problems. She was very good. About 5 years later she sent me an article in *USA Today* about Asperger syndrome. She had worked with Cameron from ages 3 to 5. We found that he was 70 percent unintelligible at age 3. We went to [local] Children's Hospital in Fresno and they sent us to the speech therapist. He [Cameron] went for speech and hearing in 1994. The school district gave the diagnosis. Indiana, at that time did not qualify Asperger's, only autism. But, the special education director knew Cameron had Asperger's so she wrote an IEP for him before the school year was ended.

Q: What went through your head when you received the diagnosis of Asperger's for Cameron?

Jen: Huge relief. We were also in the process of getting a diagnosis of autism for our other son, Jordan. We knew with a label that we could get help then.

Q: Talk about Cameron's school experience. How did/does the IEP process work for you?

Jen: The first few IEPs I made sure I had somebody with me. Other therapists for our son Jordan came with me to our IEP meetings for Cameron—probably the first 2 or 3 years. I talk to his coordinator a lot. We're on a first name basis. We don't want to sit there for 3 or 4 hours. I catch teachers in the hall or other places and discuss and have conversations with them, then bring it all (conversations) to the same place [IEP meeting]. I would make sure I had my lists going ahead of time. I always bring cookies and make compliments to people how they have helped. I give very specific and complimentary details to school personnel and also send them in a letter to the superintendent. After the compliments I can say, "But now we have this going on with him and how do we help now?" For example, the principal would ask, "He has all A's and B's, why do we need to serve him?" If he has sensory needs why would you take those supports away?

Q: Have schools been receptive to working with Cameron's (and others') unique needs?

Jen: For the most part we've had a pretty good reception. We'd ask for only one thing every year: "Can we please know who would be his teacher before school started?" The answer was always, "No." Even the special education department wanted him [Cameron] to know. The OT took him in before school started one year to meet the teacher. Middle school was a little harder to pull out of classes for services. Band really met his sensory needs. We used *Samonas Therapeutic Listening* for a couple of years at home. Saw a huge difference in him. We're not interested in intrusive interventions.

Q: What supports were already in place and what did you have to "teach" the schools? How do you have to advocate for Cameron?

Jen: School has been receptive but the school knows we have a lot of knowledge. We sit with school people and exchange knowledge. We go to conferences and trainings together. We eat and laugh together, and even though sometimes things are horrible, we get along. It's about teamwork. Getting in a contest with them once doesn't promote teamwork. So far so good. I had an OT who also had a son with Asperger's syndrome so she was able to help the school regarding sensory issues and teaching the assistants, teachers, and principal. They did get it at the end.

Q: Describe your proudest or happiest moments with Cameron.

Jen: Easy one—there's two: The little boy who was absolutely miserable at school in second grade, he had no friends, isolated himself from other kids, paced the playground at recess, in fifth grade was selected by his peers as the "Road Runner," the name for their school mascot. The "Road Runner" is an award given to the best all-around good friend to everyone, a good person and good friend, the best representative of the school and class. His class gave the award to him. The second one is marching with the high school band. He was invited as an eighth grader. He had to march to this complex huge drill. This year's show could take them to state finals at the RCA Dome. Everyone who knows him knows how incredible this is! I can't watch him without being in tears. He was voted band member of the year last year.

Q: How do you meet the needs of all members of your family?

Jen: Craig [12-year-old son] is gifted, and Jamie [ten-year-old daughter], she is neurotypical. Like anybody with four kids you take them individually, one at a time. Eric and I try to spend one-on-one time with each of them—Eric mostly with the two in the middle and I do the kids on both ends [of the sibling order]. We try to include everyone with all activities and for all to support each other. Craig will go to "sib shop" workshop. We try to do special things just for each of them—try to take their passions. Cameron is in band; Craig is into cooking and wants to be a chef. Jordan is into golf and Jamie is trying to find herself—she likes to sing and is artistic. We try to build them up on their own. We try to find balance not over one day, but over time.

Q: Is your family different from the "idealized" American family? Why and how or why not?

Jen: We laugh at what's "normal" anyway. We are as typical of a family as any other family with four kids. We go to church. The autism thing is our challenge. We deal with it. Other families have other challenges. That's how we look at it.

Q: Describe a special family memory.

Jen: We went to Florida for spring break. My uncle lives down there and likes to play golf. We drove for 16 hours in a car—it was a blast! Each kid had their own electronic device on the trip. This was the first time in years we got to spend time with family—just really neat.

Q: Do you have tips or suggestions to share regarding family life raising a child or children with ASD, for example, going to restaurants, shopping, vacations, or leisure activities?

Jen: Do it! It's hard. I was on a parent panel recently and I was asked to introduce my family first. After I talked about my family, the person next to me said, "We have it really hard." Everybody's family is hard. We had the expectations that we would just do it. We usually go to buffets rather than sit down restaurants. Jordan can't wait that long to be served. They [the kids] sort of rise to the occasion. You can't stop your whole life or you'd be miserable. They can be your life but you have to have a life, too.

Q: How do you take care of yourself?

Jen: You have to do something for yourself. I go to conferences that are uplifting like MAAP. I enjoy listening to things that are uplifting. I like photography. I will shoot pictures at the games the kids play at. I sometimes will just close my door. I can go to the grocery store by myself. Most of all I have good friends.

ANN PILEWSKIE

## LIFE, NEWLY REALIZED, ON THE SPECTRUM (ADULT)

Bleeping horns. The sound of someone eating an apple. A ticking clock. Hurried conversations. All around us, in every day, we are subjected to a barrage of sensory messages that most of us ignore without even thinking about them. Every day, most of us interact with the world around us without giving much thought to how we are doing it; it just comes naturally. This is not, however, the case for the person on the autism spectrum. Asperger syndrome is a form of autism that was not officially recognized and put into the DSM-V until 1994 (APA). There has been a huge lack of public awareness and knowledge of this disorder, although it has gotten more attention in recent years. As a result of this knowledge gap, many kids, teenagers, and adults are walking around every day carrying feelings of extreme isolation and difference from those that surround them but never quite knowing why.

I have been one of these people. I am 21; a college senior at Goucher College in Baltimore. I have a 3.7 GPA in my college and always did well in school, but all my life I have lived with the knowledge that something was "different" about me, something I couldn't quite figure out. I kept to myself as a kid. I entertained myself and lived in worlds I created for myself. I was happy enough until about the seventh grade, when an unsettling realization hit me. I realized for the first time that I had no friends. I had never had any desire for them before, but I wanted them now.

I observed other people pairing up and doing things together. I noticed them talking and laughing and walking to class together. I suddenly felt lonely. For the first time in my life, I wanted friends. But I had no idea how to get them. I had always regarded people as targets to avoid, inscrutable objects that could be potentially dangerous to me. Now I felt a desire to relate to them. It seemed, though, that I did not speak the same native language as them. I had no idea what to do with them.

I was the target of quite a bit of bullying and harassment my eighth grade year. I shrank away from people much more after this. Still, I wanted friends. In high school I got my first taste of this. My junior year and senior year, I was befriended by a few girls from my classes. For the first time in my life, I experienced what it was like to "hang out" with people, to go to their houses or just have conversations with them. Despite these burgeoning friendships, though, I still felt troubled. I wanted to know why it was so hard to make friends with my peers. I wanted to know why I still felt so isolated, like there was a thick wall between me and other people. I had a pretty good life: I had things I was interested in, people to talk to when I wanted, a family that loved me, all the things I could really want. But I became more and more desperate to find out the answers to the question of my differences that had always plagued me.

I wanted to know why I didn't dress the same as others my age, always placing comfort high above fashion. I wanted to know why I didn't have any of the same interests as my peers and why "friends" seemed to be like the seventh class in my senior year schedule. All very intangible things, and I was reassured over the years by therapists, guidance counselors, and family that there was nothing different about me, that I was just like everyone else. That I was maybe a little anxious around my peers but that I'd find friends. All I had to do was meet people with similar interests. I knew this wasn't true. I knew that I was different in some essential way, some way that I had absolutely no words for but that I felt in the deepest recesses of my heart. I knew it in the way that I felt so cut off from people—the feeling that no matter how many interests I shared with a person, we somehow had two completely different ways of communicating and would never be able to connect on the level that I needed. People tried their hardest but nobody had any answers for me, so I learned to cope. I shut out the outside world as much as possible and learned to take pleasure in my own world, in things that I found enjoyable.

The schism between the way I experienced and related to the world and the way that all of my peers experienced and related to the world kept growing and growing, and I felt more and more torn. I wanted desperately to be a part of the world around me, but found it so difficult, so cumbersome. It took so much energy. It was so much easier to retreat into my world. Yet, I knew this would lead nowhere I wanted to go; the isolation was becoming unbearable.

And then, at age 21, I learned of Asperger's syndrome, and for the first time in my life could fit my behaviors and way of experiencing the world into an already established pattern. I fit somewhere. There was a perfectly logical explanation for my difficulties. Now, instead of spending all my energies trying to shut out a world that did not understand me, I could find a segment of the world that did. I could start to forgive myself for all the transgressions I had so painfully made over the years without knowing why. I could find other people who "spoke Aspie."

Thinking back over my life up until now, I am amazed by the sheer amount of effort those with AS must make just to get through each day, by the amount of coping techniques we must intuitively come up with and practice. We are bombarded every day with so much overwhelming sensory information. Our clothes are too tight, making eye contact can literally hurt, the sounds of everyday conversation, of a clock ticking or someone tapping a pencil against the desk can drive us out of our minds. Certain smells can overwhelm us, the lights are too dim or too bright, we just don't feel comfortable in our bodies. It's very hard for us to actually relax, because there always seems to be a threat lurking somewhere.

Every interaction we have is like solving a 500-piece puzzle before the time is up. When we see a person we would like to interact with, first we must decide if we have enough energy to go through with the interaction. Whereas a large segment of the population gets energy from interaction with others, for us it can be sometimes dangerously overwhelming and depleting. It is like a forbidden fruit that we would like to enjoy but must weigh the consequences. Then we have to figure out, often in just a few seconds, what we're going to say and how we're going to say it and try to double check it before we say it to make sure, to the best of our knowledge, that it might be something that could flow reasonably into the conversation. We have to call up old scripts and decide which is most appropriate for the situation. And on top of all that, we have to make it sound as natural as we can.

If you were a native English speaker with some background in the French language, and you spent a month in France, you would find yourself trying to translate your thoughts in English to French before you spoke them. This is very similar to what happens when an AS person must talk: they have to translate their Aspie way of thinking to a more neurotypical format. This can be a difficult task if you don't know the language well; slip-ups are bound to happen. It ends up being a very time-consuming and exhausting process to continuously go through.

When I was growing up, I constantly felt like I was speaking a different language from everyone around me. I would have such a hard time conveying what seemed to be the simplest of things, and felt like I was constantly being misunderstood. What a relief it is later, then, to find in so much of the literature on Asperger syndrome those same very words: "People with Asperger syndrome speak a different kind of language than their peers." This is, of course, due to the fact that we do not understand nonverbal language. We do not pick up on those small signals, those nuances in the way you say words that are supposedly meant to carry so much meaning. We won't see the reassuring look in your face because we can't read your face. We only hear the words. When we talk, we might over-explain something due to the fact that so much of what people take for granted as being understood, we have no way of knowing is understood; we are awkward and clumsy because we are trying to put words to emotions and feelings that most people are able to communicate nonverbally.

We are creatures of habit and have a great need for structure and routine; disruptions in our routine can wreak havoc on us. There are so many things that can make us feel off balance and it can be very difficult to recover from this. I think the hardest thing for me as a person with AS is the feeling of always being on the edge. The feeling that yes, I'm coping now, but at any minute I could loose my hold and become completely overwhelmed by the world around me. This is terrifying in so many ways and something I deal with so much every day. I try to structure my days and my routines in such a way that I feel as calm and stable as possible, and I am always making sure I am engaged in some activity or another so that I give myself as little chance as possible to succumb to the terror of the unknown—but it creeps up on you during every down time that you have, and you fight it as best as you can, promising rosier visions of the future, promising that there will come a time when you aren't so scared. You learn to focus on the one or two things that made you happy in any given day and fixate on them, hold on to them for as long as possible, using them as your reason to keep fighting.

There are many little things we do to cope with all of the pressures we feel. I personally carry lavender lotion around with me everywhere; I find the scent and feel of it calms me down when I'm approaching an overload quicker than just about anything. The feeling of water against my skin is also a stimulus that is very calming to me. Recently I've figured out that water fountains tend to have much colder water than some public sinks, so I've taken paper towels and put them under the spray of the water fountain to make them as cold and reviving as possible. There are so many little things like that we notice that no one else would, so many things that we must intuit to do to help ourselves function in this world.

So many people are apt to pass off people with AS or any of a number of other disorders as somehow less intelligent or someone not worth getting to know. If they're clumsy socially, they must be clumsy mentally, right? But the fact of the matter is we have to be quite intelligent to figure out a way to deal with the foreign world in which we live. At any given moment, we are planning out everything that will happen the rest of the day so that we are not taken by surprise by anything. We are thinking ahead to try to figure out if a proposed activity will be safe for us and not contain too much sensory overload; we are figuring out how much downtime we need to program in to anything we schedule ourselves to do.

I explain all of this just to give the average person an idea of what it is like to live on the autistic spectrum, and especially an idea of what it is like to live there without knowing about AS. While it is a struggle, it is not an impossible one. There are benefits that go along with it, too: the ability to remember large amounts of information related to your interests, which could be helpful for those who manage to get a job in a field of interest to them; the ability to focus single-mindedly on a task to get it done; and a great deal of honesty, loyalty, and perseverance. AS employees are much more likely to stick to the rules and do exactly what you have told them to. People with AS won't tell you one thing one day and change their mind the next; they are unfailingly honest. They'll tell you what they mean; you won't have to play guessing games with them.

It is only by learning about each other's struggles and challenges and really trying to understand them that we can build a world that is safe for everyone to live in. A world where its inhabitants don't have to live in fear of being different, but can instead embrace it—a world where we can truly grow and improve because we are taking advantage of everyone's strengths, not just the strengths of a selective few. That is the kind of world that I want to live in. It's the kind of world that we all want to live in.

### REFERENCE

American Psychiatric Association. (1994). *Diagnostic and statistical manual of mental disorders* (4th ed., text rev.). Washington, DC: Author.

KATE GOLDFIELD

## PERCEPTIONS OF AN OLDER SIBLING

When I was a little girl, my biggest wish was to have a baby brother or sister. Actually I preferred a sister, but at age 8, after years of begging and praying every night, I would have taken either.

I remember the big day when my dad came to pick me up from school. Heather had arrived and I was given the honor of choosing her middle name. At the hospital, I helped dress Heather in her first outfit. It would be the beginning of many firsts we did together. Heather took her first steps to me. I taught her how to climb up on the couch much to my mother's chagrin. I was Heather's teacher and she was my wish come true. Being 8 years apart removed a lot of the normal sibling drama.

My mother says that she knew Heather was special, soon after she joined our lives. As a baby, I was very demanding while Heather was content most of the time. She was a very good baby and rarely cried even after undergoing surgery to correct her eye problems. Although I was young enough not to remember the steps leading up to Heather's developmental testing, I clearly remember the psychiatrist trying to explain to me that Heather had autism. I remember disagreeing with him in my strongest 10-year-old voice and personally vowing that it would not be so.

So began Heather's early interventions, both research based and "experimental." Heather started high-risk preschool at the nearby university hospital. At home, I started my own interventions. We had a thin camouflage blanket that had a slick texture on both sides. Heather loved to be wrapped up tight like a caterpillar in a cocoon. I consistently got in trouble for "tying Heather up." Heather loved it. Today we know deep pressure can be very calming for persons with ASD. My mother thought it was sibling war.

It was Heather that led me to choosing my career in the field of autism. It is my relationship with her and my experience of growing up in our family that gave me a yearning to reach out to children with autism and their families. After college, I completed my master's degree with an emphasis in autism and behavior disorders. I've taught 10 years now in the public school setting. I enjoy the opportunity to work with these amazing children and their families.

Heather is in her twenties now. Navigating the world of vocational rehab has proven difficult. Although she attends several different day programs, none of these have been individualized to meet her specific needs for gaining independence and caring for her health. Heather continues to live at home. And yes, she has limitations according to the "real world" but what does the world know?

During a recent visit with Heather, I realized how many amazing abilities she possesses. Although Heather often appears to tune out in a social setting, she is quick to notice and stop her 3-year-old nephew when he steps outside the safety ring of adults. She would actually go after Jonah, pick him up, and return him back to an area that she considered safe. Often I wouldn't realize Jonah had wandered away, until she came lugging him back with a proud look on her face, while he squealed with excitement. So much for a mother's watchful eye.

One of Heather's other amazing talents is her creativity with yarn. She can crochet anything she can imagine, without a pattern. She has created amazing doll costumes, tutus and even dollhouse curtains armed with only a crochet hook and yarn. She has crocheted newborn hats and sewn blankets that were donated to a children's hospital in memory of her nephew, Noah, who passed away before the age of two. Heather struggles with processing information yet she can follow a long string of verbalized crochet directions without any delay. Being the first born, my mother spent hours trying to teach me various handwork. I was an unwilling and difficult student and lacked the patience to participate for very long. Heather was a different story. So when it is all said and done, I think perhaps, I am the one with limitations in this crafty family.

VALERIE JANKE REXIN

# REFLECTIONS ON TEACHING CHILDREN ON THE AUTISM SPECTRUM (TEACHER)

As a teacher working in a small, private school, my experience with children who have been diagnosed with an ASD has been somewhat limited. I suspect that I have taught a number of children who may not have been diagnosed or whose parents did not share information because they were afraid of the ramifications of such labeling for their child. I also suspect that I have taught others who had received an early diagnosis and proper intervention, and were doing so well that the parents did not feel it necessary to share that information. Though I understand the dilemma of wanting to protect children from the stigma and misunderstanding that may come with such a diagnosis, it has been my experience that children who are diagnosed as early as possible, where effective therapies have been on-going, and where there is good communication between school and home, have experienced greater school success.

As I reflect on my experience with students on the spectrum, two children come immediately to mind. In both cases, the parents were well-educated and very caring people who wanted the best for their children. The children had "social problems" or were described by previous teachers as being "socially immature." Both families had sought help from their public school districts. Both were told that their children had ADD but did not meet the qualifications for special education, and, dissatisfied with this response, both families received outside evaluations and counseling for their children. Both families turned to private education, hoping that the smaller class sizes and challenging curriculum would be the answer to their child's problems. Neither child was properly diagnosed until major events at school precipitated an adequate evaluation that targeted the problems encountered by these two children. Though these children were very bright, in the end, both children ended up leaving the private school setting and were eventually diagnosed with Asperger syndrome, one at age 13 and the other at age 11. The most striking thing about this to me was that in one case in particular, the signs seemed very obvious. I had very little training or experience with ASD and yet suspected Asperger syndrome within two days of having this child in my class. It seems terribly tragic that a proper diagnosis and appropriate therapy had not begun years before when the chances for school success would have been significantly increased. Without such therapy, these two children were ill-equipped to deal with the social demands of the classroom. The impact on the other children, even with some of the valuable lessons learned, was still less than satisfactory. They were certainly no more equipped to deal with the conflicts and constant disruptions than I was. And I felt helpless to provide what I most wanted for both children: an environment in which they could thrive and succeed. With only suspicions and symptoms to go on, it was very difficult to know how to do much more than muddle through from one problem to the next.

Another student I taught was diagnosed by the first grade with a central processing disorder. I had this student in my fifth/sixth grade multiage class. His parents were very open about his needs and in constant communication with me about his progress. This consistent communication gave the therapist who was working with him the information she needed in order to target specific behaviors and problem areas. The family offered her as a resource for me, and we met several times to discuss strategies that she had found to be effective with the student over the many years she had worked with him. Through this process, the child gained much confidence and the skills he needed to succeed in an academically demanding learning environment. He had a solid group of friends who were very supportive of his learning differences, and though they were not aware of a label, they did know that their friend processed information differently than they did. Because his parents were open about this, and he was very aware of both his weaknesses and strengths, we were able together to educate his peers about how people think, learn, and communicate in different ways. Given honest information and some helpful tools for conflict resolution, the kids were able to take this in stride, and the child had several close friendships and was generally well liked by his classmates. A supportive family, on-going therapy, and a positive school environment made it possible for him to thrive socially and academically.

LYNDA M. MOORE

## SUCCEEDING IN COLLEGE (ADULT)

College can be a very daunting prospect for anyone, but if you have an autism spectrum disorder, it can be downright terrifying. Living on campus? Interacting with other people? Being away from home? It can sound like a nightmare. But if you know a few things before you start, it can become a very manageable prospect, that anyone can do, even an individual on the autism spectrum. I would like to share with you what I believe the most important tips are to succeeding in college for individuals with an autism spectrum disorder.

Most importantly, make connections with whoever you can. These will become your lifeline. Try to befriend your professors; they are often much easier to interact with than your peers. Try to choose a college small enough where you will be able to have a relationship with your professors. Stay after class and talk to them about the assignment or a particular idea you had about one of the topics from class. Comment about the weather. Ask their opinion of school-wide issues. Any kind of repeated small talk leads to a feeling of connection, and a genuine friendship. When you need to talk about more serious issues or need help with something, you will have natural allies. These connections will keep you from feeling too lonely, and give you a sense of connection to and belonging within the college. You will most likely find doing this with professors much easier than with your peers.

The second most important thing is to accept that you are different. Don't waste all your time comparing yourself to others. Know that you may appear different, talk different, walk different, and have different interests. It's not worth beating yourself up over. You've known this for a long time; it's old news. If you choose the right college, the student body won't care that you're different. Look for smaller, quirky colleges with a more welcoming student body. At my college, I was quite self-conscious my first few years, but eventually grew into myself and didn't care that I appeared different. Instead, I reveled in it. This gave me more confidence when interacting with my peers and helped me to make friends.

Take classes in what you are truly interested in, not what other people tell you to. Boredom is the most surefire way to fail academically. Follow your passions. Make the material your own. When you are assigned a project or a paper, think to yourself, "What do I want to say about the world, or myself? What do I want to find out about the world or myself? How can I express this in this paper in a meaningful way?" Find something that engages you and you will excel academically and really get something out of the process in the meantime. At my college, I really enjoyed when we got to do portfolios in my psychology classes. We were allowed to express our learning of the material in any way we wished: through essays, song lyrics, paintings, research papers, or whatever we liked. I was able to really explore myself and the world around me while doing these portfolios.

Work around sensory concerns. College can be a sensory nightmare, but only if you let it. If noise is a problem while you are taking tests, ask to take tests in a separate room or the learning center. If you have a problem with perfumes, have the teacher ask the class not to wear any. If you tend to get overwhelmed while being out and about on a busy college campus, get a Walkman or iPod to listen to while you walk around. This will soothe you and give you something to concentrate on. Figure out the way you relax best and work time into your schedule to do it. Find a nice, quiet place on campus where you can retreat when you need to. For me, that was the basement of my school library. I personally had trouble going to sleep at night when I could hear any noise at all coming from any of the other dorm rooms. So I scheduled late classes and made a point to stay up until two or three in the morning when I was sure everyone else had gone to sleep. Unorthodox, yes, but it worked throughout the time I was at my college.

Find something you enjoy, and do it regularly. Make you sure you leave time to relax. Don't stress out if you don't have anyone to do it with. There is no law stating you can't go out to dinner by yourself or to a movie alone. Sometimes, it is even more enjoyable that way. Take yourself out on the town. I used smoothies as rewards for difficult tasks, and regularly went into town by myself. I wandered around and forgot about school for a while.

Organization is important. Knowing yourself and your patterns, and having a routine, is key to succeeding. What time of day do you work best? Morning or night? Before dinner or after? Do you work best under the pressure of deadlines, or do you need to break tasks into smaller, more manageable chunks? Do you need an area with no distractions to work in, or does some amount of activity stimulate your thinking process? These are all important things to know about yourself. Have a schedule of when you will do all your work, and stick to it. Invest in binders and keep work neatly labeled where you can find it. Try to work around the same time every day.

Finally, and this is very important, ask for help if you need it. Most colleges have learning centers where you can get extra tutoring or other accommodations. Don't be afraid to be a pest when asking teachers to clarify assignments—it's better than getting a bad grade. Utilize e-mail to ask questions of professors if talking to face-to-face is too difficult. Make sure you have a source of support. The counseling center in your school can be very useful to help you deal with the myriad stresses of a college career. Make sure you have someone to talk to, whether that person is a friend, a professor, family member, or whomever.

If you follow all of those tips, I think that you will find you really enjoy your college experience. Your college years are particularly notable because not only are you learning a ton of stuff academically, but you are also growing so much as a person. You're learning how to live on your own, how to interact with others, how to discipline yourself and stay motivated. You're learning about things you are interested in, and new ways to express yourself. You're building an identity for yourself. I wish you all the luck as you travel down this important path!

Kate Goldfield

## WHICH IS IT? DISTINGUISHING TYPICAL DEVELOPMENT FROM DISABILITY-DRIVEN BEHAVIORS (MOTHER)

Our son, who has Asperger syndrome, will turn 18 in November. For what seemed like a sea of endless days and one thing after another, I am astonished at how quickly the years have passed. I can remember from the earliest days when he was a little more than 2 years old and having major meltdowns, or insisting the toy trains stay strategically across the living room floor, to the constant state of chaos and disorganization that we have now, the question has always been, "Just what can I blame on the Asperger syndrome and what is garden variety kid stuff?"

I take great comfort in knowing that I am not alone in the world with my own obsessive tendencies toward this issue, because I also work with many families whose children are in the same boat and we all ask the same thing. Since many of those children are younger, I often appear to be the one who has the most combat time, if you will. The answer is simple: ask a behaviorist and it is all environmental and learned; ask a pediatrician and it is developmental and most certainly will be grown out of at some point; and then ask your spouse or the babysitter and it is just plain WRONG. Along the way, I have catalogued most everything by one of these disciplines and come up with some general guidelines to decipher the mixed messages flying about and give each faction its due in part.

*Whose problem is it?* Now this is certainly grounded in most parenting classes, but since our kids have great difficulty assessing the cause and effect of social situations, it is often a situation where we as parents or teachers or innocent bystanders find ourselves targeted for blame in a pinch. So, if I can decide reasonably whether I am impatiently asking for compliance when an extra minute wouldn't hurt, or is my child allowing his fondness for video games to interfere with the rest of the world, I will be in a much better position to respond without making anything more unpleasant than it already is.

*Is it a "hardware" problem?* I have become a firm believer in understanding the neurological underpinnings to the best of my ability, so there are a few basic principles I allow for in my deliberations. We know that our kids just don't understand or attribute other people's motivations for their words or actions well; forming abstract concepts or the "big pictures" is quite tough sometimes and knowing that most kids on the autism spectrum have sensory processing deficits regulating their responses or being overly aware of their physical surroundings, I know that they are prone to overreacting but can be taught strategies to become more socially appropriate. So the moral of that story is this: Educate yourself thoroughly about what's going on in their heads.

*Don't forget that everyone is human.* Inappropriate behavior is never a good thing, but respectful, POSITIVE approaches are much more effective at correcting the problem and, most importantly, preserving a better relationship with your kids.

SHERRY MOYER

# Index

Page numbers in **bold** indicate main entries.

Motor skills: Asperger's disorder, 22; dyspraxia, 132; gross, 163; regression, 309–10

Motor tics, 379

Movement: catatonia, 67; coordination of, 162–63; dance therapy, 95–96; proprioception, 283; repetitive, 169, 243, 300

Moyer, Sherry, 468–69

MRI. *See* Magnetic resonance imaging

Multidimensional Anxiety Scale for Children (MASC), **226–27**

Multidisciplinary evaluation (MDE), **227**

Multidisciplinary framework, 313–18

Multidisciplinary team, **227**, 314

Multisensory association method, 27

Multistep skills, 2

Multitasking, 83

Muscle catatonia, 67

Musical savant skills, 159

Music therapist, 228–29

Music therapy, **227–29**

Mutually acceptable written agreement, **229**

Mutual regulation, 316

Myelin, 140

National Alliance for Autism Research (NAAR), 446

National Association for the Education of Young Children, 102

National Association of School Nurses, 185–86

The National Autistic Society, 430

National Human Genome Research Institute, 446

National Human Genome Research Project, 248

National Information Center for Children and Youth with Disabilities (NICHCY), 447

National Institute for Child Health and Development (NICHD), 443

National Institute of Child Health and Human Development (NICHD), 447

National Institute of Health Autism Coordinating Committee, 449

National Institute of Mental Health (NIMH), 444, 449, 450

National Institute on Deafness and Other Communication Disorders (NIDCD), 443

National Institutes of Health, 198, 444, 446, 447, 449, 450

National Organization for Rare Disorders (NORD), 447

National Research Council, 194, 262

National Service Dogs (NSD), 11

National Voter Registration Act of 1993, 405

Naturalistic approach, 201

Natural language paradigm, **231**

Needs: assistive technology, 25; underlying, 423

Negative practice, 241

Negative reinforcement, escape training, 126

Nervous system: Halstead-Reitan Neuropsychological Test Battery, 165–66; rewiring, 334; sensory integration, 333–34; stimulants, 363

Network on the Neurobiology and Genetics of Autism, 443

Neurofeedback, **231–33**

Neuroimaging, 150, **233**

Neurological condition: dual sensory loss, 390–91; dyspraxia, 132; sensory sensitivity, 338

Neurological damage, pesticides, 248

Neurological disorder, 98; Childhood Disintegrative Disorder, 72; pervasive developmental disorder not otherwise specified, 246

Neurological syndromes, nonverbal learning disability, 234–35

Neurologic organization, 243–44

Neurologist, **233**

Neurology, **233**

*Neurology* (journal), 434

Neuromotor, **233**

Neuropsychology, **233**

Neuroscience-based perspective, interventions, 140–41

*Neuroscience & Biobehavioral Reviews* (journal), 434

Neurotoxic, **233**

Neurotransmitter, 115, **234**; serotonin, 338

New England Center for Children (NECC), 428

*The New England Center for Children Research Newsletter*, 428

*New England Journal of Medicine* (journal), 434

Newsletter, **234**

NLP. *See* Natural language paradigm

No Child Left Behind Act 2001 (PL 107-110), **234**, 447

Nocturnal enuresis, 123

Noise, background, 68

No-no prompt procedures, **234**

# About the Editors, Advisory Board, and Contributors

## EDITORS

**Brenda Smith Myles, PhD,** is the chief of programs and development of the Ohio Center for Autism and Low Incidence, and an associate professor in the Department of Special Education at the University of Kansas, where she codirects a graduate program in Asperger syndrome and autism. The recipient of the 2004 Autism Society of America's Outstanding Professional Award and the 2006 Princeton Fellowship Award, she has written numerous articles and books on Asperger syndrome and autism including *Asperger Syndrome and Difficult Moments: Practical Solutions for Tantrums, Rage, and Meltdowns* (with Southwick) and *Asperger Syndrome and Adolescence: Practical Solutions for School Success* (with Adreon), the winner of the Autism Society of America's Outstanding Literary Work. Brenda has made over 500 presentations all over the world and written more than 150 articles and books on autism and Asperger syndrome. She is on the executive boards of several organizations, including the Organization for Autism Research and Maap Services, Inc. In addition, she was recently acknowledged as the second most productive applied researcher in autism spectrum disorders in the world from 1997 to 2004.

**Terri Cooper Swanson, MS Ed, MT-BC,** has worked nationally and internationally with individuals with Asperger syndrome and autism, including working with adults with disabilities at Opportunity Village in Clear Lake, Iowa, and serving as a consultant for home, school, and community-based programs. Currently, Terri is a doctoral student at the University of Kansas in the Special Education Autism/Asperger Syndrome Program where she was a Project Coordinator for the Asperger Syndrome Research Study. She has authored several research articles and book chapters, and has presented and consulted internationally on autism spectrum disorders.

**Jeanne Holverstott, MS Ed,** is the autism spectrum specialist at Responsive Centers for Psychology and Learning in Overland Park, Kansas, where she provides clinically based therapy, school consultation and advocacy, and diagnostic services. Prior to taking this position, she earned her master's degree in special education from the University of Kansas, specializing in the autism and Asperger syndrome program. Jeanne has worked for 6 years with children on the autism spectrum in a variety of settings and capacities, including as a clinician, paraeducator, discrete trial therapist, consultant, tutor, and camp counselor. Additionally, Jeanne has taught several courses and authored a number of articles about children with autism and Asperger syndrome.

**Megan Moore Duncan, BS,** is a full-time wife and mother; she is also a freelance project coordinator, writer, and speaker. In addition to volunteer work in three schools and her church, Megan's passion is to see people (especially her children) reach their full potential.

## ADVISORY BOARD

**Simon Baron-Cohen, PhD,** is a professor of developmental psychopathology at the University of Cambridge and a fellow of Trinity College, Cambridge. He is Director of the Autism Research Centre at the University of Cambridge, in the United Kingdom. Baron-Cohen has authored several books, including *Mindblindness* and *The Essential Difference: Men, Women, and the Extreme Male Brain*, and the DVD-ROM, *Mind Reading: An Interactive Guide to Emotions*.

**Pat Schissel, LMSW,** is the president of the Asperger Syndrome and High Functioning Autism Association (AHA), a parent and professional organization in New York providing groups, information, and conferences to families and professional affected by autism spectrum disorders. She is also an adjunct professor at Delphi University and the parent of an adult with Asperger syndrome.

**Stephen Shore, PhD,** diagnosed with "strong autistic tendencies," nonverbal until age 4, and recommended for institutionalization, Stephen completed a doctorate at Boston University focusing on helping people with autism develop their capacities to the fullest extent possible. Stephen is an internationally known author, consultant, and presenter.

**Pamela Wolfberg, PhD,** is a professor and director of the autism spectrum graduate program at San Francisco State University. Her research and practice center on efforts to develop inclusive peer play programs for children on the autism spectrum. She has authored numerous books, chapters, and articles and actively presents worldwide.

## CONTRIBUTORS

**Jennifer M. Akullian, MS,** is a research assistant for the Indiana Resource Center for Autism at Indiana University, where she is a doctoral student the School of Psychology.

**Ruth Aspy, PhD,** is a licensed psychologist who specializes in assessment and intervention for individuals with autism spectrum disorders. She is coauthor of *The Ziggurat Model*. Dr. Aspy speaks nationally on this and other topics.

**Lisa R. Audet, PhD, CCC-SLP,** is assistant professor of speech-language pathology at Kent State University where she developed the Pervasive Developmental Disorders certificate. For over 20 years she has worked extensively with individuals who possess severe communication disorders. Her research focuses on communication development for individuals with autism.

**Andrea M. Babkie, EdD,** is currently working as an educational consultant while editing and writing. She has served on the executive committees of several international organizations, including the Council for Learning Disabilities and the presidential chain of the Division on Developmental Disabilities of the Council for

Exceptional Children. Dr. Babkie has authored a number of professional articles and has presented nationally on a variety of topics in the field of special education.

**Bruce Bassity, RPA-C,** practices primary care medicine in rural northern New York State.

**Katie Bassity, MS,** recently completed the autism/Asperger syndrome program at the University of Kansas. She currently works as an autism consultant at the Ohio Center for Autism and Low Incidence (OCALI).

**James R. Batterson, MD,** is a child psychiatrist at Children's Mercy Hospitals and Clinics in Kansas City, Missouri, and runs a Tourette syndrome clinic, as well as working with patients with autism spectrum disorders. He has been the principal investigator for several medication trials with children and adolescents with these disorders.

**Scott Bellini, PhD,** is the assistant director of the Indiana Resource Center for Autism, and is a faculty member with the Indiana University school psychology program. His research and clinical interests include social-emotional functioning for children with autism spectrum disorders, including anxiety disorders, social skills programming, and video self-modeling.

**Josepha Ben-Arieh, PhD,** is a consultant for students with autism spectrum disorders (ASD) and Asperger syndrome. Dr. Ben-Arieh coauthored the book *Autism Spectrum Disorders: Interventions and Treatments for Children and Youth* and is the author of *How to Use Joint Action Routines.* She has presented nationally and internationally on ASD and Asperger syndrome.

**Susana Bernad-Ripoll, MS,** is a special education practicum supervisor at the University of Kansas, where she is a doctoral student in the autism/Asperger syndrome program.

**Douglas Biklen, PhD,** is Dean of the School of Education at Syracuse University. He is also Professor of Cultural Foundations of Education and Teaching and Leadership, faculty in Disability Studies and Director of the Facilitated Communication Institute at Syracuse University.

**Amy Bixler Coffin, MS,** is the education autism administrator for the Ohio Center for Autism and Low Incidence (OCALI) where she coordinates and provides professional development in the area of autism spectrum disorders for Ohio schools and families.

**Cameron Blackwell** is a 15-year-old freshman in high school, working towards an honors diploma. He was diagnosed with Asperger syndrome while in second grade. He has been very involved in his school and church, as well as attending autism-related conferences. His special passion is band. He marched with the high school band as an eighth grader and hopes to someday be a band director himself.

**Craig Blackwell** is 12 years old and in his first year of middle school. He loves cooking, fishing, gold, and anything to do with dragons. He is beginning band and enjoys attending his brother's marching band competitions.

**Eric Blackwell** is a husband and father of four children (two of whom are on the autism spectrum). He is the director of technology for a large real estate brokerage and owner of Netvantedge, an Internet company that teaches and implements search engine and e-commerce strategies for business and organization. He regularly teaches and presents on e-commerce and Internet-related subjects.

**Jen Blackwell** received her degree in education and taught students with severe emotional disabilities in a group home. Four children and two autism spectrum diagnoses later, she has returned to work in a special-needs setting, in an inclusive preschool. She and her children have served as guest speakers to education classes dealing with issues related to autism spectrum disorders.

**Jaime Blackwell,** 10 years old, is the lone daughter among all brothers. She is in her last year of elementary school and is enjoying being "Top Dog" for the school year. She loves to sing, and not only has she sung with groups at church, she has performed songs in sign language for both school and church. She loves to spend time with her friends and family.

**Marjorie A. Bock, EdD,** is an associate professor of special education at the Associated Colleges of Central Kansas where she teaches special education courses. She developed and directed the Global Rural Autism/Asperger Information Network (GRAAIN) at the University of North Dakota. She has authored several articles and presented nationally and internationally on autism spectrum disorders.

**Signe M. Boucher, BA,** is a doctoral student in the school psychology program at the University of North Carolina (UNC). She has worked in both clinical and research capacities for Division TEACCH for several years and is currently completing her internship at UNC with a focus on developmental disabilities.

**Jenny Clark Brack, OTR/L,** is a pediatric occupational therapist with over 14 years' experience in school settings. Currently she works both as a staff occupational therapist within a rural special education cooperative and as a special consultant to schools in several states. Jenny has presented nationally and has been published in several occupational therapy periodicals. She is the author of *Learn to Move, Move to Learn!*

**Stacey L. Brookens, MS,** is the director for Autism Services, Central Pennsylvania, at NHS Human Services, where she supervises the Stepping Stones Programs, the NHS Autism School in Altoona, Pennsylvania, and the Behavioral Health Rehabilitative Services for individuals diagnosed with an autism spectrum disorder.

**Martha S. Burns, PhD, CCC-SLP,** serves on the faculty of Northwestern University and the professional staff at Evanston-Northwestern Hospital, both in Evanston, Illinois. She is also Director of the Clinical Specialist Market at Scientific Learning Corporation. Dr. Burns has published widely on neuropathologies of speech and language in children and adults.

**Kari Dunn Buron, MS,** is retired from K–12 education and currently coordinating the ASD Certificate program for educators at Hamline University in St. Paul, Minnesota. She is the coauthor of *The Incredible 5 Point Scale* and the author of *When My Worries Get Too Big* and *A 5 Is Against the Law!*

**Steve Chamberlain, PhD,** is an associate professor of special education at the University of Texas at Brownville. His research interests include different ways culture influences teacher/student and teacher/parent interactions in schools, and culturally responsive assessment and instruction for students with disabilities.

**Hyun-Jeong Cho, MS,** is a second-year doctoral student in special education at the University of Kansas. Her emphasis is in self-determination and functional education. She is a graduate research assistant for Dr. Michael L. Wehmeyer.

**Yu-Chi Chou, MS Ed,** is a doctoral student at the University of Kansas in the autism and Asperger syndrome program.

**Beth Clavenna-Deane, MS,** is a graduate research assistant with the Transition Coalition at the University of Kansas. She is currently a doctoral student in the transition program. She has 13 years' experience in the special education arena as a special educator and transition coordinator for students with autism and Asperger syndrome.

**Katherine E. Cook, PhD,** is a visiting assistant professor at the University of Kansas in the Department of Special Education. Her areas of specialization include autism spectrum disorders, early childhood special education, and alternative assessment. Cook has published several articles, book chapters, and books related to autism spectrum disorders and has presented nationally.

**Virginia L. Cook,** is a doctoral candidate in special education at the University of Kansas. She works with researchers at Juniper Gardens Children's Project in Kansas City, Kansas.

**David R. Cormier, MS Ed,** is an educational consultant for Connecticut's State Education Resource Center where he coordinates the state's Focus on Autism professional development and resource initiative. He provides training and technical assistance to education professionals and families on topics including positive behavior supports, responsible inclusive practices, and differentiated instruction.

**Karla Dennis, MA, CCC-SLP,** is a speech pathologist for the Blue Valley School District in Overland Park, Kansas. She works with middle school students with a variety of disabilities, including autism spectrum disorders. Karla also has a master's degree in special education with an emphasis in autism and Asperger syndrome from the University of Kansas.

**Lynn Dudek, MS, CCC-SLP, MBA,** is a speech pathology coordinator at the Ohio Center for Autism and Low Incidence. She has supervised speech language pathologists and specialized in the treatment of individuals with autism spectrum disorders for 12 years, while also presenting on topics such as communication deficits in autism. Of particular interest to her is professional collaboration and social skills.

**Theresa L. Earles-Vollrath, PhD,** is an assistant professor at the University of Central Missouri. Dr. Vollrath previously worked as a teacher for children with autism, as a director of an autism resource center, and as an autism specialist for a public school district. She has also coauthored several books, book chapters, and articles on autism.

**Jennifer B. Ganz, PhD,** has been working in special education for 12 years as a general and special education teacher, an educational consultant, university instructor, and researcher. Ganz has authored several articles, book chapters, and books, and has presented on strategies to address social and communication skills for individuals with autism spectrum disorders.

**Peter Gerhardt, EdD,** is the president of the Organization of Autism Research, a nonprofit organization, the mission of which is to fund applied research and disseminate relevant findings in support of learners with autism spectrum disorders and their families. Dr. Gerhardt received his doctorate from the Rutgers University Graduate School of Education.

**Kate Goldfield** is a 22-year-old psychology major from Standish, Maine, who attended Goucher College in Baltimore. She has written several articles related to autism spectrum issues, and has been published in the *Baltimore Sun* and *Hartford Courant*. She has presented at autism conferences and has been involved with Asperger syndrome groups in Maine, Baltimore, and Washington, DC.

**Carol Gray** is an educational consultant and president of The Gray Center for Social Learning and Understanding in Kentwood, Michigan, a nonprofit organization serving people with autism spectrum disorders (ASD) and those who work on their behalf. Carol developed the Social Storyapproach in 1991, and is the author of several articles, chapters, and resources. She is a recipient of the Barbara Lipinski Award for her international contribution to the education and welfare of people with ASD.

**Patty Dobbs Gross** serves as Executive Director of North Star Foundation, a nonprofit organization dedicated to partnering assistance dogs with children to help them reach their social, emotional, and educational goals. She is the author of *The Golden Bridge: A Guide to Assistance Dogs for Children Challenged by Autism or Other Developmental Disabilities*.

**Barry G. Grossman, PhD,** is a licensed psychologist who specializes in assessment and intervention for individuals with autism. He provides assessment and consultation services in the public schools as well as staff development in the area of autism spectrum disorders. Dr. Grossman coauthored *The Ziggurat Model* and speaks nationally.

**Steve Gutstein, PhD,** the founder of RDI, holds a doctorate in clinical psychology and is the director of the Connections Center and board president of the Foundation for Autism Research and Remediation (FARR). Dr. Gutstein and his partner and wife of 25 years, Dr. Rachelle Sheely, have published five books and numerous article related to RDI. They travel internationally conducting workshops, training, and programs.

**Melanie D. Harms, MME, NMT, MT-BC,** is a doctoral student and graduate research assistant in the autism/Asperger syndrome program at the University of Kansas. Melanie provides music therapy services for Gardner Public Schools and serves as the Midwest representative on the American Music Therapy Association Standards of Clinical Practice.

**Rebekah Heinrichs, MSN, MS Ed,** works as an educational specialist in autism spectrum disorders and bullying prevention. She is a trained community facilitator with the Adults and Children Together (ACT) Against Violence Program and is the author of *Perfect Targets: Asperger Syndrome and Bullying*. Rebekah presents nationally on autism spectrum disorders and bullying prevention.

**Linda Hodgdon, MED, CCC-SLP,** has pioneered the development of visual strategies for supporting students with autism spectrum disorders and related communication challenges. Author of the best-seller, *Visual Strategies for Improving Communication*, Linda is a popular national and international presenter who is well-known for her practical approach to dealing with communication challenges.

**Andrea Hopf, MS,** is a doctoral student in the school psychology program at Indiana University. As a graduate assistant at the Indiana Resource Center for Autism, she collaborated on research regarding social skills assessment and intervention for children with autism spectrum disorders.

**Rose Iovannone, PhD,** is the director of a federally funded behavior research center, the Prevent-Teach-Reinforce Project, at the University of South Florida. She also serves as coprincipal investigator in the Professional Development in Autism Project. She has authored several articles and book chapters and has presented nationally on autism spectrum disorders.

**Maya Israel, MS Ed,** is a project coordinator on Project POISE (Providing Outreach Instruction for Special Educators), a special education personnel preparation grant at the University of Kansas. She is a doctoral student in the area of high incidence disabilities.

**Tyi-Sanna Jones, MS,** is a doctoral student at the University of Nevada, Las Vegas (UNLV). She teaches in the special education department at UNLV. Her research and interest areas include autism/Asperger syndrome, gifted education, and multicultural education. She has presented at national professional conferences.

**Joung Min Kim, MS,** is a doctoral student at the University of Kansas in the autism/Asperger syndrome program. She is also a graduate research assistant for the Positive Behavior Supports Project at the Juniper Gardens Children's Project.

**Jan L. Klein, MS Ed,** is a doctoral candidate in special education with a minor in multicultural education at the University of Kansas. She has presented statewide and nationally on culturally responsive teaching and minority parent participation in the special education process.

**Whitney Mitchell Krusniak, MEd,** is an educational consultant for students with autism spectrum disorders for the Ottawa Area Intermediate School District in Holland, Michigan. She is a member of Team Social Stories and has coauthored a series of articles for the *Autism Spectrum Quarterly*.

**Paul G. LaCava, PhD,** earned his degree from the Department of Special Education at the University of Kansas. He has worked as a special education teacher, inclusion facilitator, and consultant. His research interests include autism spectrum disorders, historical perspectives of disability and autism, technology, and interventions for social/emotional skills.

**Hyo Jung Lee, MA,** is a doctoral student at the University of Kansas where she worked as a project coordinator for the Asperger Syndrome Research Study, which is led by Dr. Brenda Myles. Currently, she is working at Ohio Center for Autism and Low Incidence as a research assistant.

**Lisa Ackerson Lieberman, MSW, LCSW,** is a psychotherapist with over 30 years' experience. A national speaker, she skillfully addresses issues related to living with a disability in the family. She has published numerous articles and a book, *A Stranger Among Us*, which is a comprehensive guide to hiring one-to-one providers for people with disabilities.

**Jennie Long, MS Ed,** is a doctoral student at the University of Kansas with an emphasis in autism and Asperger syndrome.

**Lisa Barrett Mann, BA,** is a former health care reporter and editor. She is currently a graduate student at the University of Kansas, studying autism and Asperger syndrome.

**Jo-Anne B. Matteo, MS, CCC-SLP,** is a consultant with Pyramid Educational Consultants, Inc. Prior to working at Pyramid, she was a speech-language pathologist and special education administrator in the Connecticut public schools for 21 years. She travels extensively doing presentations and consultation on PECS and the Pyramid Approach to Education.

**Gary B. Mesibov,** is a professor of psychology in the Departments of Psychiatry and Psychology at the University of North Carolina and Director of Division TEACCH, North Carolina's statewide program serving people with autism spectrum disorders and their families. Mesibov has authored numerous articles, chapters, and books on autism and related conditions emphasizing educational approaches and thinking and learning problems. He is also the editor of the *Journal of Autism and Developmental Disorders*.

**Tara Mihok** is a doctoral student in special education, emphasizing in autism and behavior disorders, at the University of Kansas. She has worked as an occupational therapist for four years for the Washington, DC Public Schools and a private school in Northern Virginia. Her background also includes in-depth training in the use of applied behavior analysis in the treatment of autism.

**Lynda M. Moore** is an elementary school teacher in a multi-age fifth- and sixth-grade class in Portland, Oregon, where she has taught for the past 12 years. Prior to working as a classroom teacher, Lynda worked for 3 years as part of a multidisciplinary team at Oregon Health Sciences University's Children Day Treatment Center.

**Sherry Moyer** is a regional consultant for NHS Human Services of Pennsylvania and the director of the Asperger Syndrome Coalition of the U.S. Moyer has contributed chapters to several books and speaks internationally. She is also the mother of a young adult with Asperger syndrome.

**Daniel W. Mruzek, PhD,** is an assistant professor at the University of Rochester Medical Center. He serves as Psychology Discipline Coordinator in the Leadership Education in Neurodevelopmental and Related Disabilities (LEND) program and as an investigator in the Multisite Young Autism Project, a study on early, intensive behavioral intervention for children with autism. He has authored several peer-reviewed articles and book chapters on autism and other developmental disabilities.

**Michele Mullendore, MS Ed,** is the mother of a child with autism. In addition, she is a special education teacher in the Blue Valley School District in Overland Park, Kansas. Michele joined Blue Valley several years ago where she assisted in opening the first Applied Behavior Analysis–based program for children with autism and developmental disabilities.

**Stephanie Nickelson, Ed S,** is a school psychologist, and Practicum Field Supervisor at the University of Kansas, where she is a doctoral student studying special education policy. She has previously participated in research and participated locally and nationally on neurofeedback.

**Hye Ran Park, MS,** is a doctoral student at the University of Kansas, where she is specializing in autism and Asperger syndrome.

**Jessica Kate Peters, BS,** is in the school psychology doctoral program at Indiana University, where she is focusing on children with autism and children who speak English as a second language. She is also a graduate research associate for the Early Childhood Center at the Indiana Institute on Disability and Community.

**Christine R. Peterson, PhD,** is an assistant professor of pediatrics and team leader for the autism faculty at Strong Center for Developmental Disabilities at the University of Rochester. She provides consultation and training, and conducts research on autism and developmental disabilities, with an emphasis on social communication and transition issues for higher-functioning students with autism and Asperger syndrome.

**Ann Pilewskie** is Director of Autism Services for the Ohio Center for Autism and Low Incidence.

**Carol L. Pitchlyn, MS,** is a support teacher for the Kansas City Kansas Public Schools. She earned her master's degree from the University of Kansas in autism/

Asperger syndrome studies and is currently a KU doctoral student in special education. She is a parent of an adult son with autism. She has presented nationally on families and children with disabilities.

**Kelly M. Prestia, MS Ed, OTR,** is a school-based occupational therapist in Colorado. She has worked with students with autism and related disorders in school systems for 7 years. She has authored several articles and book chapters on autism spectrum disorders.

**Valerie Janke Rexin, MS Ed,** is the autism spectrum disorder (ASD) consultant for the North Kansas City School District where she previously taught in a self-contained class for students with ASD for 10 years. She has a younger sister with autism, which sparked her initial interest in the area of autism.

**Jamie Rivetts, MS Ed,** is a clinician and consultant at Michelle Garcia Winner's Center for Social Thinking, Inc., in San Jose, California, where she leads therapy groups for children in kindergarten through high school. Jaime also consults with local school districts in the San Francisco Bay area in regard to incorporating social thinking across the student's school day.

**Lisa Robbins, MS Ed,** is full-time faculty at Missouri Western State University where she teaches early childhood and special education courses. She is also an autism consultant and provides training and consultation services to parents and school districts nationally and internationally. She is a doctoral student at the University of Kansas.

**Myrna J. Rock, BS,** has worked with clients with special needs in a variety of settings. She freelances in writing curriculums and other items.

**David A. Ruggierio, PhD,** is a thought-leader in the BrainBut Initiative at Columbia University in New York City, where he is exploring the biological basis of nurture and developing new treatments for developmental disorders including autism. He is considered a world expert on visceral brain networks and the visceral thalamic/prefrontal cortical stress axis involved in stress-related developmental disorders.

**Kristi Sakai** is the mother of Tom, Kito, and Kaede, and wife to Nubuo, all of whom have Asperger syndrome. She is the author of *Finding Our Way: Practical Solutions for Creating a Supportive Home and Community for the Asperger Syndrome Family*.

**Fiona J. Scott, PhD,** is a chartered psychologist specializing in autism spectrum disorders (ASD) based at the Autism Research Centre, University of Cambridge, and also offers independent consultation and professional training. Dr. Scott has 14 years' experience in researching assessing children and adults with ASD and is widely published in the field.

**Mark Shelley** is president of The Special Minds Foundation and Special Minds Productions. Mark is committed to developing visual-based technology tools that address everyday issues faced by families living with a diagnosis of autism spectrum disorder.

**Sheila M. Smith, MS Ed,** is a doctoral student at the University of Kansas. She has spent over 20 years as a special educator, administrator, and staff developer in New York, Georgia, Virginia, Kansas, and Ohio. She presents at local, state, national, and international conferences, and has published articles and chapters on autism spectrum disorders.

**Tristram Smith, PhD,** is an assistant professor of pediatrics at the University of Rochester Medical Center (URMC). He serves as the research director for the

Multisite Young Autism Project, which is a federally funded study on early, intensive behavioral intervention based on the UCLA/Lovaas model for children with autism. He is also an investigator in a study at the Center for Studies to Advance Autism Research and Treatment at the University of Rochester. He has authored or coauthored a number of the most widely cited studies on treatment outcomes for individuals with autism spectrum disorders.

**Paula Tallal, PhD,** is the cofounder and codirector of the Center for Molecular and Behavioral Neuroscience at Rutgers University. She has authored over 200 scientific publications and three books. She is the cofounder of Scientific Learning Corporation, the company that developed the Fast ForWord family of language and reading intervention programs.

**Raschelle Theoharris, MS,** is a doctoral student at the University of Kansas in the deaf education program.

**Kai-Chien Tien, MS Ed,** is a doctoral student in the autism/Asperger syndrome program at the University of Kansas. She completed a secondary education licensure program offered by the Teacher Training Center at the National Taiwan University of Arts and received an MS degree in special education from the University of Kansas.

**Melissa L. Trautman, MS Ed,** teaches students with Asperger syndrome in the Blue Valley School District located in Overland Park, Kansas. She is a coauthor of *The Hidden Curriculum: Practical Solutions for Understanding Unstated Rules in Social Situations*.

**Cynthia K. Van Horn, MS Ed,** is the LIFT teacher (Learning Through Intensive Functional Teaching) at Lakewood Middle School in Overland Park, Kansas. She has authored several book and video reviews and contributed to a number of book chapters. Cynthia has presented nationally on autism spectrum disorders.

**Martha G. Welch, MD,** is the codirector of the BrainGut Initiative at Columbia University in New York, where she is exploring the biological basis of nurture and developing new treatments for developmental disorders including autism. In addition to authoring research articles, book chapters, and books, she has presented nationally and internationally on autism spectrum disorders.

**Michael L. Wehmeyer, PhD,** is Professor of Special Education and Director, Kansas University of Center of Developmental Disabilities. He has authored 200 articles or chapters and 20 books on disability issues, including self-determination, universal design for learning, and technology and cognitive disabilities. He is editor-in-chief of *Remedial and Special Education*.

**Michelle Garcia Winner, MA, CCC-SLP,** specializes in helping students with social cognitive deficits. She runs a clinic, has authored numerous books, and speaks internationally. Michelle's goal is to help educators and parents appreciate how social thinking and social skills are an integral part of a student's academic as well as social experience.

**Brooke Young, MS,** is the project coordinator at the Professional Development in Autism Center, where she is a doctoral student in the autism program at the University of Kansas. Brooke has been working in the field for 15 years as a special education teacher and autism consultant.